The State and American
Foreign Economic Policy

A volume in the series

Cornell Studies in Political Economy

EDITED BY PETER J. KATZENSTEIN

A full list of titles in the series appears at the end of the book

The State and American Foreign Economic Policy

EDITED BY

G. JOHN IKENBERRY, DAVID A. LAKE,
AND MICHAEL MASTANDUNO

Cornell University Press

ITHACA AND LONDON

This book first published 1988 by Cornell University Press.

First printing, Cornell Paperbacks, 1988.
Third printing 1993.

The contents of this book first appeared in volume 42, number 1, of the journal *International Organization*.

International Standard Book Number (cloth) 0-8014-2229-9
International Standard Book Number (paper) 0-8014-9524-5
Library of Congress Catalog Card Number 88-11858

Printed in the United States of America

*Librarians: Library of Congress cataloging information
appears on the last page of the book.*

⊗ The paper in this book meets the minimum requirements of the
American National Standard for Information Sciences—Permanence
of Paper for Printed Library Materials, ANSI Z39.48–1984.

Contents

Contributors

Jeff Frieden is Assistant Professor of Political Science at University of California, Los Angeles.

Judith Goldstein is Assistant Professor of Political Science at Stanford University, Stanford, California.

Joanne Gowa is Associate Professor of Political Science at the University of Pennsylvania, Philadelphia.

Stephan Haggard is Associate Professor of Government at Harvard University, Cambridge, Massachusetts.

G. John Ikenberry is Assistant Professor of Politics and International Affairs at Princeton University, Princeton, New Jersey.

David A. Lake is Assistant Professor of Political Science at the University of California, Los Angeles.

Michael Mastanduno is Assistant Professor of Government at Dartmouth College, Hanover, New Hampshire.

Acknowledgments

The editors owe a special thanks to Stephen Krasner and Peter Katzenstein for encouragement and guidance. We thank the Brookings Institution, which provided the location for the early discussions of this project when the editors were there together as research fellows. The Woodrow Wilson School of Public and International Affairs at Princeton University funded the first gathering of the contributors in May 1985. A second conference was held at UCLA in November 1985 and was funded by the Office of International Studies and Overseas Programs. Parts of the project were also presented at the Berkeley/Stanford Colloquium on International Institutions and Cooperation and at the Program on Interdependent Political Economy at the University of Chicago. For helpful comments and suggestions, we would like to thank Beverly Crawford, Timothy McKeown, Cynthia Hody, and John Odell, all of whom participated in the initial discussions of the group, and also Arthur Stein, Peter Gourevitch, Peter Hall, and Charles Lipson.

The State and American
Foreign Economic Policy

Introduction: approaches to explaining American foreign economic policy

G. John Ikenberry, David A. Lake, and Michael Mastanduno

Despite its relative economic decline, the United States remains the dominant power in the world economy. The foreign economic actions taken by American officials, whether they involve trade, technology transfer, or the value of the dollar, continue to have profound consequences for other states in the international system, as well as for American domestic politics and economics. Thus, it is not surprising that the study of American foreign economic policy attracts considerable scholarly attention, and presently constitutes a major portion of the subfield of international political economy.

In constructing explanations of American foreign economic policy, scholars have employed a range of analytical and theoretical approaches. Three have major significance: system-centered, society-centered, and state-centered approaches. International, or system-centered, approaches explain American policy as a function of the attributes or capabilities of the United States relative to other nation-states. In this view, government officials are perceived as responding to the particular set of opportunities and constraints that America's position in the international system creates at any moment in time.[1] Society-centered approaches view American policy as either reflecting the preferences of the dominant group or class in society, or as resulting from the struggle for influence that takes place among various interest

1. Examples and discussions of system-centered approaches include Charles Kindleberger, *The World in Depression* (Berkeley: University of California Press, 1973); Robert Keohane, "The Theory of Hegemonic Stability and Changes in International Economic Regimes," in Ole Holsti, R. Siverson, and A. George, eds., *Change in the International System* (Boulder: Westview Press, 1980); Stephen Krasner, "State Power and the Structure of International Trade," *World Politics* 28 (April 1976), pp. 317–43; David A. Lake, "International Economic Structures and American Foreign Economic Policy, 1887–1934," *World Politics* 35 (July 1983), pp. 517–43; and Duncan Snidal, "The Limits of Hegemonic Stability Theory," *International Organization* 39 (Autumn 1985), pp. 579–614.

International Organization 42, 1, Winter 1988
© 1988 by the Massachusetts Institute of Technology and the World Peace Foundation

groups or political parties. In either case, this approach explains foreign economic policy essentially as a function of domestic politics.[2] Third, state-centered approaches view foreign economic policy as highly constrained by domestic institutional relationships that have persisted over time, and also by the ability of state officials to realize their objectives in light of both international and domestic constraints. This approach emphasizes the institutional structures of the state and the capacities of political and administrative officials who occupy positions within it.[3] Each of these three perspectives is well-represented in the literature, and no single approach currently dominates the field.

The contributions to this volume reflect and, in fact, highlight the existing diversity in approach. The authors place varying emphasis on the significance of state, society, and international system in their efforts to account for different aspects of American foreign economic policy. In addition, the authors reinterpret important historical episodes or circumstances of American policy that are not adequately explained in the existing literature. The failure of the United States to assume leadership in the interwar period, the persistence of a free-trade orientation in the 1970s and 1980s, and major turning points in American energy and East–West trade policy are among the issues for which the articles attempt to provide more compelling explanations.

Collectively, the evidence cumulated from the papers suggests two important findings. First, both system-centered approaches, which collapse the distinction between state and nation-state, and society-centered approaches, which tend to view the state as an arena for political conflict and a relatively passive political actor, could be enhanced by focusing more explicitly and positively on the role of state officials and institutions in the policy process.[4] The volume, as a whole, suggests that the state serves as an important independent or intervening variable between social and international forces, on the one hand, and foreign economic policy on the other.

Both system- and society-centered explanations of foreign economic policy treat the policymaking process as a "black box." Such a conception is

---

2. Society-centered approaches include E. E. Schattschneider, *Politics, Pressures and the Tariff* (New York: Prentice-Hall, 1935); Jonathan J. Pincus, *Pressure Groups and Politics in Antebellum Tariffs* (New York: Columbia University Press, 1977); Timothy McKeown, "Firms and Tariff Regime Change: Explaining the Demand for Protection," *World Politics* 36 (January 1984), pp. 215–33; and Peter Gourevitch, *Politics in Hard Times* (Ithaca: Cornell University Press, 1986).

3. On state-centered approaches, see Peter J. Katzenstein, "Conclusion: Domestic Structures and Strategies of Foreign Economic Policy," in Katzenstein, ed., *Between Power and Plenty* (Madison: University of Wisconsin Press, 1978), and *Small States in World Markets* (Ithaca: Cornell University Press, 1986); Stephen Krasner, *Defending the National Interest* (Princeton, N.J.: Princeton University Press, 1978); and G. John Ikenberry, "The Irony of State Strength: Comparative Responses to the Oil Shocks," *International Organization* 40 (Winter 1986), pp. 105–37.

4. Jeff Frieden's contribution to this volume is an exception, since it does not support this general finding.

most useful when it explains or predicts the pattern of a large number of cases across time or space. However, it becomes less useful when analysis, as in the present volume, focuses more closely on a small number of cases in a single country over time. In that event, we need to understand the policy process, and how domestic and international forces and constraints are transmitted through the black box of government. The articles in this volume provide insights about how one might disassemble the black box, as it were, to explain specific episodes of American foreign economic policy.

Second, state-centered approaches are limited in their explanatory power by the widespread conception of the American state as "weak" (that is, able to do little more than register the demands of private actors) relative to its own society. Several authors demonstrate empirically the limitations of the weak state conception, and seek to determine the sources of state strength and variations in it across time and issue-area. Overall, this volume suggests that, in American foreign economic policy, the state matters more, and in different ways, than previously has been appreciated. Greater attention, we conclude, should be devoted to the role and efficacy of the state.

The weak-state conception is useful in situating the American state relative to those in other advanced industrial countries. Yet it tells us little about variations in the role of the state across time and issue-area within a single country. The contribution of these articles is that they provide detailed analyses of when and how the American state has an impact on foreign economic policy, both as an actor and as an institution.

The remainder of this introduction elaborates the points already made. We examine the conceptual underpinnings of each of the three approaches, and how each currently explains American policy. We also discuss how each approach might be refined or modified, given the findings and arguments the authors raise.

System-centered explanations

Systemic-level theories are the most distinctively "international" approaches to the study of world politics and international political economy. Where both society- and state-centered approaches begin their analyses within the nation-state, systemic theories abstract from domestic politics and focus on the relative attributes of countries. In this perspective, theoretical propositions are derived only from the interrelationships and interactions among nation-states.[5]

In the explanation of foreign economic policy, some scholars argue that

5. See Kenneth Waltz, *Theory of International Politics* (Reading, Mass.: Addison-Wesley, 1979), and Robert Keohane, "Theory of World Politics: Structural Realism and Beyond," in Keohane, ed., *Neorealism and its Critics* (New York: Columbia University Press, 1986).

systemic theories deserve a certain primacy over other levels of analysis. As Robert Keohane writes:

> an international-level analysis . . . is neither an alternative to studying domestic politics, nor a mere supplement to it . . . On the contrary, it is a *precondition* for effective comparative analysis. Without a conception of the common external problems, pressures, and challenges . . . we lack an analytic basis for identifying the role played by domestic interests and pressures . . . Understanding the constraints imposed by the world political economy allows us to distinguish the effects of common international forces from those of distinctive national ones.[6]

The international system, in this view, is a necessary "first cut" in any analysis of international or comparative politics. As such, it can explain recurring international events and the commonalities in national foreign policies. This is important even in the study of foreign economic policy in a single nation-state, and it should lead the analyst to apply at least an implicit comparative standard.

Several systemic theories of relevance to American foreign economic policy have enjoyed prominence over the last decade. In particular, world systems theory, generally associated with the work of Immanuel Wallerstein, explains foreign economic policy as a function of the processes and contradictions within international capitalism. The literature on transnational relations and economic interdependence examines how international transactions, a systemic process, increase the sensitivity of one country to developments in a second, and thereby render foreign policy more contingent or strategic. And the burgeoning literature on international regimes suggests that they may constrain national policy and facilitate greater international cooperation. All of these literatures have helped shape the research agenda of international political economy, and are reflected in the articles to varying degrees.[7]

More centrally, the articles directly or indirectly address the theory of hegemonic stability. The theory is primarily intended to explain the rise and fall of international economic regimes, but it is also important as an explanation of foreign economic policy. In this context, the theory holds that a nation-state's position in the international economy decisively shapes its foreign economic policy. More specifically, dominant or "hegemonic" states have a strong preference for liberal economic regimes and possess the power to create and maintain such regimes, either by providing collective

6. Keohane's statement is found in "The World Political Economy and the Crisis of Embedded Liberalism," in John H. Goldthorpe, ed., *Order and Conflict in Contemporary Capitalism* (Oxford: Clarendon Press, 1984), p. 16.

7. See Wallerstein, *The Modern World System,* vols. 1 and 2 (New York: Academic Press, 1974 and 1978); on transnational relations, see Edward Morse, *Modernization and the Transformation of International Relations* (New York: Free Press, 1976), and Robert Keohane and Joseph Nye, *Power and Interdependence* (Boston: Little, Brown, 1977); on regimes, see Stephen Krasner, ed., *International Regimes* (Ithaca: Cornell University Press, 1982).

goods or by coercing reluctant states to participate. Hegemonic stability theory has been used primarily to account for the evolution of the postwar trade regime and the role of the United States in its creation and maintenance. It has also been applied to developments in other issue-areas, including energy and monetary policy. Over the past decade the theory has received considerable attention, but only mixed empirical support.[8]

Like all systemic-level theories, the theory of hegemonic stability identifies only the international constraints placed on nation-states. Without a theory of domestic political process, it is limited to explaining recurrent patterns of behavior within the international arena. If a scholar is seeking to explain foreign economic policy in a single country, the systemic approach alone is inadequate. As Kenneth Waltz points out, to explain how any single nation-state will respond to the constraints imposed by the international structure requires a theory of foreign policy.[9] The articles in this volume confirm this insight and demonstrate that it is necessary to unpack the "black box" of domestic politics.

Several articles take up historical episodes in American policy that either confound, or are not adequately addressed by, hegemonic stability theory. For example, Judith Goldstein finds that, during the 1970s and 1980s, American trade policy has remained surprisingly liberal, despite the country's relative decline within the international economy and the growing import penetration of key sectors of the American economy. Similarly, Michael Mastanduno finds that, although it was at the zenith of its hegemonic power in the 1950s, the United States could not maintain the East–West trade regime it preferred. Jeff Frieden and Stephan Haggard both examine the interwar years—a period generally stumbled over by hegemonic stability theory—and seek to understand why the United States was so slow in assuming a position of leadership, despite possessing the economic resources and stature associated with such a role.

In reinterpreting these episodes, the authors suggest, explicitly or implicitly, that hegemonic stability theory (and indeed, systemic theory more generally) should be refined to include a conception of domestic political process, and in particular the role of state officials and institutions. Goldstein's argument emphasizes the manner in which the dominant idea of liberalism became embodied in state institutions; this idea-institution nexus, in turn, has acted as a brake on protectionist pressures and has enabled the United States to maintain a generally liberal trade policy despite its relative

---

8. See Snidal, "The Limits of Hegemonic Stability Theory"; Keohane, *After Hegemony: Cooperation and Discord in the World Political Economy* (Princeton, N.J.: Princeton University Press, 1984); Timothy McKeown, "Hegemonic Stability Theory and Nineteenth-Century Tariff Levels in Europe," *International Organization* 37 (Winter 1983); and Peter Cowhey and Edward Long, "Testing Theories of Regime Change: Hegemonic Decline or Surplus Capacity?" *International Organization* 37 (Spring 1983). A good discussion of the theory is found in Robert Gilpin, *The Political Economy of International Relations* (Princeton, N.J.: Princeton University Press, 1987), pp. 85–92.

9. See Waltz, *Theory of International Politics*.

economic decline. For Mastanduno, the inability of the United States to determine alliance East–West trade policy at the peak of its hegemony derived not from its structural position or societal constraints, but from the contradictory nature of the goals of autonomous state officials. To maintain intra-alliance cohesion against the Eastern bloc and build liberal international economic regimes in the West, U.S. officials decided that they could not push the issue of East–West trade to the point at which it disrupted relations with Western Europe. Thus, while Goldstein's argument focuses on state institutions, Mastanduno emphasizes the importance of the interests and resources of state officials.

On the interwar period, Frieden resolves the paradox of the United States being able, yet unwilling, to lead by emphasizing the stalemate between nationalist and internationalist societal forces. So long as different parts of the state were captured by competing social forces, U.S. policy remained confused and contradictory. Only when internationalist forces began to dominate did American policy become more commensurate with the structural position of the United States. Haggard provides an alternative account, tracing the emergence of U.S. economic leadership not to the struggle of societal elements, but to effective institution-building at the level of the state. Haggard argues that State Department officials managed to exploit the crisis of the 1930s by centralizing control over trade policy and enhancing their own role in its formulation. In this way, state actors, in pursuit of their own interests, rendered U.S. policy consonant with America's structural position.

Finally, David Lake's contribution suggests a similar and more explicit refinement of hegemonic stability theory. He argues that executive branch officials within the state, who typically face a national electorate and are charged with the overall defense and welfare of the nation-state, are particularly sensitive to the constraints and opportunities of the international system and seek to adopt policies consistent with these "national interests." The principal political cleavage, in this view, is between the foreign-policy executive and the representative elements of the state—primarily the legislature—which reflect societally generated interests. Foreign economic policy is the outcome of a bargaining process between these two sets of actors. Thus, the extent to which systemic constraints are reflected in foreign economic policy is determined by the relative success of the foreign policy executive within the domestic political arena. This success, in turn, is conditioned by the structure of the state. In this approach, although systemic factors are clearly important, by themselves they cannot explain policy choice. The analyst must examine both the international system and the domestic political process.

These authors clearly take different approaches to explain foreign economic policy, and their arguments carry different implications for systemic-level theory. They all accept, however, that while it may be theoretically more parsimonious to collapse the concepts of state and nation-state, the explanation of particular cases requires a greater appreciation of the domestic political process, in particular the role and efficacy of the state. With the exception of Frieden, the authors contend that we can enhance our understanding of American foreign economic policy by focusing on the actions of executive officials or the organizational structure of the American state.

Society-centered explanations

According to the society-centered approach, explanations of foreign economic policy are found in the ongoing struggle for influence among domestic social forces or political groups. State officials or institutions play neither an autonomous nor significant intervening role in shaping or constraining policy. Rather, the theory explains foreign economic policy in terms of the interests and capacities of groups or coalitions competing within the policy arena.

While there are several variants of society-centered explanations, the interest group approach is particularly prominent in the foreign economic policy literature; it draws on pluralist theory and views policy as the outcome of a competitive struggle among affected groups for influence over particular policy decisions.[10] This approach assumes that interest group involvement is somewhat fluid and variable, as various types of groups (for example, industry associations, labor unions, consumer advocates) form alliances that are contingent on the particular issue at stake. As the issues change, so too do the interest group alliances. Policy outcomes on any particular issue are a function of the varying ability of groups to organize and give their interests prominence in the policy process. In this approach, government institutions essentially provide an arena for group competition, and do not exert a significant impact on the decisions that emerge.

The interest group approach has enjoyed analytic primacy in the literature on American trade policy.[11] This approach views the American state as

---

10. The classic statements of the pluralist perspective can be found in David Truman, *The Governmental Process: Political Interests and Public Opinion* (New York: Knopf, 1951), and Robert Dahl, *Who Governs?* (New Haven, Conn.: Yale University Press, 1963). Subsequent revisions of the pluralist approach dispute some of its elements, but retain the essense of the society-centered focus. See Theodore Lowi, *The End of Liberalism* (New York: Norton, 1969), and Charles Lindblom, *Politics and Markets* (New York: Basic Books, 1977).

11. See Schattschneider, *Politics, Pressures and the Tariff*; Pincus, *Antebellum Tariffs*; Peter Gourevitch, "International Trade, Domestic Coalitions, and Liberty: Comparative Responses to the Crisis of 1873–1896," *Journal of Interdisciplinary History* 8 (Autumn 1977); and Thomas Ferguson, "From Normalcy to New Deal: Industrial Structure, Party Competition, and American Public Policy in the Great Depression," *International Organization* 38 (Winter 1984). Also relevant is the growing literature on "rent-seeking" behavior. See Robert Baldwin, *The Political Economy of U.S. Import Policy* (Cambridge: M.I.T. Press, 1986), and Réal P. Lavergne, *The Political Economy of U.S. Tariffs* (New York: Academic Press, 1983).

essentially passive; it acts as a disinterested referee for competing groups, and supplies policies to satisfy the demands of successful domestic players. In this context, U.S. policy during the interwar period (most importantly, the Smoot–Hawley tariff) is explained as the consequence of protectionist sentiment generated by import-competing groups, while the rise of free trade in the postwar era is traced to the emergence of an internationalist, export-oriented coalition. As the growth of the U.S. economy has slowed in the 1970s and 1980s, import-competing interests have reemerged in the policy process, and their impact has been felt in the modification of America's free-trade stance.

In this volume, Frieden demonstrates the utility of a society-centered perspective, and uses it to develop a persuasive explanation for U.S. policy during the interwar period. Frieden highlights the inadequacy of system-centered approaches by arguing that the United States failed to assume the leadership role commensurate with its dominant economic power. He casts doubt on state-centered approaches by demonstrating that the state could not act as a coherent and purposive unit, since conflicting social groups captured significant parts of it. The state, and the foreign economic policy it pursued, largely reflected the ongoing struggle at the level of society. Frieden's overall argument suggests that the American state may be unable to exert a decisive, independent influence over foreign economic policy, particularly over issues where much is at stake and social forces are profoundly divided.

Other contributors subject the interest group approach and its application to more critical scrutiny. At a general level, they note the approach tends to lack theoretical rigor and predictive value, largely because it lacks an independent measure of group power. This creates problems when scholars working within this approach identify the dominant group or coalition at any time. Most analysts assess a given group's influence by observing the policy outcome, but this approach runs the risk of tautological reasoning. If the outcome of a group struggle can only be explained after the fact, the predictive value of the approach is severely limited, and explanations tend to take on an *ad hoc* character.[12]

More specifically, Lake, Goldstein, and Ikenberry demonstrate that state actors and institutions can play a critical role in shaping the manner and extent to which social forces can exert influence on foreign economic policy. Lake argues that the structure of societal interests facing the government is neither rigid nor predetermined, and shows that state officials can have an important impact by shaping the array of interest groups that contend over policy. In 1890, for instance, President Benjamin Harrison and Secretary of State James G. Blaine mobilized farmers, a previously latent group, and so enhanced their ability to internationalize American tariff policy. Along simi-

---

12. In his latest work, *Politics in Hard Times,* Gourevitch attempts to address this problem by developing a more structured conception of interest groups and coalitions.

lar lines, Goldstein contends that state institutions can shape interest groups' ability to gain access to the policy arena; the prevailing set of trade policymaking institutions channels American industry's demands for protectionism. Ikenberry takes this argument a step further, and demonstrates that the existing state institutions may influence the interests societal actors possess. In the energy sector, the existing regulatory apparatus had an onerous impact on some oil firms but provided substantial subsidies to others, and thus split what might otherwise have been a natural coalition of petroleum companies in favor of price decontrol.

Finally, Joanne Gowa's contribution attempts to specify more rigorously the conditions under which societal forces and state actors gain prominence in the policy process. For Gowa, the relative influence of state and society in foreign economic policy is likely to depend on whether or not the political "goods" in question (for example, trade, monetary policy) are susceptible to collective action. Their susceptibility, in turn, is a function not only of features intrinsic to the goods themselves, but also of the structure of state institutions within which these goods are situated.

These arguments suggest that the emphasis researchers place on society-centered approaches to explain American policy risks obscuring the critical intervening role that state actors and institutions may play in shaping the constellation and impact of interest groups in the policy process. An approach that focuses exclusively on societal groups captures only the "demand" for policy, but not its "supply"; to address the latter requires attention to the policymaking process.[13]

State-centered explanations

The state has long been the subject of social scientific inquiry, with strong roots reaching back to the continental European tradition of scholarship exemplified in the writings of Max Weber and Otto Hintze. Yet in American social science, as Theda Skocpol points out, the state traditionally has not been granted causal primacy, in deference to the dominance of society-centered perspectives.[14] Within the last ten years, however, there has been a strong revival of interest in the state, partly because we have come to recognize the limited explanatory power of more traditional pluralist and Marxist approaches. Within political science, the state has emerged as an important variable in the explanation of foreign economic policy in studies of both developing and advanced industrial societies.[15]

13. This point is raised by McKeown, "Firms and Tariff Regime Change."
14. Skocpol, "Bringing the State Back In: Strategies of Analysis in Current Research," in Peter B. Evans, Dietrich Rueschemeyer, and Theda Skocpol, eds., *Bringing the State Back In* (Cambridge: Cambridge University Press, 1985).
15. See Katzenstein, "Conclusion"; and Krasner, "State Power"; John Zysman, *Govern-*

In recent social science literature, two broad approaches linking the state to policy outcomes have developed.[16] First, what can be termed the institutional approach conceives of the state primarily as an organizational structure, or set of laws and institutional arrangements shaped by previous events. In this view, institutions, once formed, tend to endure. Institutional change is nonlinear, and occurs primarily at moments of significant crisis, such as in the wake of wars or depressions.[17] The persistence of institutions enables them to influence policy even after the ideas and coalitions that initially gave rise to them no longer dominate.

The second approach conceives of the state as an actor, and focuses directly on politicians and administrators in the executive as independent participants in the policy process. Its primary emphasis is on the goal-oriented behavior of politicians and civil servants as they respond to internal and external constraints in an effort to manipulate policy outcomes in accordance with their preferences. An underlying presumption is that these preferences are partially, if not wholly, distinct from the parochial concerns of either societal groups or particular governmental institutions, and are tied to conceptions of the "national interest" or the maximization of some social welfare function.[18]

Within the past decade, state-centered approaches to American foreign economic policy have incorporated notions of the state as an organizational structure and an actor. The most widely cited literature considers how the institutional characteristics of states influence the policy process and particularly the ability of state officials to formulate and implement foreign economic policy. This so-called "domestic structures" approach, advanced most prominently by Peter Katzenstein, suggests that nation-states differ in the extent to which their states and societies are centralized, and in the range of policy instruments available to state officials in the conduct of foreign economic policy. They also differ in the degree of autonomy state officials

---

ments, *Markets and Growth* (Ithaca: Cornell University Press, 1983); Peter Evans, *Dependent Development* (Princeton, N.J.: Princeton University Press, 1979); and Alfred Stepan, *The State and Society: Peru in Comparative Perspective* (Princeton, N.J.: Princeton University Press, 1978).

16. Skocpol, "Bringing the State Back In."

17. See Stephen Krasner, "Approaches to the State: Alternative Conceptions and Historical Dynamics," *Comparative Politics* 16 (January 1984), and James March and Johan Olsen, "The New Institutionalism: Organizational Factors in Political Life," *American Political Science Review* 78 (September 1984), pp. 734–50.

18. For example, Krasner suggests that the high-level government officials (i.e., "central decision-makers") are uniquely charged with protecting and promoting broad national security interests and thus are led to develop a distinctive and autonomous set of preferences. See Krasner, *Defending the National Interest.* Alternatively, it has been argued that the preservation of bureaucratic missions and the maintenance of control over annual budgetary resources may lead state officials to adopt preferences at variance with the interests of societal groups. See Graham Allison, *Essence of Decision* (Boston: Little, Brown, 1971), and Morton H. Halperin, *Bureaucratic Politics and Foreign Policy* (Washington, D.C.: Brookings Institution, 1974).

enjoy relative to societal forces. Given differences in these characteristics, different states can be placed along a continuum that ranges from "weak" to "strong" in relation to their own societies.

In this literature, a general consensus exists that the United States possesses a weak state.[19] That is, the American state tends to be decentralized and fragmented along bureaucratic or institutional lines, and state officials lack the range of policy instruments available to their counterparts in stronger states. As a result, we would expect that American state officials find it difficult to act purposefully and coherently, to realize their preferences in the face of significant opposition, and to manipulate or restructure their domestic environment.

As noted at the outset, while the weak state/strong state distinction may be appropriate for comparative purposes, it is of limited utility in the analysis of a single case. The contention that the American state is weak relative to that of France tells us little about the instruments available to state officials in the United States, and the impact of state institutions in trade as opposed to financial policy, or in the 1890s as opposed to the 1980s.[20] Consequently, many of the articles in this volume attempt to move beyond the weak-state characterization. They contend and demonstrate that the American state matters more and in different ways than the domestic structures literature generally appreciates. Neither individually nor collectively do they suggest, however, that a conception that views the American state as "strong" should replace the weak-state conception. Rather, the authors seek to develop contextual, empirically informed answers to the question of how and why the American state matters in the formulation and conduct of foreign economic policy.

As we have noted, Goldstein's argument emphasizes the tendency of state institutions to endure long after the decline of the social coalitions or international conditions that initially led to their creation. She explains the persistence of free trade in the altered circumstances of the 1970s and 1980s as a function of the legacy of institutional practices that took shape following the Great Depression and World War II and continue to influence the trade policy process. Haggard's analysis is relevant to this argument: he traces State Department efforts to rework domestic institutional arrangements to enhance executive power in the 1930s. In effect, Haggard analyzes the creation of the institutional framework that, for Goldstein, continues to influence current policy. Institutional factors also figure heavily in Ikenberry's

19. See Krasner, "United States Commercial and Monetary Policy"; Katzenstein, "Conclusion"; J. P. Nettl, "The State as a Conceptual Variable," *World Politics* 20 (July 1968), pp. 559–92; and Ira Katznelson, "Rethinking the Silences of Social and Economic Policy," *Political Science Quarterly* 101 (Summer 1986), pp. 307–25, especially 321–25.

20. Recent work by Helen Milner suggests that the weak state/strong state distinction may be problematic in the comparative context as well. See Milner, "Resisting the Protectionist Temptation: Industry and the Making of Trade Policy in France and the United States during the 1970s," *International Organization* 41 (Autumn 1987).

analysis: the structure of the existing petroleum regulatory apparatus not only constrained state officials in the 1970s, but also shaped or influenced the preferences of both energy producers and consumers. Finally, for Gowa, institutions are a mediating variable in a broader conceptualization of the foreign policy process. State institutions are an important determinant of the propensity for collective action, and thus for the relative influence of state and society, in a given issue-area.

Several of the articles suggest that institutional structures may, in fact, be malleable in the face of determined efforts by policymakers to overcome their constraining effects. Lake's discussion of the successful passage of freer trade legislation in 1913, for example, demonstrates that the supposedly rigid state structures, which would be expected to magnify the importance of domestic protectionist pressures, failed to block President Woodrow Wilson's liberal reform. Taking the line of argument a step further, Ikenberry emphasizes the ability of executive officials to disassemble the formidable regulatory apparatus that had come to characterize the U.S. energy sector. In effect, the reimposition of the market became the central tool of energy adjustment.

The relative significance of institutions in the explanation of foreign economic policy promises to be an important topic for future research and debate. The approach, and its implications, are discussed more fully in the conclusion.

For proponents of the state-as-actor approach, the state is neither the only significant actor, nor is it necessarily the most important. Also, they do not assume that the state always acts as a rational, unified entity. Nevertheless, in several of the cases that are examined in this volume, state officials do emerge as central actors, and play a critical role in shaping foreign economic policy. What resources does the state possess, and in what circumstances can it bring its influence to bear on the policymaking process? Drawing upon the cases, it is possible to identify three strategies available to state officials for expanding their influence in the policy process. The existence of such strategies and their effective use by state officials suggests that the American state, although decentralized and fragmented, is not necessarily as weak as it is portrayed in the domestic structures literature.

First, and related to the institutionalist perspective outlined above, the articles suggest that state officials can build new institutions to alter the distribution of power within the government or to achieve a specific goal. As Goldstein suggests, political change in the United States is often codified into new government institutions without displacing the older structures, creating a layered government of often contradictory mandates and goals. The actors involved, in other words, do not directly confront political conflict, but circumvent it through "state building" exercises in which the "winners" gain power and the "losers" maintain their trappings. Haggard examines an important case of state building in the Reciprocal Trade Agreements Act of

1934. In that case, state officials, prompted by the need to match the bilateral negotiating abilities of their European counterparts, effectively transferred tariff-setting authority from Congress to the Department of State, an institutional change necessary for the successful pursuit of the more liberal trade policy desired by Secretary of State Cordell Hull and other executive branch officials. Congress retained its ultimate authority over trade policy by stipulating that the executive's negotiating authority would have to be renewed every three years, but state officials were, nonetheless, able to achieve their aims.

Second, the state is situated at the intersection of the domestic and international political economies and is the principal national actor charged with the overall conduct of defense and foreign affairs. This unique position of the state gives executive officials a special legitimacy in the formulation and implementation of foreign economic policy that they lack in other, more "domestic" areas of public policy. As a result, state officials can redefine previously domestic issues as foreign policy issues, thereby legitimating a larger policymaking role. This strategy is seen most clearly in Lake's discussion of tariff policy in the early 1890s and Ikenberry's analysis of energy policy in the 1970s. Moreover, as Mastanduno's examination of the East–West trade case shows, if trade issues are judged to be of direct national security significance, state officials are likely to enjoy even greater authority. Officials can also use their unique position to enter into transnational coalitions, and thereby alter the stakes and outcome of political debate. Again, Lake finds this strategy effectively pursued in the case of reciprocity in 1890, and it plays an important role in Ikenberry's explanation of the successful passage of oil decontrol legislation. Mastanduno also finds that state officials entered into an alliance with the West Europeans to constrain Congress' more restrictive view of East–West trade issues.

Finally, state officials can mobilize otherwise inactive societal groups, with interests that complement their own, into the policy arena to offset their political adversaries. Since the structure of private interests facing the government tends to be somewhat fluid, it can itself become an object of political struggle. All actors, of course, can seek to mobilize public support for their goals. However, state officials often have an advantage in such a struggle; since, typically, they are less often identified with parochial interests, they can claim with greater justification to speak for the nation-state as a whole.

If state officials can enhance their influence in the political process by mobilizing societal groups, altering the structure of state institutions, and effectively utilizing their position as the principal makers of foreign policy, the cases in this volume also identify several conditions that limit the influence of state officials. Examining the standoff between the economic nationalists and internationalists in the 1920s and 1930s, Frieden emphasizes the difficulties of state action when societal actors are stalemated. Unable to mobilize greater support for a more liberal policy, state officials were forced to settle for a confused mix of mercantilist and liberal foreign economic policies that satisfied no one. Similarly, Mastanduno demonstrates how the pursuit of many complex objectives can create state "weakness." Torn between the desire to strengthen the Western alliance and the emerging system of free trade on the one hand, and the desire to limit the economic capability of the Soviet Union on the other, state officials were forced to acquiesce in Western Europe's preference for a less restrictive East–West trade policy. In both cases, state officials were stymied and their influence undermined.

Conclusion

While there does exist substantial divergence among the articles, a common theme emerges in most, if not all, of them. Specifically scholars need to rethink the role of the state when explaining foreign economic policy. This rethinking would enhance system-centered approaches, since it is the state that translates the constraints and opportunities of international structures into foreign economic policy. It would improve society-centered explanations, since state officials and institutions can shape the nature and role of interest groups in the policy process. Finally, moving beyond the general conception of the United States as a weak state, and examining more contextually the ways in which the state can have an impact on policy, would enhance state-centered explanations.

Following a conceptual contribution by Joanne Gowa, the remaining case studies in the volume are organized chronologically, beginning with David Lake's explanation of pre-World War I tariff policy, and concluding with Judith Goldstein's account of current trade policy. A concluding chapter by John Ikenberry returns to the themes raised in this introduction, and seeks to develop more fully the institutional approach to explaining American foreign economic policy.

Public goods and political institutions: trade and monetary policy processes in the United States Joanne Gowa

Basic analytic premises are at issue in contemporary debates about the U.S. foreign economic policy process. In dispute are the power structures alleged to govern the formation of American trade and international monetary policy. Thus, the literature supports both of these assumptions: the distribution of power is skewed towards private actors in the issue-area generally; the distribution of power varies according to issue-area. Within the camp of issue-specific power structures, as I shall discuss in more detail, support can be found for almost any assumption about the distribution of power prevailing, in the language of current debate, between "state and society."[1]

This debate echoes the long and still unresolved community power debate not only because of its manifest confusion about essential issues. The debate is as fundamental to larger issues in international relations as the community power debate was to central issues in American politics. The power structure governing U.S. foreign economic policymaking is assumed to have a strong influence on policy itself: state-centered structures, it is assumed, produce liberal trade policy; society-centered structures produce protection. As a consequence, reliable predictions about the U.S. commit-

Earlier versions of this article were presented at the 1985 annual meeting of the American Political Science Association, New Orleans, 29 August–1 September 1985, and at a UCLA conference on The American State in the International Political Economy, November 1985. For comments on the article, I am grateful to Frederick W. Frey, Avery Goldstein, Stephan Haggard, Robert O. Keohane, Jack Nagel, Paul Quirk, Peter Swenson, the participants in the UCLA conference, and four *IO* referees.

1. Despite its rapid growth, the state and society literature still lacks rigorous and consistent definitions of both of its critical variables. In general, of course, they are meant to distinguish public and private actors. This distinction is adequate for the purposes of this article, which largely challenge the microanalytic foundations of this literature. Successful research in comparative politics oriented along state and society lines, however, depends on the development of much more precise analytic and empirical referents for both variables than currently exist.

International Organization 42, 1, Winter 1988

ment to a liberal world-trading order depend partly on a better understanding of policy structures than we currently have.

In an effort to clarify ongoing debate, this article applies to the arena of U.S. foreign economic policymaking the logic of collective action, as affected by the specific institutions of the U.S. policy process. This approach requires a conception of American trade and international monetary policy as political goods whose susceptibility to collective action is a function both of characteristics inherent in those goods and of the institutional framework within which they are produced. As such, this article employs and extends arguments linking issue-areas and political processes that have been advanced in different contexts by Theodore J. Lowi, William Zimmerman, and James Q. Wilson.[2] To the extent that this analysis is persuasive, it suggests the need for a differentiation of political process in foreign economic policy based on variables associated with organizational choice within politically determined constraints.

As will become apparent, an analysis of the collective action problems posed by monetary and trade policy seems to challenge fundamentally the logic of the existing state and society literature. Paradoxically, however, this logic is partly resurrected when attention shifts to the institutional framework within which collective action occurs. Some discussion of the state of the art in explanations of foreign economic policymaking and of the logic of collective action must precede this argument.

The U.S. policy process: divergent views

In *Between Power and Plenty,* Peter J. Katzenstein argues that the relationship between state and society determines foreign economic policy in some historical periods. "The domestic structure of the nation-state," he contends, "is a critical intervening variable without which the interrelation between international interdependence and political strategies cannot be understood." Katzenstein arrays six advanced industrialized nations along a continuum from strong to weak states in relation to their societies, and places the United States at the weak-state end of the continuum. There (and in Britain), he asserts, ". . . the coalition between business and the state is relatively unfavorable to state officials and the policy network linking the public with the private sector is relatively fragmented."[3]

2. Theodore J. Lowi, "American Business, Public Policy, Case-Studies, and Political Theory," *World Politics* 16 (July 1964), pp. 677–715; James Q. Wilson, *Political Organizations* (New York: Basic, 1973), chap. 16; William Zimmerman, "Issue Area and Foreign-Policy Process: A Research Note in Search of a General Theory," *The American Political Science Review* 67 (December 1973), pp. 1204–12. For a recent typology that explicitly includes public goods, see Leonard Champney, "Public Goods and Policy Types," paper prepared for the annual meeting of the American Political Science Association, New Orleans, 29 August–1 September, 1985.

3. Peter J. Katzenstein, ed., *Between Power and Plenty: Foreign Economic Policies of*

Although Katzenstein maintains that "state power . . . varies according to whether one analyzes the definition of objectives or the implementation of foreign economic policy," he does not distinguish state strength along the more conventional issue-area lines.[4] Some of the contributors to his book, however, do. In discussing the American case, Stephen D. Krasner, for example, asserts that the state is much stronger in the arena of international monetary policy than in the arena of foreign trade policy. "The laws and practices affecting America's foreign commercial policy," he observes, "illustrate the fragmentation and diffusion of power that can exist for particular issue-areas in the American political system. The problem has been much less acute for monetary policy," where, according to Krasner, "U.S. leaders . . . have had a relatively free hand. . . ."[5]

Neither Katzenstein's emphasis on domestic structures nor Krasner's insistence on distinguishing between money and trade has been universally acclaimed. Arguing that power is not a highly fungible resource, John Zysman objects to Katzenstein's approach: ". . . a government's ability to act in one policy arena will be very different from its ability to act in another. . . . The policy tasks in each sector vary, as does the pattern of interest organization. Consequently, a state's 'strength'—the ability to formulate and implement policy—varies with its capacity to execute these different tasks."[6]

Krasner has been attacked from both sides: although they agree that the power of the state varies across issue areas, some scholars dispute his view that the U.S. state is weak in trade, while others object to his view that it is strong in international monetary policy.[7] Thus, Judith Goldstein argues, for example, that the weakness of the American state in foreign commercial policy has been exaggerated: the persistence of a liberal U.S. trade policy, despite domestic opposition to that stance, she maintains, "suggests an ability on the part of the U.S. government to retain its autonomy from society. That autonomy is a result of the ideological adherence of central decision makers to the tenets of free trade."[8] A detailed study of the politics

Advanced Industrialized States (Madison: University of Wisconsin Press, 1978), pp. 3, 21. In a more recent work, Katzenstein applies a similar analytic framework to Switzerland and Austria, arguing that "liberal capitalism" in the former and "democratic socialism" in the latter condition the different responses of each to changing international markets. See his *Corporatism and Change: Switzerland, Austria, and the Politics of Industry* (Ithaca and London: Cornell University Press, 1984).

4. Katzenstein, *Between Power and Plenty*, p. 20.

5. Stephen D. Krasner, "United States Commercial and Monetary Policy: Unravelling the Paradox of External Strength and Internal Weakness," in ibid., pp. 64, 66.

6. John Zysman, *Governments, Markets, and Growth: Financial Systems and the Politics of Industrial Change* (Ithaca and London: Cornell University Press, 1983), p. 297.

7. Krasner himself has argued that the U.S. state is strong in the area of foreign raw materials investment. See his *Defending the National Interest: Raw Materials Investment and U.S. Foreign Policy* (Princeton, N.J.: Princeton University Press, 1978).

8. Judith L. Goldstein, "A Domestic Explanation for Regime Formation and Maintenance: Liberal Trade Policy in the U.S.," paper prepared for delivery at the annual meeting of the

of U.S. trade from 1953 to 1962 also demonstrated to the satisfaction of its authors that the influence of special interest groups on American trade policy has been overstated.[9]

On the monetary side, conversely, some observers contend that the U.S. state has evidenced less autonomy than might be expected of a strong state. They do not agree among themselves, however, on the factors that allegedly limit the American state's power in this policy arena. Thus, Jeff Frieden asserts that bankers, in particular, have played a large role in setting U.S. international monetary policy; I have argued that the size and structure of the domestic economy constrains the freedom of American officials in this sphere of policy.[10]

Were Krasner's original argument compelling or the counterarguments it provoked consistent with each other, both heat and light might have been shed on the character of the U.S. foreign economic policymaking process. Neither, however, has been wholly the case. Krasner argues that the American state is more powerful in establishing monetary than trade policy in large part because the monetary policymaking process is more insulated. "Decisions about monetary policy," he contends, "have been taken in the White House, the Treasury Department, and the Federal Reserve Board, arenas that are well insulated from particular societal pressures."[11] Yet, in the next breath, Krasner seems to suggest that institutional insularity *per se* is less significant in explaining the difference than the relatively greater activity of pressure groups in trade: "Private actors rarely saw how monetary decisions related to their specific interests and therefore did not press for greater access to the decision-making system."[12]

Krasner attributes the observed activity pattern of pressure groups partly to their inability to relate international monetary policy easily to their own tangible economic interests.[13] Krasner's emphasis on the intellectual barriers to interest group activity in monetary policy is typical of other work on U.S. foreign economic policy formation. John S. Odell observes, for example:

American Political Science Association, Washington, D.C., 30 August–2 September 1984, pp. 13–14. For a further development of her general argument and an empirical test of it, see her "The Political Economy of Trade: Institutions of Protection," *American Political Science Review* 80 (March 1986), pp. 161–84.

9. Raymond A. Bauer, Ithiel DeSola Pool, and Lewis Anthony Dexter, *American Business and Public Policy: The Politics of Foreign Trade,* 2d ed. (Chicago: Aldine-Atherton, 1972).

10. Jeff Frieden, "The Internationalization of U.S. Finance and the Transformation of U.S. Foreign Policy, 1890–1940," paper prepared for delivery at the annual meeting of the American Political Science Association, Washington, D.C., 30 August–2 September, 1984; Joanne Gowa, *Closing the Gold Window: Domestic Politics and the End of Bretton Woods* (Ithaca and London: Cornell University Press, 1983).

11. Krasner, "United States Commercial and Monetary Policy," p. 65.

12. Ibid.

13. Krasner also notes, however, the role of the norm of fixed exchange rates in establishing the pattern of interest group activity, an important observation to which I will return.

Here we have [three] counterintuitive cases in which interested groups did not act on behalf of their supposed interests. What accounts for these cases? One ready explanation would be the esoteric nature of the subject of international monetary policy and ignorance on the part of group leaders. Put another way, the causal chains from dollar devaluation to group welfare are multiple and difficult for even specialists to weigh, contrary to simple assumptions about group interest. In contrast, group leaders more readily grasp the net consequences of raising and lowering trade barriers for their sectors, and they are therefore far more active on trade policy.[14]

Robert O. Keohane, Joseph S. Nye, and I have also linked the scarcity of interest groups in the international monetary policy process to the nature of monetary policy itself.[15]

When interest groups are routinely engaged on other issues as seemingly arcane as international monetary issues, however, it is not easy to attribute the absence of pressure group activity to the esoteric nature of its subject. The Occupational Safety and Health Administration (OSHA), for example, is beset by group pressures whenever it proposes changing the permissible level of industrial chemicals in the workplace; congressional representatives contemplating seemingly obscure details of banking deregulation also experience interest group pressures. International monetary policy should be no more intellectually inaccessible to the groups it affects than other issues, which are hopelessly obscure only to those without a clear stake in them. The rise in the dollar exchange rate during the early 1980s, moreover, provided anecdotal evidence that export- and import-competing industries clearly understood the relationship between their shrinking market shares and U.S. exchange-rate policy.

Thus it seems unlikely that intellectual barriers to entry can explain the differences that are alleged to exist between the U.S. trade and monetary policy processes. Nor, in fact, does it seem likely that the conventional distinction between commercial and financial policy actually distinguishes correspondingly different political processes: these can vary not only *between* money and trade but also among issue-areas *within* monetary and trade policymaking. Frieden's observations of a weak state in the arena of international debt, for example, may be perfectly consistent with Krasner's emphasis on a strong state in exchange-rate policy. Similarly, state strength in American commercial policy may be a function of the particular trade

14. John S. Odell, *U.S. International Monetary Policy: Markets, Power, and Ideas as Sources of Change* (Princeton, N.J.: Princeton University Press, 1982), p. 347. As is true of Krasner, however, Odell's explanation is not monocausal: he also attributes the relative scarcity of pressure group activity to norms that established a "taboo" against pressures for devaluation, to the availability of alternatives to devaluation, and to the nature of the U.S. economy. See ibid., p. 347.

15. Robert O. Keohane and Joseph S. Nye, *Power and Interdependence: World Politics in Transition* (Boston: Little, Brown, 1977); Gowa, *Closing the Gold Window,* p. 134.

policy at issue. We can distinguish these issues and structures analytically
by relying on insights that are drawn from the literature on collective action
and embedded within the institutional framework of U.S. foreign economic
policymaking.

The logic of collective action

Contrary to at least the conventional interpretation of pluralist theory, Mancur Olson argued in 1965 that the expectation that groups would act effectively on their shared interests rested on a fallacious assumption.[16] Interest
groups supposedly exist to secure collective goods for their members. Paradoxically, however, collective goods greatly inhibit group activity. Olson
points out that this occurs because collective or public goods possess two
attributes that distinguish them from private goods: 1) they exhibit "non-
rivalry" in consumption (that is, one individual's consumption of the good
does not interfere with any other individual's ability to consume it); and 2)
they are "non-excludable" (that is, it is either "impossible, or at least very
costly" to prevent any individual from consuming the good, once it is supplied, whether or not he has paid for it[17]).

These characteristics imply, Olson observed, that each potential member
of a large group will refuse to pay his share of the costs of producing the
group's good. Rational individuals will seek to "free ride" on the contributions of others in the group, and the collective good, without certain
countervailing conditions, is therefore unlikely to be provided at all. This
sometimes unfortunate outcome is attributable to two factors: the cost of an
individual's contribution is likely to exceed the benefit returned to him as a
result of his contribution; and the "inconsequentiality problem" or the assumed independence of individual decisions in large groups.[18]

Thus, large groups are unlikely to successfully provide themselves with
collective goods unless they can overcome the free-rider problem. This can
occur, Olson asserts, through two routes: the use of selective incentives or
coercion. Large groups can induce individuals to contribute to common
purposes if group membership makes the individual eligible to receive selec-

16. Mancur Olson, *The Logic of Collective Action: Public Goods and the Theory of Groups*
(Cambridge: Harvard University Press, 1965).

17. Robin W. Boadway and David E. Wildasin, *Public Sector Economics,* 2d ed. (Boston:
Little, Brown, 1984), p. 57.

As Duncan Snidal argues, non-excludability implies non-rivalry. See Snidal, "Public Goods,
Property Rights, and Political Organizations," *International Studies Quarterly,* 23 (December
1979), pp. 534–44.

18. For Olson's discussion of large groups, see his *Logic of Collective Action.*

tive incentives—"gains that are private or subject to some form of exclusion"[19]—that exceed the cost of contribution. Large groups can also induce contributions if group membership is compulsory: the introduction of closed shops, for example, led to a rapid increase in unionization.[20]

Small groups encounter less difficult collective action problems. Brian Barry observes that "where the beneficiaries form a small group in close contact with one another, the assumption that . . . [individuals'] decisions are independent of one another cannot be upheld."[21] Moreover, in a small group, the individual's share of the incremental increase in the collective good his contribution produces may exceed the costs of that contribution. Thus, a small group may successfully organize itself for collective action, although the level of collective goods produced is likely to be suboptimal.

Basing an analysis even in part on the logic of collective action requires some sensitivity to the weaknesses of this analytic framework. The utility function that Olson attributes to individuals deciding whether to contribute to the production of collective goods is clearly too narrow to capture the interests of actors in all political and social situations.[22] Olson is vulnerable as well on the issue of selective incentives: if members join an organization that supplies collective goods because of the selective incentives it offers, it seems reasonable to assume that another organization not burdened with supplying collective goods would be able to supply the private goods more cheaply.[23] Russell Hardin points out, in addition, that while the provision of selective incentives or the "by-product theory . . . can make sense of contributions to an ongoing political organization, it does not seem to explain how it is that many groups got started in the first place," nor does "political entrepreneurship" provide a suitable substitute.[24]

More fundamental, perhaps, is the charge that the logic of collective ac-

19. V. Kerry Smith, "A Theoretical Analysis of the Green Lobby," *American Political Science Review* 79 (March 1985), p. 132.

20. Olson, *The Logic of Collective Action*, p. 68.

21. Brian Barry, *Sociologists, Economists, and Democracy* (London: Macmillan, 1970), p. 25.

22. See Russell Hardin, *Collective Action* (Baltimore: Johns Hopkins University Press for Resources for the Future, 1982), p. 72; and John Mark Hansen, "The Political Economy of Group Membership," *American Political Science Review* 79 (March 1985), p. 82.

23. George J. Stigler, "Free Riders and Collective Action: An Appendix to Theories of Economic Regulation," *Bell Journal of Economics and Management Science* 5 (Autumn 1974), p. 360.

24. Hardin, *Collective Action*, pp. 34, 36. Hardin comments:

. . . the incentive of personal career may seem more suited to explaining ongoing than newly emerging organizations. Jimmy Hoffa owed his great power in the Teamsters Union in large part to his efforts to strengthen and expand the union, thereby enhancing the prosperity of its members. One may be less inclined to suppose that, say Joe Hill, the 'poet laureate' of the Wobblies who was executed in Utah in 1915 on a murder charge that was believed by many to be a frame-up for his strike activities, was motivated by his own career prospects as an eventual union leader (p. 36).

tion predicts much more severe social and political problems than actually exist. The "basic 'economic man' model . . . correctly identifieś the 'free rider' problem as absolutely crucial," notes Howard Margolis, "but it rather overkills this issue. The conventional economic model not only predicts (correctly) the existence of problems with free riders but also predicts (incorrectly) such severe problems that no society we know could function if its members actually behaved as the conventional model implies they will."[25] Analogously, Barry argues that such relatively widespread phenomena as voting make no sense when viewed in terms of Olson's logic; similar arguments could be made about social revolutions and urban riots.[26]

Although "the logic" of collective action, at least as Olson expressed it, does not seem to hold universally across all contexts, it nonetheless does provide a powerful explanation of collective action (or its absence) in some important situations. The theory seems least vulnerable to criticism when we apply it to the context within which it was originally advanced: economic interest groups. Since these groups are the focus of this article, an application of even a theory of collective action that is somewhat limited empirically may prove useful.

Collective action in money and trade

We can easily explain prevailing patterns of interest group activity in the U.S. foreign economic policy process by examining the very different collective action problems presented by trade and monetary policy. The concentration ratios in U.S. industry that permit small groups to organize successfully for collective action does not by itself distinguish commercial from financial policy. Because it is more excludable, however, trade policy presents fewer problems for collective action than does monetary policy. As a consequence, interest groups are far more active in it, and the trade policy process appears more fragmented than does its financial counterpart.

Industrial concentration in the United States potentially offers a small group solution to the collective action problems that confront interests with a stake in foreign economic policy. This conclusion follows from the definition of a small group, in which the number of potential members of any group is less critical to determining whether it is "small" or "large" than is the size of any subgroup that would benefit if it alone provided all of the group's good—the size of what Thomas Schelling refers to as a "k" group.[27]

25. Howard Margolis, *Selfishness, Altruism, and Rationality: A Theory of Social Choice* (Cambridge: Cambridge University Press, 1982), p. 6.

26. Barry, *Sociologists, Economists, and Democracy*, chap. 2. For an attempt to explain contributions to urban riots within a collective action framework, see T. David Mason, "Individual Participation in Collective Racial Violence: A Rational Choice Synthesis," *American Political Science Review* 78 (December 1984), pp. 1040–56.

27. See Hardin, *Collective Action*, p. 41.

Thus, as George Stigler points out, "the small number solution has a wider scope than a literal count of numbers would suggest. The size distribution of individuals is highly skewed when these individuals have a size dimension (sales of firm, property of family). The large individuals in a group may therefore properly view themselves as members of a small number industry if their aggregate share of the group's resources is large." For industry, using the Herfindahl measure of concentration, Stigler adds that "many, many industries fulfill in good measure the small number condition."[28]

Highly concentrated industries may satisfy the small number condition conducive to collective action, but this fact does not by itself distinguish the monetary from the trade arena in terms of predictions of pressure group activity. *A priori,* there is no reason to expect that industries with an interest in trade policy would be more highly concentrated than industries affected by international monetary policy: indeed, in many cases, the sets of industries affected by either policy would be identical. Observable variations in pressure group activity must instead be a function partly of differences in the "excludability" of political goods sought in each issue-area.

The excludability of non-rivalrous goods can vary: as Michael Laver notes, "goods may be more or less excludable, the degree of 'excludability' being measured by the costs of exclusion, relative to the benefits to the excluder." Laver asserts that control over exclusion can theoretically be exercised even over the service provided by a lighthouse, which is a frequently cited example of a pure public good: ". . . I could surround the entire area within which the lighthouse was visible with a minefield, and issue the directions for safe passage only to those whom I wished to use it. . . ."[29]

The political goods an industry receives as a result of collective action may be excludable partly as a consequence of variations among firms in the product mixes they produce. As Stigler observes:

28. Stigler, "Free Riders and Collective Action: An Appendix to Theories of Economic Regulation," p. 362.

The Herfindahl index is "the sum of squares of the sizes of firms in an industry where size is the percentage of total industry assets." See Kenneth W. Clarkson and Roger Leroy Miller, *Industrial Organization: Theory, Evidence, and Public Policy* (New York: McGraw-Hill, 1982), p. 72.

29. Michael Laver, "Political Solutions to the Collective Action Problem," *Political Studies* 28 (June 1980), p. 198. Laver adds about the lighthouse, however: ". . . in practice, this would probably be unfeasible, and almost certainly not economically worthwhile."

In fact, lighthouses once produced private goods in England: shipowners were "assessed . . . at the docks. Ordinarily only one ship was in sight of the lighthouse at a particular point in time. The light would not be shown if the ship (which was identified by its flag) had not paid." Edwin Mansfield, *Microeconomics: Theory/Applications,* 5th ed. (New York: Norton, 1985), p. 494.

For an extensive discussion of the early British lighthouse system that allegedly demonstrates that economists are wrong when they point to a lighthouse as an example of a public good requiring government supply, see R. H. Coase, "The Lighthouse in Economics," *Journal of Law and Economics* 17 (1974), pp. 357–76, quotation at 376.

The smaller firms in an industry seldom make the full range of products: they specialize in a narrower set of products. Hence, if they are not represented in the coalition, they may find that their cheap ride is to a destination they do not favor. The proposed tariff structure may neglect *their* products; the research program may neglect *their* processes; the labor negotiations may ignore *their* special labor mix.[30]

Trade legislation in the United States provides another route to excludability. This legislation routinely incorporates several provisions sanctioning protection against imports that, in effect, transform the public good (or ill) of free trade into a partly excludable good. Escape clauses, peril points, and national security clauses, for example, have all been written into legislation at various times in the postwar period. All these provisions permit protection against import competition to be extended on an industry basis.[31] In addition, specific trade acts sometimes prohibit tariff concessions on the products of particular industries: the Trade Expansion Act of 1962, for example, "actually exempted a small number of industries from [tariff] cuts, mainly the 14 industries which had received escape clause treatment before 1962 . . . , and petroleum and certain petroleum products which had received special status under the national security clause in 1959. . . ."[32]

The avenues of protection provided by Congress and implemented by the executive branch suggest that trade policy can be and has become in some instances a highly excludable good. The Short Term Arrangement on textiles concluded in 1961 specified sixty-four categories of cotton textiles; the orderly marketing agreements (OMAs) concluded in footwear in the late 1970s covered "all nonrubber footwear except zoris, disposable paper footwear, and wool felt footwear."[33] That small or even privileged groups are, as a consequence, empowered to pursue their collective interests in import protection is also suggested by the experience with voluntary export restraints (VERs) in steel: in 1984, Bethlehem Steel and the United Steelworkers of America filed an escape clause petition, opposed by other steel producers, that resulted eventually in the government's approval of relief to the steel industry.[34] The successful petition for import protection filed in 1982 by

---

30. Stigler, "Free Riders and Collective Action," p. 362. Emphasis in original.

31. The escape clause (introduced in 1951) permits tariff concessions to be withdrawn if they increase imports, causing, or threatening to cause, serious injury to an industry; the peril point (introduced in 1948, eliminated in 1949, reintroduced in 1951, and eliminated again in 1962) required the establishment of a level below which tariffs for a particular industry could not be reduced; the national security clause (introduced in 1955) allows almost any measure necessary to protect national security. Réal P. Lavergne, *The Political Economy of U.S. Tariffs: An Empirical Analysis* (Toronto: Academic, 1983), p. 34.

32. Ibid., p. 28.

33. David B. Yoffie, *Power and Protectionism: Strategies of the Newly Industrializing Countries* (New York: Columbia University Press, 1983), pp. 85, 189.

34. A privileged group is one in which one member has enough interest in the collective good that he will supply it even if he bears its entire cost.

Other producers opposed escape clause action because they were concerned that it might end

Harley-Davidson, the only American manufacturer of large motorcycles, suggests that control over exclusion can sometimes be extensive enough to transform trade policy into a private good.[35]

I am not suggesting that collective action by industries seeking protection from imports is easily achieved or ultimately successful. Control over exclusion is rarely extensive enough to eliminate the public character of trade policy: a protectionist coalition's ability to keep free-riding firms from consuming the benefits of import protection, for example, will vary with the extent to which the products of those firms are substitutes for the products of firms within the coalition.[36] It will also vary with the height of barriers to entry into the industry.[37]

Nor do opportunities for small group action guarantee the successful organization of those groups. Even in theory, small groups may fail to act effectively because their members cannot agree on an acceptable distribution of the costs or benefits of collective action. A small group also almost inevitably confronts free-rider problems, making the group itself unstable unless discount rates and valuations of the good do not vary at all among its members.[38] In practice, moreover, small groups in industry may be more difficult to organize than concentration ratios suggest, in part because industries (and even individual firms) are not always homogeneous with respect to interests in trade protection: highly competitive and declining firms within a single industry will not find common ground in import protection. Nor, as empirical studies demonstrate, is the political process responsive solely to interest group pressures.[39]

---

the 1982 U.S.-EEC steel trade agreement. See Robert S. Walters, "Industrial Crises and U.S. Public Policies: Patterns in the Steel, Automobile, and Semiconductor Experiences," in W. Ladd Hollist and F. LaMond Tullis, eds., *International Political Economy Yearbook*, vol. 1. (Boulder: Westview, 1985), p. 164.

35. Technically, because any manufacturer of large motorcycles gained the same protection, trade policy in this instance was not a private good. In practice, however, the only consumer of the protection granted was Harley-Davidson.

36. As observed by Robert E. Baldwin in remarks at a National Bureau of Economic Research (NBER) Conference on the Political Economy of Trade Policy, Dedham, Mass., 10–11 January, 1986.

37. For an analysis of the underexplored issue of the life cycle of import protection that emphasizes the influence on that cycle of the height of entry barriers, see Vinod Aggarwal, Robert O. Keohane, and David B. Yoffie, "The Evolution of Cooperative Protectionism," paper presented at a NBER Conference on the Political Economy of Trade Policy, Dedham, Mass., 10–11 January 1986.

38. Laver, "Political Solutions," pp. 203–4.

39. In a recent attempt to explain the inter-industry pattern of U.S. import protection, Robert E. Baldwin tests five different models against various indicators of U.S. protection. He concludes that the pattern cannot be adequately explained by models that are based on short-run self-interest, including pressure group models. He emphasizes, however, that "an eclectic approach to understanding [U.S. trade policy] . . . is the most appropriate one currently." The relative explanatory power of different models, he argues, cannot be accurately assessed "until the various models are differentiated more sharply analytically and better empirical measures for distinguishing them are obtained. . . ." See his *The Political Economy of U.S. Import Policy* (Cambridge, Mass: MIT Press, 1985), p. 180.

On the other hand, the contrast between trade and international monetary policy in terms of ease of organization for collective action remains instructive. Consider exchange rates, for example. For those groups hurt by the rise in the effective exchange rate of the dollar—whether under Bretton Woods or the subsequent floating-rate system—a dollar devaluation was a distinctly non-excludable good: no individual could be prevented from benefiting from the change, whether or not he had contributed to it. Thus, there was no conceivable excludability for groups adversely affected by the overvaluation of the dollar.

Nor does it seem possible that any small group could organize for collective action on exchange rates: it seems highly implausible that the benefits to members of any small group would exceed their costs in seeking the public good of a lower dollar exchange rate. Given that particular groups can seek import relief to compensate for exchange-rate change, action on exchange rates seems even less probable. Again, although there has been some pressure group activity on U.S. exchange-rate policy in the very recent past, what remains most impressive—as perhaps with riots and revolutions—is not how much, but how little activity has occurred, given the damage that the rise of the dollar during the early 1980s inflicted on export and import-competing industries.

A first cut suggests, then, that the relative costs of collective action might explain why interest groups more strongly impact U.S. trade than U.S. international monetary policy. Deeper analysis makes it clear, however, that a sharp distinction between costs of group action in trade and money is misleading: neither policy arena, in reality, imposes homogeneous opportunities or constraints on collective action by groups that have a stake in the process. This heterogeneity offers some leverage for explaining why observers differ among themselves about the power of actors in the U.S. foreign economic policy process.

Disaggregating trade policy, for example, suggests that the costs of collective action can vary widely even in an arena some observers consider a paradigmatic case of interest group vulnerability. Logically, barriers to pressure-group entry into the policy process should be much higher when a major shift in trade policy is under consideration than when a more narrowly drawn policy is at stake. Proposed shifts from protection to free trade or from a unilateral to a multilateral process of tariff determination should impose prohibitive costs on group activity, because they confront affected interests with the classic problems of collective action that afflict large groups. OMAs, VERs, and similarly scaled trade issues, on the other hand, seem expressly designed to facilitate pressure-group formation. As a consequence, the trade process will not be populated uniformly by pressure

Baldwin also provides an excellent review of recent empirical efforts to explain U.S. tariffs in his "The Political Economy of Protection," in Jagdish N. Bhagwati, ed., *Import Competition and Response* (Chicago: University of Chicago Press, 1982), pp. 263–86.

groups, and the roles that public and private actors play, even within the realm of trade policy, will vary. Thus, Goldstein can accurately attribute "essentially liberal" policy to the major role of the state in the U.S. policy process, while, with equal accuracy, Krasner can insist that interest groups enjoy easy access to, and significant influence over, the policy process.

We can apply a similar analysis to international monetary policy. Thus, exchange rates, international reserve creation, and the nature of the monetary system are high-cost collective action issues: each affords few opportunities for excluding free riders or for organizing small groups. This is not true, however, of either capital controls or international debt. For example, capital controls need not be applied uniformly: when the United States imposed the Interest Equalization Tax in 1964, it exempted Canada, Japan, and the less developed countries. Although no firm evidence exists on this point, investment banks with large stakes in these markets might have contributed to this outcome.[40] International debt also presents opportunities for exclusion, as the lead banks may exclude from subsequent loan consortia banks that refuse to participate in collective action in this area. In addition, the concentration of foreign lending among U.S. banks permits small groups to form on issues related to foreign lending.[41]

In general, then, the costs of collective action presented by specific issues would appear to provide a more compelling basis for distinguishing the power of actors in the foreign economic policy process than would either institutional insularity or intellectual barriers to group action. On logical grounds alone, "weak" states should be no more pervasive in trade than "strong" states are in monetary policy: the power of actors will vary instead as the public character of political goods varies. However sparse, available data do suggest that the political processes relevant to specific issues may less resemble others *within* than across the conventional divide of trade versus monetary policy.[42]

Implicit in this argument is a fundamental challenge to the state and society literature. The argument suggests that the state–society relationship is not as fundamental to political analysis as is the potential for collective action that inheres in particular political goods. Because the power of state

40. This example should not be weighted heavily. The exemptions seem to have been more closely related to national security than to industry interests.

41. In the United States, "the 25 largest banks account for over three-quarters of U.S. overseas bank lending. For these banks, foreign business averages nearly half of total business." Jeff Frieden, "International Finance and Domestic Politics: Financial Internationalization and the United States," mimeo, May 1985, p. 13, cited by permission.

42. Some evidence suggests, for example, that both capital controls and international debt issues have precipitated more interest group activity than have other issues within the sphere of international monetary policy. See Odell, *U.S. International Monetary Policy*; Keohane and Nye, *Power and Interdependence*; and Gowa, *Closing the Gold Window*. Although much more evidence is available on the relationship between interest groups and trade policy (see note 39), few definitive conclusions have emerged, and attempts to compare rigorously trade and monetary policy processes seem nonexistent.

and society apparently derives from existing collective action problems that vary widely across issues, the logic of state and society interpretations appears flawed. The distribution of power over policy becomes a function not of macro but of microanalysis: power can be inferred less accurately from domestic structures than from the degree of publicness inhering in particular political goods.

As with other issue-area typologies, however, this one cannot stand alone. In reality, whether a political good is public, private, or somewhere in between does not inhere only in the good: it is also a function of existing markets in these goods, and these are established by political institutions.

Institutions and markets for political goods

Because they typically analyze choice among available alternatives, most economists and rational choice theorists do not closely examine how any given set of alternatives is itself determined.[43] Among the more powerful determinants of any particular array of choices are institutions—the rules organizing, as Alexander James Field puts it, "the interaction of two or more individuals. A hospital, school, army, firm, or church is an institution, but the essence of these organizations lies not in the physical buildings associated with these entities, but in the rules, formal and conventional, which organize the behavior of individuals within them."[44]

Institutions strongly influence the character of political goods and associated patterns of interest group activity. Whether a good is public or private is not only a function of its attributes; it is also a function of the institutional framework that produces it. Political rules of the game, in part, establish whether the government controls exclusion over what could be treated as non-excludable goods. As Duncan Snidal argues, few goods are unalterably non-excludable: "Shipping lanes, lighthouse beams, or TV signals seem to display extreme publicness. But techniques ranging from demands for tribute by Barbary Coast pirates to ship licenses to cable television reveal our ingenuity in assigning property rights and achieving some degree of exclusion."[45] Whether potentially public goods are treated as such is determined

43. Douglass C. North observes that institutions "establish the cooperative and competitive relationships which constitute a society and more specifically an economic order. When economists talk about their discipline as a theory of choice and about the menu of choices being determined by opportunities and preferences, they simply have left out that it is the institutional framework which constrains people's choice sets." *Structure and Change in Economic History* (New York: Norton, 1971), p. 201.

44. Alexander James Field, "The Problem with Neoclassical Institutional Economics: A Critique with Special Reference to the North-Thomas Model of Pre-1500 Europe," *Explorations in Economic History* 18 (April 1981), p. 183, note 13.

45. Snidal, "Political Organizations," p. 545.

by political institutions, or what Snidal refers to as the prevailing system of property rights: that *"system of mechanisms which serves to permit exclusion of goods and uniquely to determine the beneficiaries of (and losers from) that exclusion."*[46]

Brief reflection clearly shows that the public character of the specific goods of trade and monetary policy resides as much in the political institutions that produce them as in the goods themselves. Foreign economic policy can be administered as a public good, from which exclusion is impossible, or as, in Snidal's term, a "quasi-public good," "an erstwhile public good [that] has had payment and exclusion mechanisms attached to it by a central authority structure."[47] Thus, we can imagine a political universe in which trade policy is not excludable at all, just as it is possible to imagine a regime in which excludability is pervasive. The former would not sanction any exceptions to free trade, for example, and the latter would provide protection against import competition on demand. Similarly, we can conceive of domestic political regimes in which exchange-rate policy is administered as a public good, and of regimes in which exchange controls transform it into a highly excludable good.

Nor need imagination serve as the only way to examine the influence of institutional variation on the public character of political goods, even within a single country. In the United States in 1930, the concentration of power over tariffs in Congress suppressed the public character of "national" trade policy: the Smoot–Hawley tariff of that year came close to the sum of individual industry demands, accurately mirroring dominant attitudes at the time.[48] By 1934, however, Congress had shifted much of its tariff authority to the executive branch and sanctioned a negotiated approach to tariff-setting; both moves restored some of the public character to trade policy and thus "substantially reduced the probable impact of pressure groups" on U.S. tariff levels.[49]

On a smaller scale, we can also observe changes over time in the political market for U.S. international monetary policy, with corresponding changes in the costs to affected interests of collective action on particular issues. The public character of monetary policy was enhanced when the Nixon administration abandoned the capital controls used by successive administrations in the 1960s and early 1970s, which eliminated a feasible target for interest group activity. But costs of collective action in other areas—notably exchange rates—have fallen in the recent past, although for reasons that em-

---

46. Ibid., emphasis in original.
47. Ibid., pp. 558–59.
48. Similarly, in the 1820s, congressional responses to claims for protection were "conditioned by belief [sic] in the efficacy of protection and its proper place in the development and defense of the nation." Jonathan J. Pincus, *Pressure Groups and Politics in Antebellum Tariffs* (New York: Columbia University Press, 1977), p. 169.
49. Lavergne, *Political Economy*, p. 20.

phasize the importance of international, rather than domestic institutions as the source of variation in the public character of political goods. Almost until the collapse of the Bretton Woods system, its fixed exchange rates and the dollar's value were regarded as immutable: as Krasner observes, ". . . until the late 1960s, virtually all sectors of the American elite regarded both the value of the dollar and fixed exchange rates as graven in stone and beyond the tampering of mere mortals."[50] In contrast, under a floating exchange-rate system, the value of the dollar came to be considered of legitimate concern to both Congress and industry. Thus, the costs of collective action in exchange-rate policy have fallen over time within the United States—however, because that policy is largely the residual of domestic macroeconomic policy, they remain prohibitive for interest groups other than those "piggybacking" on the activities of other groups.

Because of their influence on the public or less-than-public character of political goods, institutions strongly impact interest groups' potential for effective action. Within the United States, the public or private character of trade and monetary policy has shifted over time, as institutional structures have changed. This shift implies that, while an analysis of incentives for collective action may yield information about the distribution of power prevailing in various areas of foreign economic policy at any time, it will not address other important questions about the process: the pattern of incentives itself, for example, can be explained only by understanding the creation and evolution of the political institutions that establish incentives for collective action as a by-product of public goods definition.[51]

This emphasis on institutions as a determinant of collective action costs partially restores the logic of state and society analyses with, however, some significant caveats. The power of states and societies to determine foreign economic policy is conditioned by constraints on the publicness of political goods that either inhere in or are imposed on the goods by international and domestic political institutions. If issues cannot stand alone as predictors of foreign economic policy processes, neither can states and societies.

Conclusion

Because of important variations within each broad issue-area, efforts to distinguish power structures in U.S. foreign economic policy exclusively on the basis of differences between trade and monetary policy are destined to

50. Krasner, "Commercial and Monetary Policy," pp. 65–66.

51. For an analysis that emphasizes the fundamental changes in appropriate conceptions of and policy responses to issues that occur when they are seen over rather than at a single point in time, see John Gerard Ruggie, "Social Time and International Policy: Conceptualizing Global Population and Resource Issues," in Margaret P. Karns, ed., *Persistent Patterns and Emergent Structures in a Waning Century* (New York: Praeger, 1986), pp. 211–36.

prove futile. The alleged intellectual inaccessibility of international monetary policy is not the critical barrier to interest group activity: it is much more likely that the insuperable obstacles are the public character and invulnerability to small group action of *some* issue-areas within monetary policy. Analogously, debates about power structures in trade need to focus more closely on particular issues within the broad category of commercial policy. Major decisions on national trade policy present very different incentives for collective action than do more narrowly drawn decisions. This implies a weak logical foundation to any argument that posits a uniform distribution of political power across the entire U.S. trade policy process.

In short, an analysis of incentives for collective action seems likely to identify power structures in foreign economic policymaking more accurately than either institutional insularity or subject matter. Largely anecdotal evidence from the United States suggests that policy processes do conform to expectations generated by this analytic framework: thus, interest groups are active on international debt and banking issues, as Frieden observes; they appear virtually nonexistent in U.S. exchange-rate policy, as Krasner and others observe; their presence is marked in escape clause actions. Some cross-national data also suggest a relationship between incentives for group activity and foreign economic policy processes: Katzenstein's study of seven small European states, for example, effectively links highly public liberal trade policies to high degrees of democratic corporatism.[52] Whether the hypotheses that can be derived from this framework can be successfully operationalized and tested remains to be seen, but no insuperable obstacles are apparent.

Even as it stands, however, an analysis of incentives for organizational action raises red flags both for issue-area typologies and for state and society models. Emphasis on the variable publicness of trade and monetary policy tends to vitiate the logic of state and society distinctions; attention to the role of political institutions in establishing the public or "quasi" public character of goods in the political marketplace partly—but only partly— resurrects it. The U.S. case raises warning flags for both because it reveals that the defining characteristics of issues are neither obvious nor immutable, and it simultaneously demonstrates how easily "weak" states can metamorphose into "strong" states as the public character of political goods varies.

Because we assume that power structures influence policy content, their clarification is of more than academic interest. By rendering trade policy an excludable good, the current U.S. system awards interest groups an influence over public policy that, predictably, leads to a host of exceptions to liberal trade; these exceptions are not found in systems that constrain interest groups more heavily. The future of the U.S. commitment to a liberal

52. Peter J. Katzenstein, *Small States in World Markets: Industrial Policy in Europe* (Ithaca and London: Cornell University Press, 1985).

world trading order consequently depends in part on the evolution of its foreign economic policymaking system. As long as U.S. presidents remain committed to the existing international economic order, and as long as Congress does not radically change prevailing exclusionary mechanisms, the United States is unlikely to abandon the premise of free trade that constrains, however imperfectly, protectionist pressures. Changes in either, however, would alter the U.S. commitment to liberal trade.

Thus, foreign economic policy processes in the United States, and elsewhere to a less significant extent, play a more significant role in determining the nature of the international economic order than is sometimes acknowledged. Complex interactions among domestic policy processes, international power, and political outcomes create high risks for hypotheses, including those described in this article, whose explanatory or predictive power rests almost exclusively on variables that look either outward to the international system or inward to the domestic policy process.

The state and American trade strategy in the pre-hegemonic era David A. Lake

Trade policy is commonly seen as a product of domestic interest group politics. Despite the obvious economic distortions introduced by trade barriers, protectionism recurs, we are often told, because producers organize more readily than consumers and dominate the political process. In this "demand side" explanation of protection, the state is seen as the empty receptacle of societal bargaining with no independent voice or role.

This article seeks to challenge the analytic primacy accorded to domestic interest groups, and to develop the preferences and role of the state in the formulation of trade policy. I focus on trade *strategy,* where strategy is used in its game theoretic sense to indicate contingent or interdependent decision-making among self-seeking nation-states.[1] All trade policy is strategic, at the most basic level: every import is someone else's export. Every change in policy, including both increases in protection and free trade, affects the utility of others. Trade strategy, in the narrower sense I use, however, refers to policies contingent upon the actions of other nation-states or explicitly intended to manipulate the preferences and policies of others.

Interest-group explanations typically overlook this strategic dimension of trade policy. When focusing on Congress and the domestic political bargains

An earlier version of this article was presented at the annual meeting of the American Political Science Association, New Orleans, 29 August–1 September, 1985. Parts of this essay are drawn from my *Power, Protection and Free Trade: International Sources of U.S. Commercial Strategy, 1887–1939* (Ithaca, N.Y.: Cornell University Press, forthcoming 1988). I would like to thank Beverly Crawford, Jeff Frieden, Judith Goldstein, Joanne Gowa, Cynthia Hody, G. John Ikenberry, Wendy K. Lake, Michael Mastanduno, Timothy McKeown, John Odell, and four anonymous reviewers for their many helpful comments. They are, of course, absolved from responsibility for any and all shortcomings that remain. The generous financial support of the Academic Senate and International Studies and Overseas Programs at the University of California, Los Angeles, is gratefully acknowledged.

1. See Avinash Dixit, "Strategic Aspects of Trade Policy," mimeo, Princeton University, January 1986; see also the growing literature on "strategic trade policy." For a review, see Gene M. Grossman and J. David Richardson, "Strategic Trade Policy: A Survey of Issues and Early Analysis," in Robert E. Baldwin and J. David Richardson, eds., *International Trade and Finance,* 3d ed. (Boston: Little, Brown, 1986), pp. 95–114.

International Organization 42, 1, Winter 1988

inherent in the legislative process, tariff-making often appears as anything but rational and sensitive to strategic concerns. This article, on the other hand, makes two general analytic claims that dispute this received wisdom. First, even in the late nineteenth and early twentieth centuries, when interest groups clearly dominated the congressional tariff-making process, an important *strategic* component nonetheless existed. Second, state leaders within the executive branch most clearly recognized and acted upon strategic trade concerns. In developing these arguments, I examine two important policy innovations: the "internationalization" of the tariff between 1887 and 1894, when the tariff was reconceptualized from an instrument of domestic protection into a lever to further open the markets of Latin America for United States exports; and the fight for, and eventual triumph of, "freer trade" in 1913.

American trade policy in the late nineteenth and early twentieth centuries is a least likely crucial case study for both of the arguments I develop. Given the generally acknowledged importance of interest groups, Congress' domination of the policy process, the weak executive,[2] and the distributive nature of the trade issue-area, trade policy is not likely to be strategic, and to the extent that it is, the executive is likely to be rather inconsequential. In the cases below, however, both these expectations are overturned.

This article is divided into three major sections. The first develops a simplified model of the roles and interests of society and the state in the trade policymaking process. Sections 2 and 3 examine the McKinley Tariff of 1890 and Wilson–Gorman Tariff of 1894, and the Payne–Aldrich Tariff of 1909 and Underwood Tariff of 1913, respectively. The conclusion summarizes the issues raised in the cases and examines their implications.

The state, private interests, and trade policy

Trade policy is typically perceived, at least in the United States, as the essence of domestic politics. E. E. Schattschneider and his followers generalized his case study of tariff-making in 1930 into a theory of interest group politics.[3] Likewise, Theodore Lowi used trade policy as the springboard for his typology of public policy.[4] Within this perspective, trade policy is dominated by private, societal interests while the government—often equated with the legislature—is passive. As Frank W. Taussig, author of the classic

2. In the historiography of American trade policy, the critical role played by Woodrow Wilson in the passage of the Underwood Tariff of 1913, which I shall discuss, is often treated as an anomaly. While Wilson's case is perhaps more self-evident than others, I argue that Wilson's actions were merely part of a larger history of important executive intervention in the process of trade policymaking.

3. E. E. Schattschneider, *Politics, Pressures and the Tariff* (New York: Prentice-Hall, 1935).

4. Theodore Lowi, "American Business, Public Policy, Case-Studies, and Political Theory," *World Politics* 16 (December 1964), pp. 677–715.

study of American tariffs, wrote in discussing the Payne–Aldrich Tariff of 1909, "There was the same pressure from persons engaged in industries subject to foreign competition, the same willingness to accede to their demands without critical scanning."[5] As Taussig implies, "society-centered" approaches to trade policy explain protection from the demand side. Private interests demand; the government then willingly supplies.

The society-centered or demand side explanation of protection is most clearly developed in endogenous tariff theory.[6] Assuming that individuals are rational utility maximizers, and recognizing that a tariff approximates a "public good" benefiting all producers of a protected item whether or not they participate in efforts to obtain it, this approach explains the structure of protection across industries as a result of two factors: the costs of organizing for collective action and the intensity of desire, related to the comparative disadvantage of the industry. As the cost of protection (that is, higher intermediate and final goods prices) are dispersed while the benefits (that is, higher producer profits) are concentrated, endogenous tariff theorists conclude that a small number of homogeneous and geographically concentrated producers facing significant import competition are most likely to organize and articulate their demands to the legislature. In this framework, articulation is akin to success. As Timothy McKeown writes, "The arguments are predictive only under 'normal' conditions—i.e., when the government is responsive to these societal demands."[7]

Recent quantitative tests of endogenous tariff theory have found, however, that interest-group pressures, while important, do not fully explain the pattern of protection. The cases examined below suggest a similar conclusion. Real P. Lavergne and Robert E. Baldwin both argue that we must also examine the "principled behavior" of the state to provide a more complete explanation.[8] Yet the origin and nature of this principled behavior, and the role and interests of the state, remain theoretically underdeveloped.

Whereas society-centered explanations focus on demands, state-centered approaches concentrate on the "supply side." State-centered approaches do not ignore the demands placed upon the government by society, but they do assert that the state is at least relatively autonomous and an active participant in the policymaking or supply process. The government, therefore, does not simply respond to societal demands. Rather, the state possesses

5. Frank W. Taussig, *The Tariff History of the United States,* 8th ed. (New York: Putnam, 1931), p. 407.

6. This literature is now quite large. See, in particular, Richard E. Caves, "Economic Models of Political Choice: Canada's Tariff Structure," *Canadian Journal of Economics* 9, no. 2 (1976), pp. 278–300; and Jonathan J. Pincus, *Pressure Groups and Politics in Antebellum Tariffs* (New York: Columbia University Press, 1977).

7. "Firms and Tariff Regime Change: Explaining the Demand for Protection," *World Politics* 36 (January 1984), p. 216.

8. Réal P. Lavergne, *The Political Economy of U.S. Tariffs* (New York: Academic Press, 1983). Robert E. Baldwin, *The Political Economy of U.S. Import Policy* (Cambridge: MIT Press, 1985).

interests and makes choices that are central to understanding policy. In this perspective, analyzing the demand for and supply of protection is necessary to provide a complete explanation of trade policy.

In the analysis of trade policy, the state can be usefully disaggregated into two principal components.[9] The representative element of the state includes the legislature, which serves as the principal link of the state to society, and the "constituent" agencies, such as the Departments of Agriculture, Commerce, and Labor in the United States. Following the endogenous tariff theories already discussed, I assume that legislators are primarily motivated by the desire for re-election and are therefore responsive to societal demands.[10] Thus, individual members of the legislature, in one form or another, represent constituencies organized on a geographic basis. Where the legislature is organized into substantive committees, these subunits also serve to represent functional societal interests. Constituent agencies are of lesser importance, but serve a similar function as the legislature. Possessing narrow institutional mandates, these agencies are easily "captured" by the interests they are designed to serve.[11] Capture can occur directly, through the appointment of interested personnel, or indirectly, as decision-makers come to identify their own career interests and success with the well-being of their constituents. As the principal link between state and society, the representative elements are the least autonomous parts of the state. Indeed, they can be understood as merely reflecting the interests of society.

The foreign policy executive constitutes a second component of the state.[12] Defined as the high-ranking bureaucrats and elected executive

9. The conception of the state I develop reintroduces a degree of bureaucratic and "intra-branch" politics into the study of the state. On the former, see Graham T. Allison, *Essence of Decision* (Boston: Little, Brown, 1971); and Morton H. Halperin, *Bureaucratic Politics and Foreign Policy* (Washington, D.C.: Brookings Institution, 1974). For the latter, see Robert A. Pastor, *Congress and the Politics of U.S. Foreign Economic Policy, 1929–1976* (Berkeley: University of California Press, 1980).

Another important element of the state may be the economic agencies, such as the Treasury Department, Office of Management and Budget, and the Federal Reserve Bank in the United States. Compared to the constituent agencies, the economic agencies possess broad, society-wide institutional mandates. Most of these agencies are primarily concerned with the macroeconomy, and specifically growth, employment, and inflation, or, before the Keynesian revolution, the stability of the government budget and money supply. Other economic agencies, however, such as the Japanese Ministry of International Trade and Industry, are also concerned with the long-term economic development of the country. Whether focusing on the macroeconomy or economic development, these broader mandates allow the economic agencies to avoid capture by particularistic interests, rendering the agencies at least relatively autonomous.

10. This assumption is central to Anthony Downs, *An Economic Theory of Democracy* (New York: Harper, 1957), and is now widely accepted in public choice models of politics. See also David Mayhew, *Congress: The Electoral Connection* (New Haven: Yale University Press, 1975).

11. On bureaucratic capture, see Marver H. Bernstein, *Regulating Business by Independent Commission* (Princeton, N.J.: Princeton University Press, 1955); and Grant McConnell, *Private Power and American Democracy* (New York: Knopf, 1967), pp. 246–97.

12. This distinction between the executive and legislature is hardly novel. See Baldwin, *The Political Economy of U.S. Import Policy,* and Pastor. But the argument I present departs from the existing literature and gives form and content to executive preferences by deducing them from the constraints and opportunities of the international economic structure.

officials charged with the overall conduct of defense and foreign affairs, the foreign policy executive sits at the intersection of the domestic and international political systems and regulates interactions between the two.[13] Most importantly, the foreign policy executive is the sole authoritative foreign policymaker and the only national actor mandated to preserve and enhance the position of the nation-state within the anarchic and competitive international system. It is charged, in other words, with husbanding the nation-state's wealth and power, given the interests and actions of other countries.

This unique position of the foreign policy executive renders it particularly sensitive to strategic trade considerations and, in turn, to the international economic structure that shapes these national trade interests.[14] The societal pressure brought to bear on the policymaking process through the representative element of the state *must* differ from the strategic preferences and desires of the foreign policy executive for two reasons. First, societal interests cannot cumulate into strategic trade preferences. Producer groups possess relatively narrow interests. They support protection if facing import competition in their own markets, and oppose it only if threatened with retaliation on their products abroad. Groups have little incentive to oppose protection on their own products if another industry is likely to bear the costs of foreign retaliation. In the pursuit of national wealth and power, and in responding to its national rather than regional electorate, the foreign policy executive must take precisely these sorts of trade-offs into account and make judgments about what is good for the country as a whole. It must also choose the appropriate means to obtain these goals, given the opposition or resistance of foreign national and state actors. Thus, if collective action problems exist, as they surely do, and only *some* groups mobilize or become manifest, there is no reason to assume that the "bottom-up" interests of society will be identical to the "top-down" strategic trade preferences of the foreign policy executive. Indeed, the greater the problems of collective action within society, the more these two interests must diverge.

Second, to the extent that the executive's strategic trade preferences are shaped by considerations of relative advantage over other countries, as might be expected within an anarchic and competitive international environment, the interests of the representative and foreign policy elements of the

13. Otto Hintze first made this point in "Military Organization and the Organization of the State," in Felix Gilbert, ed., *The Historical Essays of Otto Hintze* (New York: Oxford University Press, 1975).

14. The concept of the international economic structure is developed in David A. Lake, "International Economic Structures and American Foreign Economic Policy, 1887–1934," *World Politics* 35 (July 1985), pp. 517–43; "Beneath the Commerce of Nations: A Theory of International Economic Structures," *International Studies Quarterly* 28 (July 1984), pp. 143–70; and *Power, Protection, and Free Trade: International Sources of U.S. Commercial Strategy 1887–1939* (Ithaca, N.Y.: Cornell University Press, forthcoming 1988). In the cases I shall discuss, I empirically develop the link between the international economic structure and national trade strategies. One can agree with the argument about the role of the foreign policy executive without necessarily accepting the theory of international economic structures, although I obviously believe the two are mutually reinforcing.

state must also diverge. In the pursuit of material interests, no group in society—even encompassing coalitions—has any incentive to maximize the *relative* resources or power of the nation-state. Group interests may, at times, complement this power interest, but they possess very different roots.

I do not argue that the executive is entirely free from societal constraints. Presidents and prime ministers must periodically stand for election. Yet where the representative element of the state can be best understood as acting in the interests *of* society, to use Pareto's famous distinction, the executive acts in the interests *for* society.[15] The executive is responsible to all of society, charged with responsibility for foreign affairs, and is specifically concerned with strategic trade considerations.

Given the existence of competing trade interests within the domestic political arena, the foreign policy executive will rarely be able to translate its strategic trade preferences directly and unilaterally into policy. In few countries is trade policy entirely within the purview of the foreign policy executive. Trade strategy affects society and the representative element of the state can be expected to block, or at least partially undermine, foreign policy initiatives. Foreign policy leaders are dependent, as a result, upon the support, or at least the acquiescence, of society and the representative element of the state.

To achieve its strategic trade preferences, the foreign policy executive must bargain with the politically mobilized groups in society as manifested in the representative element of the state. Many contextual factors ultimately determine how the conflict between these sets of interests is resolved, and how successfully the executive realizes its aims. Two intervening variables, however, are important in the cases discussed below.

Most fundamentally, the bargaining process is influenced by the distribution of authority within the state, as codified into existing laws and institutions and referred to here as state structure.[16] State structure does not necessarily determine the outcome of the bargaining process between the representative and foreign policy elements of the state. By specifying which elements of the state possess authority over an issue and which actors can legitimately be involved in the political process, on the other hand, state structure does create a set of constraints within which the bargaining process occurs and a pattern of politics that endures over time.

The decentralized structure of the American state and the constitutional delegation of authority over international commercial policy to Congress

15. Stephen D. Krasner, *Defending the National Interest: Raw Materials Investments and U.S. Foreign Policy* (Princeton, N.J.: Princeton University Press, 1978), p. 12.

16. Peter J. Katzenstein, "Conclusion: Domestic Structures and Strategies of Foreign Economic Policy," in Katzenstein, ed., *Between Power and Plenty: Foreign Economic Policies of Advanced Industrial States* (Madison: University of Wisconsin Press, 1978).

isolates the foreign policy executive from the trade policymaking process. Even with the passage of the Reciprocal Trade Agreements Act in 1934, an event often interpreted as signaling the enhancement of the executive's role in trade policy, the foreign policy executive has still been dependent upon continued grants of authority from the legislature. In the time period I examine, moreover, Congress reigned supreme in the international commerce arena and the foreign policy executive deliberately had to penetrate an otherwise closed policymaking process. The principal task for foreign policy leaders during this period, then, was to gain legitimacy in and access to the trade policymaking arena. Given its unique position and interests, on the one hand, and its limited access, on the other, we can expect two patterns of politics or bargaining. First, the foreign policy executive will use its position at the intersection of the domestic and international political systems to redefine issues as foreign policy concerns and build transnational coalitions that support its preferred policies. Second, it will mobilize new or existing societal groups with complementary interests into the political system to gain access to the representative element of the state. In short, the American foreign policy executive is expected to use its position to appeal to the public, define the political debate, and conduct foreign policy to build support for its strategic goals.

At a more proximate level, presidential or executive leadership is also important in explaining the outcome of the bargaining process between the representative and foreign policy elements of the state. Presidents bring to office differing conceptions of appropriate executive–legislative roles and varying degrees of political acumen. While it is difficult to generalize about these idiosyncracies, a president who has a strong view of his policymaking role or highly developed political skills is clearly more likely to attain his goals when faced with legislative opposition.

To sustain the conception of trade politics that I advance, it is not necessary to demonstrate that society plays no role in the formulation of policy. Clearly policy does respond, at least in part, to societal demands. This idea is incorporated into the argument already set forth. It is necessary to show, however, that societal demands alone cannot account for observed policies, and that the foreign policy executive acted in the expected manner to shape the adopted policy.

I now turn to an examination of the foreign policy executive's role in formulating American trade strategy in the country's pre-hegemonic era. Each of the following sections proceeds in three steps. First, I outline the structure of the international economy and the corresponding strategic trade preferences of the relevant nation-states. Second, I identify the trade strategy interests of the foreign policy executive in each tariff act and the extent to which these interests are reflected in the final policy. Third, I briefly examine the reasons for the success or failure of the executive in realizing its objectives.

Internationalizing the tariff, 1887–1894

Between 1887 and 1894, foreign policy leaders reconceptualized American trade strategy and "internationalized" the tariff. Following the Civil War, protection was paramount; all other trade issues were subordinated to the need for domestic tariff protection. Beginning in 1887, however, a new consensus emerged among foreign policy leaders on the need for a more differentiated policy in which the tariff would continue to protect American industry from import competition *and* assist in the expansion of exports, particularly to Latin America, through selected reductions in duties on raw materials. By internationalizing the tariff, foreign policy decision-makers sought to redirect the trade of their southern neighbors—previously dominated by Great Britain—away from Europe and towards the United States. Foreign policy leaders, in other words, attempted to preserve America's protective system while changing the policies and actions of other countries through manipulations of the tariff.[17]

This important policy innovation cannot be explained simply by the desires and actions of domestic interest groups. While several sectors ultimately benefited from the innovation, many beneficiaries initially opposed the new strategy. Other supporters were mobilized into the tariff-making process only under the vigorous encouragement of foreign policy leaders (discussed below). The new trade strategy, in short, was conceived and orchestrated by the foreign policy executive.

During the late nineteenth century, the international economic structure and the trade strategy preferences of other countries were particularly propitious for the United States. America's rising relative labor productivity and growing international competitiveness combined to create new export opportunities. Manufacturers could now compete with their European counterparts on an equal footing, while American farmers continued to make the nation the bread basket of the world. Foreign policy leaders recognized the potential gains to the United States if they broadened and deepened this process of ongoing export expansion by further opening up foreign markets. At the same time, foreign policy leaders did not believe that a general reduction in American protection was necessary to accomplish this goal.

The ability of the United States to simultaneously pursue export expansion and import protection depended upon the structure of British hegemony. Although no longer as dominant as it was earlier in the century, Britain was still the largest and most productive country within the international economy. Britain's position and role as hegemonic leader had two implications for American trade strategy. First, the United Kingdom strongly preferred universal free trade, but, in seeking to lead by example, it was willing to tolerate protection abroad rather than retaliate in kind. This

---

17. The trade strategy discussed in this section is developed in significantly more detail in chap. 3 of my book, *Power, Protection, and Free Trade*.

dominant British strategy of free trade at home enabled the United States (and others) to safely free ride on the United Kingdom's leadership. As Britain's dominant strategy removed any fear of retaliation, the United States was able to insulate itself from British competitors while confidently continuing to ship over half of its exports to the United Kingdom.

Second, Britain also pursued a policy of free trade in its colonies and in other areas of the developing world.[18] The United Kingdom encouraged "open door," or non-discriminatory, tariffs; promoted a dependence on exports of raw materials and imports of finished products; and, through foreign investment, established the infrastructure necessary for foreign trade.

Like Britain, the United States singled out Latin America as an area of fruitful expansion, at least in part because of the region's relatively high level of economic development and well-established patterns of trade.[19] Also important for the United States was the region's geographic proximity, which provided an economic advantage while fitting into a larger political strategy of American regional dominance.[20]

Most American products entered Latin American markets on relatively equal terms with those of Britain and other European producers. In several cases, particularly in railroad equipment and construction and shipbuilding, equality of opportunity was insufficient to displace the special trading relationships between British producers and their Latin American consumers. In these areas, the United States sought more favorable or preferential access to the market. In other instances, most notably agriculture, Europeans had not developed the market or established trade because they lacked a comparative advantage. In these areas, the United States had to cultivate its own export markets without European assistance. The road towards United States export expansion in Latin America, in short, had already been paved; the United States merely needed to extend and reshape it to fit its own requirements.

Thus, as a result of the structure of British hegemony and the trade strategies followed by other countries, the United States had few incentives to reduce its own high tariffs. Britain would not retaliate, and export expansion to Latin America required only selective concessions on items of interest to the countries of that region, primarily raw materials. The contradiction between simultaneous export expansion and import protection could be easily overcome through a differentiated tariff that maintained the existing struc-

---

18. See Albert H. Imlah, *Economic Elements in the Pax Britannica: Studies in British Foreign Trade in the Nineteenth Century* (Cambridge: Harvard University Press, 1958); S. B. Saul, *Studies in British Overseas Trade, 1870–1914* (Liverpool: Liverpool University Press, 1960).

19. See, for example, Carlos F. Diaz Alejandro, *Essays on the Economic History of the Argentine Republic* (New Haven, Conn.: Yale University Press, 1970), pp. 1–66.

20. On American policy towards Latin America, see Walter LaFeber, *The New American Empire* (Ithaca, N.Y.: Cornell University Press, 1963).

ture of protection while encouraging exports through selective reductions in duties.

Two nearly identical versions of the strategy of export expansion and import protection were adopted between 1887 and 1894. Both centered on continued high industrial tariffs while reducing duties on a limited number of raw materials exported by Latin America. Within this common framework, however, differences were evident at the margin. Democrats supported an extensive platform of duty-free raw materials, but removed only the tariff on raw wool in the Wilson–Gorman Act of 1894. This would, the party argued, expand American exports—primarily agricultural products, steel, and railroad materials—to the wool-producing areas of the world, although *de facto* the policy was limited to Latin America's southern cone.[21] Republicans, on the other hand, advocated bilateral reciprocity treaties between the United States and various Latin American nations, in which the former would admit sugar, coffee, tea, and raw hides free of duty while the latter would grant, in return, preferential duties on a specified list of American agricultural and manufactured items. This policy was embodied in the McKinley Act of 1890 and the several reciprocity agreements negotiated in its wake.

Both these specific policies, and the larger trade strategy they reflect, originated within the foreign policy executive. The reconceptualization of the tariff from an instrument of protection into a tool of both protection and export expansion began with President Grover Cleveland. In his 1887 annual message to Congress, Cleveland called for duty-free raw materials to cheapen the costs of manufacture, lower prices, and increase exports. The duty-free raw materials platform had been articulated as early as 1866 by David Ames Wells, then commissioner of revenue. Nonetheless, Cleveland was the first high-level politician to endorse the proposal, a move that startled Congress and the nation. Developed within a small group of advisors during a meeting at the president's summer retreat, "Oak View," the 1887 tariff message was recognized by supporters and detractors alike as a bold stroke of executive leadership that reshaped the political agenda.[22] Roger Q. Mills, chairman of the House Ways and Means Committee, soon introduced Cleveland's proposal in Congress. The Mills Bill, as it was known, passed in the Democratic House, but was defeated in the Republican-dominated Senate for largely partisan reasons.

Cleveland's proposal formed the basis for the "Great Debate" in the presidential election of 1888, in which challenger Benjamin Harrison defeated the incumbent. James G. Blaine, the new secretary of state, soon proposed a policy that paralleled the Democrat's "duty-free raw materials" platform.

Blaine, a moderate protectionist, had long been interested in expanding

21. Lake, *Power, Protection and Free Trade*, chap. 3.
22. See Tom E. Terrill, *The Tariff, Politics, and American Foreign Policy, 1874–1894* (Westport, Conn.: Greenwood Press, 1973), pp. 109–40.

trade to Latin America. In 1889, after defeating Cleveland for the presidency, Harrison asked Blaine to preside over the State Department, not only because of the secretary's position within the Republican Party, but also because of their similar views on foreign affairs, particularly commerce with Latin America.[23] Indeed, during the 1888 campaign, Harrison echoed Blaine's well-known views on expansion, declaring that "we do not mean to be content with our market. We should seek to promote closer and more friendly commercial relations with the Central and South American States."[24]

After the election, Blaine immediately began organizing an International American Conference—invitations had already been issued by Cleveland. In the conference, Blaine proposed the creation of an inter-American customs union, an idea that was rejected by the conference in favor of bilateral reciprocity treaties between interested countries of the region. Failing in his grander proposal, Blaine then focused his attention on the concept of reciprocity.[25]

While the International American Conference was in session, the House of Representatives began debating a new tariff bill drafted by Republican William McKinley of Ohio, then chairman of the House Ways and Means Committee. In this bill, McKinley proposed to take the duty off raw sugar and coffee, "necessities" of life that the United States did not produce in sufficient quantities to meet the home demand, impose duties on raw hides for the first time in twenty-five years, and raise the tariff on raw wool. The latter two actions, Blaine feared, would needlessly antagonize the Latin American nations, with whom he was then actively negotiating; the former would take away his only bargaining chip, as over 87 percent of Latin American exports already entered the United States duty-free.[26] Blaine succeeded in maintaining hides on the free list and in moderating the increased duty on raw wool, but he failed to convince Congress on the importance of using sugar, coffee, and other products as instruments of reciprocity. The House passed the McKinley bill on 21 May 1890 without provision for reciprocity. Blaine then turned his attention to the Senate, and appeared before the Finance Committee in an emotional plea for reciprocity. Despite his efforts, the committee reported the bill to the full Senate with free sugar and without provision for reciprocity.

23. Most telling in this regard is a letter from Harrison to Blaine dated 17 January, 1889, reprinted in Albert T. Volwiler, *The Correspondence Between Benjamin Harrison and James G. Blaine, 1882–1893* (Philadelphia: American Philosophical Society, 1940), pp. 44–45.

24. Cited in Terrill, *The Tariff, Politics, and American Foreign Policy*, p. 134.

25. For a discussion of the International American Conference and its results, see Alice Felt Tyler, *The Foreign Policy of James G. Blaine* (Minneapolis: University of Minnesota Press, 1927), pp. 165–90.

26. Terrill, *The Tariff, Politics, and American Foreign Policy*, pp. 162–63; Tyler, *James G. Blaine*, pp. 184–87; and David Saville Muzey, *James G. Blaine: A Political Idol of Other days* (New York: Dodd, Mead, 1935), pp. 437–51.

The congressional leadership resisted reciprocity for three reasons. First, Blaine could not guarantee that under his plan sugar would enter free of duty. Raw sugar was the single largest revenue item in the tariff, providing 23 percent of all tariff revenue and 13 percent of all federal government revenue in 1888. The growing federal budget surplus in a deflationary era was the Achilles' heel of protectionists; tariff reformers, including Cleveland, had used the issue to good effect. By placing sugar on the free list, protectionists hoped to reduce the surplus and remove an important issue from partisan debate.[27] Fearful of leaving domestic sugar growers unprotected, however, Congress also provided a direct subsidy of approximately $7 million a year to these producers, both to solidify their political support and further reduce the budget surplus.

Second, congressional leaders failed to see the importance of foreign markets. McKinley stated this most directly:

> We do not depreciate the value of our foreign trade; we are proud of it. It is of great value and must be sacredly guarded, but what peculiar sanctity hangs about it which does not attach to our domestic trade? . . . If our trade and commerce are increasing and profitable within our own borders, what advantage can come from passing it by, confessedly the best market, that we may reach the poorest by distant seas?[28]

Third, congressional leaders appear to have believed that, even if exports required stimulation, the tariff was not the proper instrument. As McKinley declared in his opening speech on the bill, "I am not going to discuss reciprocity . . . I leave that to the illustrious man who presides over the State Department under this Administration and to my distinguished friend, the Chairman of the Committee on Foreign Affairs of this House [Mr. Hitt]. This is a domestic bill; it is not a foreign bill."[29]

On 4 June, Blaine sent Harrison the final report of the International American Conference, which contained the recommendation on reciprocity, along with a letter in which he detailed the impediments to trade with South America and demonstrated that European trade in the region was increasing while the trade of the United States was decreasing. The United States, he argued, would be the greatest beneficiary of reciprocity. President Harrison submitted Blaine's letter and the report to Congress on 19 June, under a cover letter in which he threw his full support behind reciprocity.

Blaine then stepped up his efforts to publicize reciprocity, taking his case directly to the public through letters and public speeches. In a widely reprinted letter written to Senator William R. Frye, Blaine stated that:

> I do not doubt that in many respects the tariff bill pending in the Senate is a just measure and that most of its provisions are in accordance with

27. Muzzey, *James G. Blaine*, p. 442.
28. *Congressional Record*, 51st Congress, 1st session, 1890, pp. 4253–54.
29. Ibid., p. 4250.

the wise policy of protection; *but there is not a section or a line in the entire bill that will open a market for another bushel of wheat or another barrel of pork.*[30]

Blaine's efforts now began to meet with considerable success. At least one member of the House Ways and Means Committee, who was from a Western state and a bitter opponent of reciprocity, complained that "Blaine's plan has run like a prairie fire all over my district."[31]

Meanwhile, President Harrison, through quiet behind-the-scenes diplomacy, searched for compromise language which would allow for both free sugar and reciprocity. On 25 July, Senator Nelson Aldrich, on behalf of the Senate Finance Committee, introduced an amendment, apparently drafted within the White House, that fulfilled this task.[32] It was adopted with few revisions on 10 September. The House continued to resist the concept of reciprocity, however, and acceded to the Senate amendment only after several conference committee meetings and seven days' of Republican caucuses.

While Cleveland's plan for tariff reform had not been clearly spelled out in the 1884 election and no strong actions were taken during the early years of his administration, he nonetheless staffed his first cabinet with committed tariff reformers.[33] Cleveland was often criticized for delaying the 1887 tariff message. Yet Cleveland believed that if he "had announced the policy earlier the country would not have been ready for it."[34] His stand was at least partially vindicated by his successful re-election to the presidency in 1892.

Cleveland was also committed to expanding exports to Latin America. Cleveland issued the invitations for the International American Conference, at which Blaine presided. During his second administration, Cleveland first appointed as secretary of state Walter O. Gresham (1893–95) and later Richard C. Olney (1895–97). Both men were committed expansionists who—with the president's backing—led the nation into an extremely active political role in Latin America. During this administration, the United States intervened in the Brazilian Revolution of 1894, the dispute over the Mosquito Coast in Nicaragua, and the Venezuelan Boundary Crisis of 1895–96 to limit and reduce British influence in the hemisphere and expand American commercial and political ties in the region.[35]

The 1894 tariff was drafted by Democrat William L. Wilson of West Vir-

30. Ibid., pp. 4253–54. Emphasis added.

31. Quoted in Muzzey, *James G. Blaine*, p. 447; and Gail Hamilton, *Biography of James G. Blaine* (Norwich, Conn.: Henry Bull, 1895), p. 687. This quotation has been widely reprinted. The original source, the speaker, and the context are never identified.

32. On Harrison's role in drafting the reciprocity amendment, see Harrison to Blaine, 23 July 1890, in Volwiler, *Correspondence*, pp. 111–12.

33. Terrill, *The Tariff, Politics, and American Foreign Policy*, pp. 109–11.

34. George F. Parker, *Recollections of Grover Cleveland* (New York: Century, 1909), p. 104.

35. LaFeber describes three episodes in American expansion, pp. 210–29 and 242–83.

ginia, chairman of the House Ways and Means Committee and a Cleveland
intimate who had participated in the 1887 Oak View conference. As passed
by the House, the Wilson tariff contained the full list of duty-free raw materials requested by the president. The bill encountered considerably stronger
resistance in the more protectionist Senate.[36] In the upper house, the Democrats possessed only a slim majority, which had already been weakened by
the deep conflict over the repeal of the Sherman Silver Purchase Act in 1893.
The Wilson bill, as passed by the House, removed the subsidy to domestic
sugar producers, but left raw sugar on the free list to avoid abrogating the
reciprocity agreements signed under the McKinley Act. Two senators from
Louisiana strongly resisted the proposal, and their votes were necessary for
the passage of the bill. Their opposition, as well as that of others who desired
similar treatment for the industries in their states, initiated the usual logrolling politics.[37] Under the leadership of Democrat Arthur Gorman of Mary-
land, whom Wilson believed was beholden to the trusts, either through
bribery or financial interest,[38] the Senate passed a considerably narrowed
duty-free raw materials measure by a 39 to 34 margin.

The House–Senate conference committee then deadlocked on the measure. The House held to its broader duty-free raw materials bill, while the
Senate—hemmed in by continued fears of defections from its slim majority—insisted upon its more circumscribed version. Cleveland, hoping to
break this impasse in favor of the House bill, took the unprecedented step of
intervening in the proceedings of the conference committee. This strategy
backfired, as might have been foreseen by a more skilled political tactician.
On 2 July, Cleveland sent a letter to Wilson that was read into the *Congressional Record*. The letter, widely seen as direct criticism of the Democratic members of the Senate, merely stiffened the resolve of the upper
house and made any compromise appear as humiliation. In order to pass any
bill at all, the House was eventually forced to acquiesce in all of the 634
Senate amendments.[39] Torn between wanting to veto the bill and desiring to

36. The Senate was traditionally more protectionist than the House, even though economic
interests tend to be more concentrated in the latter. Three explanations are generally given: 1)
the Senate is a more individualistic institution with weaker committee chairs, 2) debate is
unlimited, 3) an unlimited number of amendments are permitted on the Senate floor. See
Baldwin, *Political Economy*, pp. 15–17; and Pastor, *U.S. Foreign Economic Policy*, pp. 162–63.
37. See Robert McElroy, *Grover Cleveland: The Man and the Statesman*, vol. 2 (New York:
Harper, 1923), p. 111.
38. Wilson wrote that "my services on the Conference Committee on the Tariff Bill gave me
enough glimpses of [Gorman's] conduct in that contest to assure me that he was the bribed
attorney of the Sugar Trust and of other trusts or jobbers, who wished their interests taken care
of in the tariff revision." Festus P. Summers, *The Cabinet Diary of William L. Wilson, 1896–
1897* (Chapel Hill: University of North Carolina Press, 1957), p. 60.
39. In nearly every tariff bill in American history, the conference committee has, in a very
real sense, written the final bill. Often, what emerged from the conference room bore little
resemblance to the two versions of the bill that went in. By accepting all the Senate amendments, the House circumvented this normal process of consensus building. It also resulted in
numerous "jokers" becoming law even though that was not intended. Senator John Sherman of

keep free wool and other reforms, Cleveland eventually allowed the bill to become law without his signature.

While the new internationalized trade strategy of the Harrison and Cleveland administrations resonated well with, and ultimately benefited, several important producer groups, we cannot explain the transformation of policy simply in terms of domestic interest group pressures. First, important beneficiaries of the new strategy actively opposed it. This is seen most clearly in the duty-free wool provision of the Wilson–Gorman Act. Tariffs on raw wool were the linchpin of the protectionist system. The United States was a high cost producer of raw wool. Even under high protection, American woolgrowers could not meet the domestic demand, and a significant quantity of raw wool continued to be imported. By raising domestic wool prices, however, the tariff made it economical for many small farmers scattered throughout the Northeast and Midwest to keep sheep to supplement their otherwise meager monetary incomes. The duty on raw wool was the only item in the tariff that yielded a real benefit to the agricultural sector and helped mitigate farm oppostion to the tariff as a whole. The acquiescence, indeed support, of the woolen manufacturers for the duty on raw wool was obtained through the "mixed" tariff system. The manufacturer received both a specific duty, nominally equivalent to the tariff on raw wool but normally containing an extra measure of protection, and an *ad valorem* duty to protect the manufacturing process. Under this system of mixed duties, both the woolgrower and the manufacturer could be benefited without apparent cost to the other. The Wilson–Gorman Act removed the duty on raw wool and the compensating specific duty entirely. While the manufacturers, in theory, continued to receive as much protection as before—and could now expand their foreign sales with more competitive prices—a key link in the protectionist coalition uniting farmers and manufacturers was severed. To ensure continued protection for their products in the future, the woolen manufacturers bitterly opposed Cleveland's plan for duty-free raw materials. If a single brick were removed from the tariff wall, then the whole edifice, protectionists feared, might come tumbling down.

Secondly, other beneficiaries mobilized in support of the new trade strategy only when actively encouraged by foreign policy leaders. The duty-free raw materals proposal was not on the national political agenda before Cleveland's 1887 annual message. Likewise, farmers supported Blaine's reciprocity plan and mobilized into the tariff-making process only after the secretary of state went directly to the public to circumvent the usual protectionist

---

Ohio remarked that "there are many cases in the bill where enactment was not intended by the Senate. For instance, innumerable amendments were put on by the Senators on both sides of the chamber . . . to give the Committee of Conference a chance to think of the matter, and they are all adopted, whatever may be their language or the incongruity with other parts of the bill." Cited in Henry Jones Ford, *The Cleveland Era* (New Haven, Conn.: Yale University Press, 1919), p. 199.

coalition. Without the initiative and advocacy of the foreign policy leaders, the transformation in American trade strategy would most likely not have occurred.

Despite this social resistance and indifference, the foreign policy executive was relatively successful in enacting its trade strategy preferences into law. While Blaine did not receive everything he wanted, the final legislation did meet his most important objectives. The executive could then use sugar, coffee, tea, and even hides in the negotiation of reciprocity treaties with no congressional limitations. While sharing the same objectives, the Democratic duty-free raw materials platform was less successful legislatively than the Republican policy of reciprocity. Wool was the only important raw material placed on the free list in 1894. Yet given the crucial role of the tariff on raw wool in cementing the protectionist coalition, this was still a major accomplishment.

The success of the foreign policy executive in enacting its trade strategy preferences into policy appears to depend upon three factors. First, it was able to mobilize previously latent interest groups, particularly farmers, into the tariff-making process. This was especially important in Blaine's appeal for reciprocity. Second, Cleveland first redefined the tariff as an issue of export promotion and foreign policy; and Blaine, in 1890, created a transnational coalition with the Latin Americans that raised the stakes of a congressional defeat of reciprocity. Each leader thus used his position within the foreign policy executive to enhance his influence over the tariff-making process. Third, Cleveland demonstrated effective executive leadership in his startling 1887 annual message, as did Blaine in his shrewd manipulation of public opinion. This contrasts with Cleveland's heavy-handed and ill-chosen intervention in the proceedings of the conference committee in 1894, which helped seal the defeat of the more extensive duty-free raw materials plan passed by the House.

The triumph of freer trade, 1909–13

American trade policy in the immediate pre-World War I period, and particularly the important change between the protectionist Payne–Aldrich Act of 1909 and the freer trade Underwood Act of 1913, indicates the importance of shifting international constraints on trade strategy and state action. As I have noted, British hegemony had been declining since the 1870s. In tandem with Britain's declining hegemony, a movement for tariff reform (that is, protection) had begun to emerge by the mid-1890s.[40] Led by Colonial Secretary Joseph Chamberlain, the Imperial Preference movement gathered in-

---

40. On the Imperial Preference movement in Great Britain before the war, see George Peel, *The Tariff Reformers* (London: Methuen, 1913); and Alan Sykes, *Tariff Reform in British Politics, 1903–1913* (Oxford: Clarendon Press, 1979).

creasing strength in the early twentieth century. It was strong enough by 1903 to split the Conservative party, costing it the parliamentary election of 1906, but still the tariff reformers remained a minority and failed to gain the unequivocal support of party leader Arthur Balfour by the time the Payne–Aldrich Act was passed in 1909.

While it could not do so with quite the impunity as before, the United States could still free ride on British free trade in 1909. Of more concern to foreign policy decision-makers at the time were the increasingly discriminatory trade barriers of continental Europe, which often singled out American products for unfair treatment.[41] To combat these rising barriers, foreign policy leaders proposed, and the Payne–Aldrich Tariff included, a maximum-minimum tariff schedule that threatened penalty duties if the Europeans continued to discriminate against American products. With the maximum-minimum weapon and its promise of success, and Britain's continuing, albeit weakening, commitment to free trade, American foreign policy leaders saw little reason for tariff restraint at home. And little restraint was found in the final bill, in which the tariff on dutiable imports was reduced from a high of 47.6 percent in the Dingley Act of 1897 to 41.0 percent—a rate similar to that found in the Wilson–Gorman Act of 1894.

The roots of the Payne–Aldrich Tariff, and particularly its maximum-minimum schedule, can be traced to the foreign policy executive under President Theodore Roosevelt. While similar measures had been used in Europe for over two decades, the precise origin of support for the maximum-minimum schedule in the United States remains unknown. By the middle of the first decade of the twentieth century, however, two important and related sources of support clearly existed. The first group of supporters were the political and economic expansionists closely associated with Roosevelt's inner circle or "tennis cabinet." Within this circle, Henry Cabot Lodge—a leading member of the Senate Finance Committee in 1909—was strongly advocating a maximum-minimum schedule to the president as early as June 1905.[42] The second supporter was Elihu Root, then secretary of state and later—during the deliberations on the Payne–Aldrich bill—senator from New York. Upon completing a tour of South America in the summer and fall of 1906, Root came out in support of the maximum-minimum schedule in an address before the Trans-Mississippi Commercial Congress:

> A single straight-out tariff was all very well in a world of single straight-out tariffs; but we have passed on, during the course of years, into a world for the most part of maximum and minimum tariffs, and with our single-rate tariff we are left with very little opportunity to reciprocate good treatment from other countries in their tariffs and very little opportunity to defend ourselves against bad treatment.[43]

41. See Lake, *Power, Protection and Free Trade,* chap. 4.
42. *Selections from the Correspondence of Theodore Roosevelt and Henry Cabot Lodge,* vol. 2 (New York: Scribner, 1925), p. 129.
43. Philip C. Jessop, *Elihu Root,* vol. 2 (New York: Dodd, Mead, 1938), p. 215.

With support from Roosevelt and Root, the 1908 Republican National Convention, chaired by Lodge, included the proposal for a maximum-minimum schedule in a more general call for tariff reform.

Neither President William Howard Taft or his secretary of state, Philander C. Knox, were deeply involved in the passage of the Payne–Aldrich Act. Taft did call for lower duties, and was disappointed when he could not fully achieve them. Nonetheless, he later canvassed the country seeking to build support for the "best tariff bill that the Republican party has ever passed."[44] As in the question of lower duties, Taft did not possess strong views on the question of the maximum-minimum schedule. Rather, he supported the proposal as a continuation of the Roosevelt program to which he was pledged.

By 1912, on the other hand, the United Kingdom's waning international position was clearly manifested in the rapid growth of British support for protectionism. Bonar Law—a committed tariff reformer—replaced Balfour; the protectionists now dominated the party; and the Conservatives appeared sure to win the next election. Law's rise to party leader and his expected election as prime minister meant that, for the first time since the 1840s, a staunch protectionist could soon be leading the government. In a dramatic change from 1909, Britain's almost century-old commitment to free trade was clearly in jeopardy.[45] This is not to argue, however, that Law and other tariff reformers, or Britain generally, eschewed a desire for free trade abroad. Britain's trade strategy preferences became a mirror image of America's. The tariff reformers desired modest tariffs at home to protect key industries, increase British exports to the colonies through imperial preferences, and enable the country to strike better bargains with its more protectionist trade rivals. But as the latter two motivations suggest, the tariff reformers remained fundamentally committed to export expansion.

Thus, around 1912, the United States could no longer free ride on Britain's leadership; the two countries now confronted a classic Prisoner's Dilemma: they could agree to adopt mutual free trade or mutual protection, but they could not simultaneously obtain their first choices of protection at home and free trade abroad. The choice confronting the United States after 1912 was either to compromise protection at home for continued export expansion and, more specifically, access to the British market, or accept greater restraints on its exports. Given the country's position as the most productive nation-state in the international economy and the export advantages this entailed, America's trade strategy preferences clearly argued for continued export expansion, and the United States, under the leadership of Woodrow Wilson, chose the route of freer trade.[46]

44. On Taft's role in the passage of the Payne–Aldrich Act, see Paolo E. Coletta, *The Presidency of William Howard Taft* (Lawrence: University Press of Kansas, 1973), pp. 45–75. The quotation is found on p. 73.
45. See Peel, *Tariff Reformers*; and Sykes, *Tariff Reform*.
46. See Lake, *Power, Protection and Free Trade*, chap. 5. In Britain, however, the war

Wilson campaigned in 1912 on a platform of vigorous tariff reduction. The Underwood Tariff Act of 1913 was based upon the principle of a "competitive tariff," which would allow the importation of foreign goods to compete with American producers.[47] The concept of competition was critical: the tariff was not to be abolished or set so low that it would severely damage an industry, but it was to be low enough to allow substantial importation.[48] In fact, the Underwood Act was expected to increase imports by approximately $123 million, or 7.4 percent of all imports in 1912.[49] In the Underwood Act, the tariff on dutiable goods was reduced from 41.0 percent to 26.8 percent, and the average rate of duty on all imports was lowered from 20.0 to 8.8 percent, the lowest rates in any American tariff bill between the Civil War and World War II. As the British magazine *The Economist* wrote, the Underwood bill was "the heaviest blow that has been aimed at the protective system since the British legislation of Sir Robert Peel between 1842 and 1846."[50]

Two mutually reinforcing issues were central to the Underwood tariff debate, both within the country at large during the 1912 election and in the government while the bill was under consideration.[51] The congressional debate centered primarily on trusts. By sheltering the domestic market from imports, the protective tariff was thought to encourage the process of industrial concentration. Lower tariffs, which would provide new competition for the trusts within the American market, were at least partly intended to halt and, hopefully, reverse this process. As a "progressive" candidate, Wilson also emphasized the trust issue. More imporantly for my argument, however, Wilson also reasoned that the structure of the international economy had changed and that the United States must adapt its policies accordingly. First, he argued, the rapid economic development of the country, through which the United States was outstripping the progress of its European rivals, had altered both the economic structure of the country and America's interests within the global economy. Without specifically mentioning Great Brit-

---

disrupted the normal course of trade politics. The McKenna duties, designed to raise revenue for the war effort, were adopted in 1915.

47. See Asher Isaacs, *International Trade, Tariff, and Commercial Policies* (Chicago: Irwin, 1948), p. 215.

48. House Ways and Means Committee, *A Bill to Reduce Tariff Duties, to Provide Revenue for the Government, and for Other Purposes: A Report to Accompany H.R. 3321*, 63d Congress, 1st session, 1913, pp. xvi–xvii.

49. The figure of $123 was often cited in the debates. See, in particular, the opening speech of F. M. Simmons, chairman of the Senate Finance Committee, *Congressional Record*, 63d Congress, 1st session, 1913, p. 2552. Total imports for 1912 were $1,653.3 million. *Statistical Abstract of the United States* (Washington, D.C.: GPO, 1916), p. 328.

50. *The Economist*, 12 April 1913, p. 867.

51. Considerable debate in Congress also occurred over the role of the Democratic caucus in the tariff-making process. At the root of this Republican disgruntlement lay the frustration of its party allies in the business community. Where in the past business had faced a friendly Ways and Means Committee, it now confronted a committee committed to rolling back the favors the business people had previously enjoyed.

ain, Wilson raised this theme in many of his speeches on the tariff. In his first message to Congress, Wilson said:

> It is clear to the whole country that the tariff duties must be altered. They must be changed to meet the radical alteration in the conditions of our economic life which the country has witnessed within the last generation. While the whole force and method of our industrial and commercial life were being changed beyond recognition the tariff schedules have remained what they were before the change began, or have moved in the direction they were given when no large circumstance of our industrial development was what it is to-day. Our task is to square them with the actual facts.[52]

Similarly, early in 1912 campaign, Wilson argued:

> [N]ow we are getting very much interested in foreign markets, but the foreign markets are not particularly interested in us. We have not been very polite, we have not encouraged the intercourse with foreign markets that we might have encouraged, and have obstructed the influence of foreign competition. So these circumstances make the tariff question a new question, our internal arrangements and new combinations of business on one side and on the other our external necessities and the need to give scope to our energy which is now pent up and confined within our own borders.[53]

Second, Wilson believed that America's economic progress in 1912 was even more constrained by the policy of protection than it had been in the past. In the campaign, Wilson said that "if prosperity is not to be checked in this country we must broaden our borders and make conquest of the markets of the world. That is the reason why America is so deeply interested in . . . breaking down . . . that dam against which all the tides of our prosperity have banked up, that great dam which runs around all our coasts and which we call the protective tariff."[54]

Third, given the changing nature of the international economy, Wilson asserted that the United States could no longer be a reclusive nation. American policies did effect other nation-states, he noted, and they could be expected to retaliate. "[A]ll trade is two-sided. You can't sell everything and buy nothing. You can't establish any commercial relationships that aren't two-sided. And if America is to insist upon selling everything and buy nothing, she will find that the rest of the world stands very cold and indifferent to her enterprise."[55] Accordingly, the Underwood Act was designed, in the

52. Arthur S. Link, ed., *The Papers of Woodrow Wilson (WWP)*, vol. 27 (Princeton, N.J.: Princeton University Press, various years), p. 270.
  53. *WWP*, vol. 23, pp. 641–42.
  54. *WWP*, vol. 25, p. 38.
  55. *WWP*, vol. 25, p. 341.

words of Wilson's congressional supporters, to free "the highways of trade"[56] and take advantage of "our great national opportunities in the markets of the world."[57]

While many groups in society recognized the need for tariff reductions, it is difficult to explain the outcome entirely in terms of interest group pressures. The economic and, by extrapolation, political importance of export dependent industries—the strongest societal supporters of freer trade—remained relatively constant over the first decade of the twentieth century.[58] Two years after the passage of the protectionist Dingley Tariff of 1897, approximately 57.5 percent (by value of manufactured output) of American industry exported more than 5 percent of its production, and only one sector, chemicals, comprising 4.7 percent of manufacturing, exported more than 10 percent of its output. By 1909, the proportion of American manufacturers who exported 5 percent or more of their production had risen only marginally to 63.6 percent, and no sector exported more than 10 percent of its output. Moreover, relatively little had changed in the structure and international orientation of American industry between 1909 and 1913.[59]

In addition, the protectionist coalition still dominated Congress, and the bill emerged from the legislature in its freer trade form only under the exertions of Wilson, who played a critical role in the successful passage of the Underwood Act. Soon after the November election, Oscar W. Underwood—chairman of the House Ways and Means Committee and one of Wilson's principal rivals for the 1912 nomination—and the Democratic members the committee began drafting a new tariff bill. The draft was completed before the inauguration, and Wilson saw it for the first time only after the committee had completed its deliberations. In an effort to make the measure more palatable to a wider cross-section of legislators, Underwood had backed away from the sweeping reform promised in the campaign. Wilson insisted that the committee hold firm, and in particular demanded the bill include free food, sugar, leather, and wool. Although he threatened to veto the bill unless these goods were admitted free of duty, Wilson compromised on sugar, allowing the duty to be gradually eliminated over three years.[60]

When Democratic support wavered under these demands, Wilson quickly acted to force congressional adherence to the Democratic party's pledge of

56. *Congressional Record,* 63d Congress, 1st session, 1913, p. 662.
57. Ibid., p. 2553.
58. William H. Becker, *The Dynamics of Business–Government Relations: Industry and Exports, 1893–1921* (Chicago: University of Chicago Press, 1982).
59. These figures are derived from those in *Foreign Commerce and Navigation of the United States* (Washington, D.C.: GPO, selected years) and the *Abstract of the Census of the United States* (Washington, D.C.: GPO, selected years). For a more detailed discussion of these data, see Lake, *Power, Protection and Free Trade,* chap. 2.
60. Arthur S. Link, *Wilson: The New Freedom* (Princeton, N.J.: Princeton University Press, 1956).

tariff reform. First, in a bold initiative, Wilson appeared before Congress to argue for the Underwood Act, both dramatizing the importance of the issue and building support for the proposed measure. Not since Jefferson had any president spoken before Congress. While many critics deemed this inappropriate interference in legislative affairs, Wilson's tactic was well received on the whole and demonstrated the president's deep commitment to the bill.[61]

Second, in an attempt to create party discipline, the absence of which Wilson the scholar had decried as the principal weakness of the American political system, the president made support for the Underwood Act a test of party loyalty. Once the measure was approved by the House and Senate Democratic caucuses, Wilson insisted that individual members adhere to all of its provisions, even though they might disagree with individual duties in the bill. Wilson's letter to Senator John Randolph Thornton of Louisiana—one of only two Democratic senators to eventually vote against the bill—is similar to many others in this regard:

> Undoubtedly, you should have felt yourself perfectly free in the caucus to make every effort to carry out the promises you had made to your own people, but when it comes to the final action, my own judgment is perfectly clear. No party can ever for any length of time control the Government or serve the people which can not command the allegiance of its own minority. I feel that there are times, after every argument has been given full consideration and men of equal public conscience have conferred together, when those who are overruled should accept the principle of party government and act with the colleagues through whom they expect to see the country best and most permanently well served.[62]

By making the tariff a party issue, Wilson alienated several progressive Republicans who would otherwise have supported the measure.[63] Without strict party discipline, on the other hand, the bill might not have passed at all, or it might have passed only in a form unacceptable to Wilson.

Despite Wilson's shrewd manipulation of the public arena and the party, senatorial support for the bill was by no means certain. Given the large Democratic majority in the House, few lobbyists believed they could overturn the expected outcome. With only a six-vote majority in the Senate, however, the pressure groups hoped the traditionally more conservative and protectionist upper house would accede to their pleas for continued tariffs. When the bill reached the Senate, rumors—most likely stimulated by the lobbyists now descending on Washington—began to circulate on Capitol Hill that Wilson was willing to compromise on his earlier demands. To combat the influence of the lobby, Wilson initiated his third and perhaps

61. Arthur S. Link, *Woodrow Wilson and the Progressive Era, 1910–1917* (New York: Harper, 1954), pp. 35–36.
62. *WWP*, vol. 28, p. 35.
63. Link, *Wilson: The New Freedom*, p. 185.

most unusual tactic. Appealing to the public and his progressive supporters in particular, the president denounced the tariff lobby:

> I think that the public ought to know the extraordinary exertions being made by the lobby in Washington to gain recognition for certain alterations in the tariff bill. Washington has seldom seen so numerous, so industrious, or so insidious a lobby. . . . It is of serious interest to the country that the people at large should have no lobby and be voiceless in these matters, while great bodies of astute men seek to create an artificial opinion and to overcome the interests of the public for their private profit. It is thoroughly worth the while of the people of this country to take knowledge of this matter. Only public opinion can check and destroy it.[64]

Wilson's remarks were greeted skeptically at first. *The New York Times* noted that it was possible that "the President has mistaken for lobbying the ordinary, usual, and perfectly legitimate measures taken by protected interests to present their case to Congress."[65] Expecting to reveal the president's charges as groundless, the Republicans proposed hearings into the activities of the lobby, which were then expanded into an investigation of the financial holdings of senators themselves.[66] While the investigation found few patently illegal activities, it did reveal numerous conflicts of interest created by legislators holding stock or other interests in industries seeking protection and considerable expenditures designed to influence public and legislative opinion.[67] In the end, the president was more than vindicated. Under the light of public scrutiny, the usual logrolling was blocked. Indeed, the bill actually emerged from the Senate with lower duties than contained in the House version, an event which had never before occurred.

Wilson's success in realizing Democratic pledges for tariff reform contrasts sharply with Taft's failure to meet his more modest promises in 1909. This difference is often attributed to the two presidents' leadership styles, which no doubt played a role in establishing the final outcome. Taft's political ineptitude is easily documented, while Wilson's advocacy of a strong president acting as a leader of his party is displayed both in his academic writings and political practice. Like Blaine, Wilson effectively blocked the dominant protectionist coalition by appealing directly to the public and mobilizing his progressive supporters into the tariff-making process.

Despite these differences in executive leadership, however, changes in Great Britain's international economic structure and strategic trade preferences are critical in understanding the differences between the Payne–Aldrich and Underwood Acts. As British trade preferences rapidly evolved

---

64. Quoted in Richard Hofstader, ed., *The Progressive Movement, 1900–1915* (Englewood Cliffs, N.J.: Prentice-Hall, 1963), pp. 156–57.
65. Quoted in Link, *Wilson: The New Freedom*, p. 187.
66. Ibid., p. 189.
67. Ibid., pp. 189–90.

in a more protectionist direction between 1909 and 1913, new constraints were placed on American trade strategy. The United States could no longer safely free ride, and now had to accommodate its principal trading partner's mixed interests in protection at home and free trade abroad by reducing its own tariff rates. Wilson's ambition was by necessity larger than Taft's.

Conclusion

That the foreign policy executive is an important actor in the national security issue-area is readily accepted by most international relations scholars. Foreign policy decision-makers, after all, make war, develop strategic nuclear doctrine, conduct diplomacy, and handle crises with little input from society. On these issues, the rational actor or bureaucratic politics models appear as valid simplifications of reality. The importance of the executive is also accepted, although to a slightly lesser degree, in the area of monetary policy.[68] Because the money supply, interest rates, and exchange rates typically affect broad social aggregates in relatively symmetrical ways and do not normally generate intense political cleavages, the executive appears at least relatively autonomous, and therefore central to the policy process. Most scholars are reluctant, however, to attribute a similar role to the foreign policy executive in the area of trade policy.

This article has sought to challenge the analytic primacy granted to private or societal interests in the study of American trade policy. I have argued that private interests alone cannot account for the internationalization of the tariff in the early 1890s or the turn towards freer trade between 1909 and 1913. Rather, both these policy innovations were influenced by changing international constraints and the trade strategies of other countries, as recognized and acted upon by foreign policy leaders. In these cases, the foreign policy executive led society.

The importance of the foreign policy executive in the formulation of trade policy results from two factors. First, many domestic coalitions potentially exist. As Arrow's paradox and coalition theory indicate, even under rather weak and plausible assumptions, majorities and coalitions are likely to be unstable.[69] The structure of interests facing the government is not rigid or

68. Krasner, "U.S. Commercial and Monetary Policy," and Joanne Gowa, "Public Goods and Political Institutions: Trade and Monetary Policy Processes in the United States," this volume, argue that the state is more autonomous and important in the monetary than in the trade issue-area. John Odell, *U.S. International Monetary Policy: Markets, Power, and Ideas as Sources of Change* (Princeton, N.J.: Princeton University Press, 1982), finds the three concepts listed in the subtitle important in explaining monetary policy. All three are consistent with a "statist" approach, although Odell does not use the term. Odell also finds that domestic politics and bureaucratic politics are relatively unimportant.

69. Kenneth Arrow, *Social Choice and Individual Values*, 2d ed. (New Haven, Conn.: Yale University Press, 1963). See also Robert Abrams, *Foundations of Political Analysis* (New York: Columbia University Press, 1980), pp. 41–101 and 235–79.

predetermined. Instead, it resembles a clay which the relatively autonomous elements of the state can—within limits—mold and shape in ways they desire. To the extent that society is open to manipulation, the role of the foreign policy executive is magnified in importance. Particularly important is the foreign policy executive's ability to mobilize latent or previously neutral societal groups into the political processes so that they offset entrenched interests at moments of significant policy change. Wilson's criticism of the tariff lobby, specifically directed at mobilizing his progressive supporters, is a clear example of this pattern. It was also Blaine's goal in his appeal to the public about reciprocity. By highlighting the export advantages that farmers were likely to receive from reciprocity, Blaine sought to weaken the position of the staunch protectionists in Congress.

Second, the unique position of the foreign policy executive at the intersection of the domestic and international political systems generates several entries into the otherwise closed congressional policymaking process. The foreign policy executive can redefine domestic political issues as foreign policy issues.[70] This process is seen clearly in the reconceptualization of the tariff between 1887 and the early 1890s. Even after this reconceptualization had occurred, Wilson continued to emphasize the foreign policy and export expansion implications of tariff reform in 1913. By redefining domestic issues as foreign policy issues, the foreign policy executive legitimates its participation in the policymaking process and increases its influence in its own society. The foreign policy executive is also in a unique position to enter into legitimate transnational coalitions. By agreeing to the recommendations of the International American Conference on reciprocity as an official representative of the United States, Blaine effectively increased his bargaining leverage relative to the protectionist forces in Congress. If Congress then failed to adopt reciprocity, it would risk disappointing the same Latin American countries that the United States had so recently attempted to court.

The cases I have examined reveal that the state is not an empty shell in which social forces compete. American trade policy does not simply result from interest group pressures. Rather, the foreign policy executive has identifiable interests and actively participates in the trade policymaking process. Drawing upon its unique position between the international and domestic political systems and its ability to mobilize societal actors, the foreign policy executive can achieve its goals despite resistance from society. The extent of this success, on the other hand, is conditioned by presidential or executive leadership (critical to the successes of Blaine and Wilson and the difficulties encountered by Cleveland and Taft), and state structure.

The argument I have presented suggests that political institutions may be

70. In his contribution to this volume, John Ikenberry, "Market Solutions for State Problems: The International and Domestic Politics of American Oil Decontrol," finds a similar pattern.

more malleable than "institutionalist" accounts of trade policy have recognized.[71] For instance, Wilson clearly and rapidly overcame the American system of protection and its entrenched protectionist interests when the international constraints facing the United States required a break with tradition and the adoption of a new American trade policy. In this case, the supposedly rigid state structures that magnify the importance of domestic protectionist pressures failed to exert their constraining effects.

This article also suggests that the foreign policy executive can be usefully conceptualized as a link between the international and domestic political systems. There is an important and unanswered question common to all realist and neorealist theories of international politics:[72] By what agent or process are systemic constraints and opportunities communicated or translated into observable public policies? While most realists do not assert that the international system is wholly determining, and they are aware that domestic politics exert an impact upon policy, the relationship between the systemic and national levels of analysis in this literature remains ambiguous. The argument I have developed helps clarify this relationship. Because of its concern with national power and wealth, the foreign policy executive is particularly sensitive to the constraints and opportunities of the international system and the strategic preferences of other countries. Thus, it acts as a conduit through which systemically generated incentives pass into the sphere of domestic politics. This conceptualization highlights the role of the foreign policy executive as a crucial actor linking the systemic and national levels of analysis.

71. See, for example, Judith Goldstein, "Ideas, Institutions, and American Trade Policy," this volume.
72. See Kenneth Waltz, *Theory of International Politics* (Reading, Mass.: Addison-Wesley, 1979).

Sectoral conflict and U.S. foreign economic policy, 1914–1940   Jeff Frieden

The period from 1914 to 1940 is one of the most crucial and enigmatic in modern world history, and in the history of modern U.S. foreign policy. World War I catapulted the United States into international economic and political leadership, yet in the aftermath of the war, despite grandiose Wilsonian plans, the United States quickly lapsed into relative disregard for events abroad: it did not join the League of Nations, disavowed responsibility for European reconstruction, would not participate openly in many international economic conferences, and restored high levels of tariff protection for the domestic market. Only in the late 1930s and 1940s, after twenty years of bitter battles over foreign policy, did the United States move to center stage of world politics and economics: it built the United Nations and a string of regional alliances, underwrote the rebuilding of Western Europe, almost single-handedly constructed a global monetary and financial system, and led the world in commercial liberalization.

This article examines the peculiar evolution of U.S. foreign economic policy in the interwar years, and focuses on the role of domestic socioeconomic and political groups in determining foreign policy. The American interwar experience powerfully demonstrates that the country's international position and economic evolution do not sufficiently explain its foreign policy. Indeed, although the contours of the international system and the place of the United States in it changed dramatically during and after World War I, these changes had a very different impact on different sectors of

The author would like to acknowledge the comments and suggestions of Beverly Crawford, Robert Dallek, Amy Davis, Barbara Geddes, Judith Goldstein, Joanne Gowa, Stephan Haggard, John Ikenberry, Robert Jervis, Miles Kahler, Paul Kennedy, Robert Keohane, Charles Kindleberger, Steve Krasner, David Lake, Mike Mastanduno, William McNeil, John Ruggie, Stephen Schuker, Jack Snyder, Arthur Stein, and Richard Sylla.

International Organization 42, 1, Winter 1988

American society. World War I dramatically strengthened the overseas economic interests of many major U.S. banks and corporations, who fought hard for more political involvement by the United States in world affairs. Yet domestically oriented economic groups remained extremely powerful within the United States and sought to maintain a relatively, isolated America. Through the 1920s and early 1930s, the two broad coalitions battled to dominate foreign economic policy. The result was an uneasy stand-off in which the two camps entrenched themselves in different portions of the state apparatus, so that policy often ran on two tracks and was sometimes internally contradictory. Only the crisis of the 1930s and the eventual destruction of most of America's overseas competitors led to an "internationalist" victory that allowed for the construction of the American-led post-World War II international political economy.

The problem

To virtually all observers then and since, at the end of World War I the United States seemed to dominate the international political economy. It had financed the victorious war effort and provided most of the war materiel that went into it; its industry was by far the world's largest and most productive. Despite its traditional economic insulation, the sheer size of the U.S. economy made the country the world's largest trading power. The center of world finance had shifted from London to New York. The United States clearly had the military, industrial, and financial capacity to impose its will on Europe. Yet after World War I the United States, in the current arcane iconography of the field, did not play the part of international economic hegemon, arbiter and bankroller of the world economic order. The United States was capable of hegemonic action, and President Woodrow Wilson had hegemonic plans, but they were defeated. The problem was not in Europe, for although the British and French were stronger in 1919 than they would be in 1946, they could hardly have stood in the way of American hegemony. Indeed, European complaints about the United States after World War I were in much the opposite direction: the Europeans bitterly protested America's *refusal* to accept the responsibilities of leadership. The Europeans charged that the United States was stingy with its government finance, hostile in its trade policy, scandalous in its refusal to join the League of Nations, unwilling to get involved in overseeing and smoothing Europe's squabbles. The British and French tried for years to entice and cajole a reluctant America into leadership. America would not be budged, at least until 1940.

The world's most powerful nation pursued a contradictory and shifting set of foreign economic policies. The country both asserted and rejected world leadership, simultaneously initiated and blocked efforts at European stabilization, and began such major cooperative ventures as the League of Nations and the Dawes Plan only to limit its participation in these American initiatives in ultimately fatal ways. The analytical problem bedevils both economic determinists and political Realists. For those who believe in the primacy of international power politics, it is difficult to explain why a United States able to reconstruct the world political system was unwilling to do so. For those who look at economic affairs first and foremost, America's unchallenged position as the world's leading capital exporter should have accelerated the trend towards trade liberalization and international monetary leadership begun before World War I; instead, the pendulum swung back towards protectionism and little public U.S. government involvement in international monetary issues.

The relevant international relations literature, faced with such analytical anomalies, generally falls back on vague reference to domestic constraints in explaining U.S. foreign economic policy in the interwar period. Charles Kindleberger, whose comparison of the era with the *Pax Britannica* and *Pax Americana* is the foundation stone for most international relations thinking on the interwar years, cites E. H. Carr approvingly, to the effect that "in 1918, world leadership was offered, by almost universal consent, to the United States . . . [and] was declined," and concludes that "the one country capable of leadership [i.e. the United States] was bemused by domestic concerns and stood aside."[1]

Seen from the perspective of American domestic politics, however, the problem is quite reversed. In the context of traditional American apathy or even hostility towards world affairs, the interwar years saw an amazing flurry of global activity by the country's political, economic, and cultural leaders. Against the backdrop of the longstanding indifference of most of the American political system to events abroad, the level of overseas involvement in the 1920s and 1930s appears both startling and unprecedented.[2]

The contradictory role of the United States in the interwar period can be traced to the extremely uneven distribution of international economic interests within American society. America's international economic position did change during and after World War I, yet overseas assets were accumulated by a very concentrated set of economic actors. This left most of the U.S. economy indifferent to foreign economic affairs, while some of the country's leading economic sectors were both deeply involved and deeply concerned with the international economy. American foreign policy was thus torn between insularity and internationalism; the segments of the foreign-policy

---

1. Charles Kindleberger, *The World in Depression 1929–1939* (Berkeley: University of California Press, 1973), pp. 297–99. The Carr citation is from his *The Twenty Years Crisis, 1919–1930* (London: Macmillan, 1939), p. 234. A popular British satirical history of the 1930s, under the heading "A Bad Thing," summarized the results of the Great War somewhat more succinctly: "America was thus clearly top nation, and History came to a ." Walter Sellar and Robert Yeatman, *1066 And All That* (New York: Dutton, 1931), p. 115.

2. Robert Dallek, *The American Style of Foreign Policy* (New York: Knopf, 1983) is a good survey of traditional American insularity.

bureaucracy that reflected internationally oriented interests tried to use American power to reorganize the world's political economy, while portions of the government tied to domestically oriented sectors insisted on limiting America's international role. The crisis of the 1930s dissolved many of the entrenched interests that had kept policy stalemated and allowed a new group of political leaders to reconstitute a more coherent set of policies.

This article builds on the work of historians investigating the interwar period[3] and on the contributions of other social scientists concerned with the relationship between the international and domestic political economies. The work of Charles Kindleberger and Peter Gourevitch, among many others, has shown the importance of sectoral economic interests in explaining domestic politics and foreign policymaking in advanced industrial societies. Both Gourevitch and Thomas Ferguson have used a sectoral approach to elucidate domestic and international events in the 1930s. The present article is thus an attempt to build on existing sectoral interpretations of modern political economies, and an extension of the approach to problems in international relations.[4]

The argument summarized

Between 1900 and 1920, the United States went from a position of relative international economic insignificance to one of predominance. A major inter-

---

3. The historical literature on the period is so enormous that it is feasible only to cite the most recent important additions. Two review essays and a forum are a good start: Kathleen Burk, "Economic Diplomacy Between the Wars," *Historical Journal* 24 (December 1981), pp. 1003–15; Jon Jacobson, "Is There a New International History of the 1920s?" *American Historical Review* 88 (June 1983), pp. 617–45; and Charles Maier, Stephen Schuker, and Charles Kindleberger, "The Two Postwar Eras and the Conditions for Stability in Twentieth-Century Western Europe," *American Historical Review* 86 (April 1981). Other important works include Denise Artaud, *La question des dettes interalliées et la reconstruction de l'Europe* (Paris: Champion, 1979); Frank Costigliola, *Awkward Dominion: American Political, Economic, and Cultural Relations with Europe 1919–1933* (Ithaca, N.Y.: Cornell University Press, 1984); Michael J. Hogan, *Informal Entente: The Private Structure of Cooperation in Anglo-American Economic Diplomacy, 1918–1928* (Columbia: University of Missouri Press, 1977); Melvyn Leffler, *The Elusive Quest: America's Pursuit of European Stability and French Security, 1919–1933* (Chapel Hill: University of North Carolina Press, 1979); William McNeil, *American Money and the Weimar Republic* (New York: Columbia University Press, 1986); Stephen Schuker, *The End of French Predominance in Europe* (Chapel Hill: University of North Carolina Press, 1976); and Dan Silverman, *Reconstructing Europe after the Great War* (Cambridge: Harvard University Press, 1982). Many of the leading scholars in the field summarize their views in Gustav Schmidt, ed., *Konstellationen Internationaler Politik 1924–1932* (Bochum, W. Ger.: Studienverlag Dr. N. Brockmeyer, 1983).

4. Charles Kindleberger, "Group Behavior and International Trade," *Journal of Political Economy* 59 (February 1951), pp. 30–46; Peter Gourevitch, "International Trade, Domestic Coalitions, and Liberty: Comparative Responses to the Crisis of 1873–1896," *Journal of Interdisciplinary History* 8 (Autumn 1977), pp. 281–313; Peter Gourevitch, "Breaking with Orthodoxy: the Politics of Economic Policy Responses to the Depression of the 1930s," *International Organization* 38 (Winter 1984), pp. 95–129; Thomas Ferguson, "From Normalcy to New Deal: Industrial Structure, Party Competition, and American Public Policy in the Great Depression," *International Organization* 38 (Winter 1984), pp. 41–94.

national borrower and host of foreign direct investment before 1900, by 1920 the United States was the world's leading new lender and foreign direct investor. The development of American overseas investments was in itself unsurprising, and in this the United States simply repeated the experience of other developed countries. Yet the rapidity of the country's shift from a major capital importer and raw-materials exporter to the leading exporter of capital, largely because of the peculiarities of the international economy in the ten years after 1914, was quite extraordinary. Even as a few major American economic actors were catapulted into global economic leadership, most of the economy remained as inward-looking as ever. This division in American economic orientation was at the root of the foreign-policy problems of the 1920s and 1930s.

As American industry and finance matured and the country became richer in capital, many large American corporations and banks looked abroad for markets and investment opportunities. United States overseas investment thus grew gradually from the 1890s until the eve of World War I. As Table 1 indicates, American foreign direct investment was appreciable by 1900; it was concentrated in raw materials extraction and agriculture in the Caribbean basin. By 1912, foreign direct investment was quite substantial and overseas lending had become of some importance; the focus was still the Caribbean area.

The gradual expansion of American overseas investment, especially overseas lending, was given a tremendous shove by World War I. The war forced several belligerent countries to borrow heavily from the United States, and previous borrowers from European capital markets now turned to the United States to satisfy their needs for capital. As Table 1 shows, American holdings of foreign bonds soared from less than 5 percent of total American holdings of non-government bonds in 1912 to nearly 17 percent in 1922. Foreign direct investment also grew rapidly, as European preoccupation with war and reconstruction cleared the way for many American corporations to expand further into the Third World and, after the war ended, in Europe itself. The 1920s saw a continuation of the wartime increase in overseas American lending and investment. American overseas investment in industrial production—especially manufacturing and utilities—and petroleum grew particularly rapidly.

By 1929 American overseas private assets—direct and portfolio investments, along with other assorted long- and short-term assets—were twenty-one billion dollars. Overseas investments in 1929 were equivalent to over one-fifth of the country's gross national product, a level that was reached again only in 1981.[5]

Although America's overseas investments were substantial by the 1920s, they were very unevenly distributed among important sectors of the U.S.

5. For figures on U.S. foreign private assets, see Raymond Goldsmith, *A Study of Savings in the United States,* vol. 1 (Princeton, N.J.: Princeton University Press, 1955), p. 1093.

TABLE 1. *Indicators of the importance of U.S. foreign investment,*
1900–1939 (in millions of dollars and percent)

	1900	1912	1922	1929	1933	1939
1. U.S. foreign direct investment	751	2,476	5,050	7,850	7,000[e]	6,750
2. Domestic corporate and agricultural wealth[a]	37,275	75,100	131,904	150,326	109,375	119,324
3. Row 1 as a percent of Row 2	2.0%	3.3%	3.8%	5.2%	6.4%	5.7%
4. U.S. foreign bondholdings[b]	159[d]	623	4,000	7,375	5,048[f]	2,600[g]
5. U.S. holdings of non-government bonds[c]	5,151	14,524	23,687	38,099	37,748	32,502
6. 4/5, percent	3.1%	4.3%	16.9%	19.4%	13.4%	8.0%

a. Net reproducible tangible wealth of U.S. corporations and agriculture.
b. Due to the different sources used, figures here conflict with those in Table 4; those of Table 4 are probably more reliable, but to ensure comparability Goldsmith's figures are used throughout the table.
c. Excludes only holdings of securities issued by U.S. federal, state, or local governments.
d. Includes stocks (for 1900 only).
e. Author's estimates.
f. Figures are for 1934, from Foreign Bondholders Protective Council, *Annual Report for 1934* (Washington, D.C.: FBPC, 1935), p. 224. This includes only bonds being serviced; a more reasonable measure would include the market value of bonds in default. If this averaged 30% of par value, figures for 1933–34 would be $5,954 million and 15.8% for rows 4 and 6, respectively.
g. Figures for 1939 holdings of foreign bonds are from Goldsmith and are probably understated.
Sources. Foreign investment: Raymond Goldsmith, *A Study of Saving in the United States,* vol. 1 (Princeton, N.J.: Princeton University Press, 1955), p. 1093.
Domestic data: Raymond Goldsmith, Robert Lipsey, and Morris Mendelson, *Studies in the National Balance Sheet of the United States,* vol. 2 (Princeton, N.J.: Princeton University Press, 1963), pp. 72–83.

economy. Tables 2 and 3 illustrate that, while overseas investment was extremely important for the financial community and some industrial sectors, most other sectors' foreign assets were insignificant. American foreign investments in mining and petroleum were considerable, both absolutely and relative to capital invested in corresponding activities within the United States. Foreign investment was also of great relative importance to corporations in machinery and equipment (especially electrical appliances), motor vehicles, rubber products, and chemicals. Yet these sectors, which accounted for well over half of all overseas investment in manufacturing, represented barely one-fifth of the country's manufacturing plant; far more American industries were quite uninvolved in overseas production.

Although only a few industries had major foreign operations, foreign lending was a favorite activity on Wall Street. As Table 3 shows, between 1919 and 1929 new foreign capital issues in New York averaged over a billion

TABLE 2. *Foreign direct investment and book value of fixed capital of selected U.S. industries, 1929 (in millions of dollars and percent)*

Sector	A Foreign direct investment	B Book value of fixed capital	A/B in percent
Mining and petroleum[a,b]	$2,278	$12,886	17.7%
Public utilities, transport and communications	1,625	41,728[c]	3.9%
Manufacturing	1,534	23,672	6.5%
Machinery and equipment	444	1,907	23.3%
Motor vehicles	184	1,232	14.9%
Rubber products	60	434	13.8%
Chemicals	130	1,497	8.7%
Foodstuffs	222	4,001	5.5%
Lumber and products	69	2,001	3.4%
Metals and products	150	4,788	3.1%
Textiles and products	71	2,932	2.4%
Stone, clay and glass products	23	1,451	1.6%
Leather and products	4	269	1.3%
Agriculture[d]	875	51,033	1.5%

a. Figures for total manufacturing do not include petroleum refining, which is included under "Mining and petroleum."

b. Figures for domestic mining and petroleum invested capital are for the book value of capital including land but excluding working capital.

c. Value of plant and equipment.

d. Domestic invested capital is reproducible tangible assets of agricultural sector.

Sources. Foreign direct investment: U.S. Department of Commerce, *American Direct Investments in Foreign Countries* (Washington, D.C.: GPO, 1930), pp. 29–36.

Domestic fixed capital: Daniel Creamer, Sergei Dobrovolsky and Israel Borenstein, *Capital in Manufacturing and Mining* (Princeton, N.J.: Princeton University Press, 1960), pp. 248–51, 317–18; Melville J. Ulmer, *Capital in Transportation, Communications and Public Utilities* (Princeton, N.J.: Princeton University Press, 1960), pp. 235–37; Raymond Goldsmith, Robert Lipsey and Morris Mendelson, *Studies in the National Balance Sheet of the United States* vol. 2 (Princeton, N.J.: Princeton University Press, 1963), pp. 78–79.

dollars a year, over one-sixth of all issues (excluding federal, state, and local securities); in a couple of years the proportion approached one-third. The United States was the world's principal long-term lender, and foreign lending was very important to American finance.

The reasons for the uneven pattern of overseas investment are fairly straightforward. It is not surprising that a capital-starved world would turn for loans to the capital-rich United States, especially to the Northeastern financial powerhouses. Foreign direct investment, on the other hand, responded to more specific incentives. Tariff barriers, which proliferated after World War I, forced former or prospective exporters to locate production facilities in overseas markets; often the advantages of local production were great even in the absence of tariffs. Foreign direct investment was thus largely confined to firms with specific technological, managerial, or market-

TABLE 3. *New corporate and foreign capital issues in New York, 1919–1929 (in millions of dollars and percent)*

	A All corporate issues	B Foreign issues	B/A in percent
1919	$2,742	$771	28.1%
1920	2,967	603	20.3%
1921	2,391	692	28.9%
1922	2,775	863	31.1%
1923	2,853	498	17.5%
1924	3,831	1,217	31.8%
1925	6,219	1,316	21.2%
1926	8,628	1,288	14.9%
1927	9,936	1,577	15.9%
1928	9,894	1,489	15.0%
1929	11,604	706	6.1%
Total, 1919–1929	63,840	11,020	17.3%
Annual average, 1919–1929	5,804	1,002	17.3%

Source. United States Department of Commerce, *Handbook of American Underwriting of Foreign Securities* (Washington, D.C.: GPO, 1930), pp. 32–37.

ing advantages, such as motor vehicles, electric appliances and utilities, and petroleum, as well as in the extraction of resources available more readily abroad. There was little overseas investment by industries producing such relatively standardized goods as steel, clothing, and footwear; they generally had little exporting experience, and few advantages over firms in their lines of business abroad. Thus the major money-center investment and commercial banks were highly international, as were the more technologically advanced manufacturing and extractive industries; traditional labor-intensive industries, which were by far the majority, were little involved in foreign investment.

American industrial export interests were similar to its foreign investments. The major industrial sectors with overseas investments were also the country's leading industrial exporters, as product-cycle theory would predict.[6] Refiners of copper and petroleum, and producers of machinery and equipment, motor vehicles, chemicals, and processed food were all major exporters as well as major foreign investors. The only important exceptions to the general congruence of trade and asset diversification were the steel industry and some agricultural interests, especially in the South. Neither steel producers nor, of course, cotton and tobacco farmers had many overseas investments. To a large extent, then, the trade and foreign investment line-ups were complementary.[7]

6. The classical explanation of the process is Raymond Vernon, "International Investment and International Trade in the Product Cycle," *Quarterly Journal of Economics* 80 (May 1966), pp. 190–207.
7. On agricultural and industrial trade preferences in the 1920s, see Barry Eichengreen, "The

Sectors with major overseas investment interests would be expected to have a different foreign economic and political outlook than sectors with little or no international production or sales. Internationally oriented banks and corporations would be generally favorable to freer trade, the former to allow debtors to earn foreign exchange and the latter both because intra-firm trade was important to them and because they tended to fear retaliation. Internationally oriented sectors could also be expected to support an extension of American diplomatic commitments abroad, both specifically to safeguard their investments and more generally to provide an international environment conducive to foreign economic growth. Those sectors that sold but did not invest abroad would be sympathetic to American attempts to stabilize foreign markets, but might oppose international initiatives that reinforced competing producers overseas. Economic sectors with few foreign assets or sales could be anticipated to support protectionist policies in their industries, because they were not importing from overseas subsidiaries, tended to be less competitive, and had few worries about retaliation. Such sectors would be unsupportive of major American international involvement that might strengthen real or potential competitors of U.S. industry.

Two broad blocs on foreign economic policy did indeed emerge after World War I, and their preferences were more or less as might have been predicted. One group of economic interests was "internationalist": it supported American entry into the League of Nations, U.S. financing of European reconstruction, commercial liberalization, and international monetary and financial cooperation. The other cluster of economic interests was the "isolationists": it opposed the League and American financing of Europe, called for renewed trade protection, and was indifferent or hostile to global financial and monetary accords.[8] The two sets of policy preferences were competing rather than complementary, and although there were some actors in a middle ground, the extreme unevenness of American overseas economic expansion meant that preferences tended to harden in their opposition.

The central dilemma of U.S. foreign economic policy for fifteen years after World War I was the great economic strength of two opposing sets of economic and political actors, neither of which was powerful enough to vanquish the other. Among the consequences of interest to the analyst of international relations is that the state *did not* undertake to impose a foreign policy derived from America's international position upon recalcitrant domestic actors; instead, the central state apparatus found itself torn between

Political Economy of the Smoot–Hawley Tariff," Discussion Paper No. 1244, Harvard Institute for Economic Research, May 1986.

8. Opposition to the League was indeed led by a prominent nationalist Massachusetts senator whose adamant insistence on protecting manufactured goods while allowing the free import of inputs was ably captured by "Mr. Dooley," who noted that "Hinnery Cabin Lodge pleaded f'r freedom f'r th' skins iv cows" in ways that "wud melt th' heart iv th' coldest mannyfacthrer iv button shoes." Cited in John A. Garraty, *Henry Cabot Lodge* (New York: Knopf, 1953), p. 268; the book contains ample, and somewhat weightier, evidence of Lodge's economic nationalism.

conflicting interests. The various economic interests entrenched themselves in the political arena and found allies within the government bureaucracy, so that domestic sociopolitical strife was carried out *within* the state apparatus. The Federal Reserve System and the State Department were dominated by economic internationalists, whether of the Wilsonian or Republican variants; the majority of the Congress, and the powerful Commerce Department, were more closely aligned with the economic nationalists who might support limited measures to encourage American exports but stopped there.

The result was a foreign policy that was eminently contradictory and volatile. The same administration encouraged foreign lending and trade protection against the goods of the borrowers, worked for international monetary cooperation and sought to sabotage it, struggled to reinforce European reconstruction and impeded it at crucial junctures. This was not due to policy stupidity but to the underlying differences in international outlook of powerful domestic socioeconomic groups. The period is thus a useful and illuminating illustration of the interaction of international and domestic sources of foreign policy.

Although it concentrates on the analytical issues of the 1920s and early 1930s, the article shows how after 1933 the world crisis served to thaw some of the policy paralysis that had characterized the postwar Republican administrations. The international and domestic crisis both changed the relative strength of important social actors and allowed policymakers to reformulate their relationship to these social actors.

The remainder of this article analyzes the development of American foreign economic policy from 1914 to 1940 in the light of the preceding considerations. The analysis focuses on the interests and activities of America's international bankers. The nation's international financiers were both the most internationally oriented group of economic actors in the United States at the time (as they are today) and the most powerful and prominent members of the internationalist coalition. Their trajectory demonstrates the general lines of the approach taken here quite well, and also clarifies the role of the differentiated state apparatus in the evolution of U.S. foreign economic policy after World War I. The article does not present a complete account of the period in question—this would require a much more detailed discussion of, among other things, overseas events, America's economic nationalists, and institutional and bureaucratic developments—but it does discuss enough of the era to show how a fuller analysis could be developed.

The emergence of American economic internationalism, 1914–1933

For fifty years before World War I, the American political economy was oriented to the needs of domestic industry. The war accelerated a process already underway, the expansion of international investments by one segment of the U.S. business community. Along with this economic change came the development of a new set of political interests that challenged the previous pattern of foreign economic policy. In the fifteen years after World War I, the economic internationalists developed great, if quite private, influence over foreign policy, but lost many public political battles. Until the Depression, American foreign economic policy was divided between measures to support "nationalist" industries and most of agriculture and those preferred by "internationalist" banks, industries, and some export agriculture.

From the Civil War until the early 1900s, however, the country's foreign economic policy was clearly designed to serve domestic industry, mostly home production for the home market and some exportation. The strategy adopted had a number of aims and evolved over time, as David Lake has demonstrated.[9] Raw materials available overseas needed to be developed and imported. Industrial goods, especially the products of basic industry, needed to find overseas markets. American tariffs on raw materials might come down, but the American market was essentially closed to industrial goods.

In this picture, America's embryonic international bankers played a subsidiary but important role. They financed overseas raw materials developments and facilitated the transport and sale of raw materials to American industry. They lent dollars to overseas consumers of America's basic industrial products—railways, railroad and subway cars, mining equipment, ships. And, of course, they financed much of the domestic expansion and merger activity of the industrial combines.

World War I was a turning-point in the evolution of American international economic interests. During the war and the period immediately following it, New York became the world's center for long-term lending. Amerian financial supremacy drew America's internationally oriented business people and politicians into world leadership during the war and in the postwar reconstruction of Europe, a role that was to be severely hampered by the strength of economic nationalists within the United States.

The outbreak of hostilities caused financial chaos on European money markets. Panic was only narrowly averted in New York, but by early 1915 the New York market had been stabilized and was the only fully functioning major capital market in the world. Originally the Wilson administration had indicated that it considered the extension of all but short-term loans to the warring powers by American financiers "inconsistent with the true spirit of neutrality." But as the fighting continued, the belligerents began to place major orders in the United States to supply their industries and compensate

9. David Lake, "The State and American Trade Strategy in the Pre-Hegemonic Era," in this volume.

for their lagging agricultures. American munitions exports went from $40 million in 1914 to nearly $1.3 billion in 1916; all merchandise exports increased from $2.4 billion in 1914 to $5.5 billion in 1916, from about 6 to about 12 percent of gross national product. Because imports remained near prewar levels, between 1914 and 1917 the United States averaged an astounding annual trade surplus of $2.5 billion, more than five times the immediate prewar average.[10]

The Allies, who accounted for most of this export expansion (the Central Powers were effectively blockaded), financed some of their American purchases by selling back to United States investors about $2 billion in American securities between the beginning of the war and U.S. entry. This was insufficient, of course, and soon the Wilson administration reversed its earlier financial neutrality. In October 1915, J. P. Morgan and Co. underwrote a $500 million loan to the English and French governments. Because of the opposition of neutralists and anti-Russian, German-American, and Irish-American forces, Morgan was only able to secure the full amount with some difficulty.[11]

Despite widespread hostility to their efforts, the New York bankers continued to finance the Allies. In addition, their longstanding ties with the big industrial combines placed the bankers well to arrange for Allied purchases and shipping. Thus Morgan acted during the war as the purchasing agent in the United States for the British and French, and in the three-year period up to June 1917, these purchases amounted to over one-quarter of all American exports.[12]

The Allies' financial requirements increased as the war dragged on, as did American sympathy for the Allied cause. Morgan led a series of syndicates in a further $250 million loan to England in August 1916, another of $300 million in October 1916, a $250 million issue in January 1917; France floated a $100 million bond in March 1917. All told, between January 1915 and 5 April 1917, the Allies borrowed about $2.6 billion: Great Britain and

---

10. George Edwards, *The Evolution of Finance Capitalism* (London: Longmans, 1938), pp. 204–5, and U.S. Department of Commerce, *Historical Statistics of the United States* (Washington: GPO, 1960), pp. 139, 537. The definitive work on the period is Kathleen Burk, *Britain, America and the Sinews of War, 1914–1918* (Boston: Allen & Unwin, 1985). See also David Kennedy, *Over Here: The First World War and American Society* (New York: Oxford University Press, 1980); John T. Madden, Marcus Nadler, and Harry C. Sauvain, *America's Experience as a Creditor Nation* (New York: Prentice-Hall, 1937), pp. 44–46; Alexander Dana Noyes, *The War Period of American Finance* (New York: Putnam, 1926), pp. 113–18; William J. Schultz and M. R. Caine, *Financial Development of the United States* (New York: Prentice-Hall, 1937), 503–4.

11. Harold Nicolson, *Dwight Morrow* (New York: Macmillan, 1935), pp. 171–75.

12. Cleona Lewis, *America's Stake in International Investments* (Washington, D.C.: Brookings Institution, 1938), p. 352. See, for a discussion of the experience, Roberta A. Dayer, "Strange Bedfellows: J. P. Morgan and Co., Whitehall, and the Wilson Administration During World War I," *Business History* 18 (July 1976), pp. 127–51.

France \$2.11 billion, Canada and Australia \$405 million, Russia and Italy \$75 million.[13]

Upon American entry into the war, private lending to the belligerents essentially ceased. Instead, between May 1917 and April 1919, the U.S. government issued four "Liberty Loans" and one postwar "Victory Loan," and used the proceeds to lend the Allies \$9.6 billion.[14] American banks also took the opportunity to establish or drastically expand their branches in France to service the hordes of arriving American troops.[15]

Private lending resumed almost as soon as wartime conditions ended, as Table 3 indicates. Especially after the 1924 Dawes Plan, which symbolized for many the economic stabilization of Europe, lending boomed. As can be seen in Table 4, in the early 1920s American lending also shifted away from the wartime allies and towards "non-traditional borrowers": Germany, Canada, Italy, smaller Western European countries, the more commercially important countries of South America, and the Dutch East Indies. United States banks also expanded their branch network overseas from 26 in 1914 to 154 in 1926. As we have mentioned, direct investment abroad by American corporations also rose very rapidly, from \$2.7 billion in 1914 to \$7.9 billion in 1929.

The rapid overseas expansion of United States businesses after 1914 led to the maturation of an outward-looking, internationalist perspective, especially on the part of the international bankers. The leaders of American finance took a new, broader view of the world in which they had invested and decided that, as Woodrow Wilson said in 1916, "We have got to finance the world in some important degree, and those who finance the world must understand it and rule it with their spirits and with their minds."[16]

Apart from the general expansion of their lending, the bankers' customers had changed. No longer were the loans going to specific raw-materials projects or railroad development. The new debtors of the 1920s were more advanced nations; many of them, like Germany, were major competitors of U.S. industry. Concern about American tariffs on manufactured goods was thus logical. The debtors were also usually governments, and the close ties the bankers were building with, for example, Central and Eastern European

---

13. Lewis, *America's Stake*, p. 355; Nicolson, *Dwight Morrow*, pp. 177–82; Vincent P. Carosso, *Investment Banking in America: A History* (Cambridge, Mass.: Harvard University Press, 1970), pp. 205–14. For a thoughtful survey of the political effects, see John Milton Cooper, Jr., "The Command of Gold Reversed: American Loans to Britain, 1915–1917," *Pacific Historical Review* 45 (May 1976), pp. 209–30.

14. This is Lewis's figure; *America's Stake*, p. 362. Others give different amounts. See, for example, Noyes, *The War Period*, pp. 162–93; Schultz and Caine, *Financial Development*, pp. 525, 533–42; Hiram Motherwell, *The Imperial Dollar* (New York: Brentano's, 1929), p. 85.

15. Charles Kindleberger, "Origins of United States Direct Investment in France," *Business History Review* 48 (Autumn 1974), p. 390.

16. Scott Nearing and Joseph Freeman, *Dollar Diplomacy* (New York: Huebsch, 1925), p. 273.

TABLE 4. *American portfolio of foreign securities, 1914–1935 (in millions of dollars; excludes inter-government war debts)*

	1914	1919	1924	1929	1935
Europe	196	1,491	1,946	3,473	2,586
Austria	1	0	27	72	57
Belgium	0	12	181	214	152
Czechoslovakia	—	0	32	32	30
Denmark	0	15	89	165	135
Finland	—	0	29	63	32
France	10	343	449	343	158
Germany	23	2	132	1,019	829
Great Britain	122	891	414	287	42
Hungary	—	0	9	63	57
Italy	0	38	41	365	271
Netherlands	0	0	99	62	132
Norway	3	5	97	185	151
Poland	0	0	30	132	97
Russia	29	127	104	104	104
Sweden	5	20	66	196	213
Switzerland	0	35	116	49	0
Yugoslavia	0	0	18	50	47
Other Europe[a]	3	3	13	72	79
Canada	179	729	1,551	2,003	1,965
South America	43	113	464	1,294	1,241
Argentina	26	58	188	370	344
Bolivia	8	10	38	62	59
Brazil	6	41	146	325	320
Chile	1	1	53	238	237
Colombia	0	1	15	167	146
Peru	2	0	9	77	74
Uruguay	0	2	15	45	51
Venezuela	0	0	0	10	10
Caribbean Region	310	305	390	430	434
Cuba	35	33	76	95	115
Dominican Republic	5	6	15	19	16
Haiti	0	0	17	15	10
Mexico	266	265	270	266	261
Central America	4	2	12	35	32
Asia	217	227	519	926	772
Australia	0	1	24	241	253
China	7	20	23	23	21
Dutch East Indies	0	0	150	175	25
Japan	184	166	234	387	384
Philippines	26	40	88	100	89
Other and international	0	0	0	18	29
Total	945	2,862	4,870	8,144	7,026

Source. Adapted from Cleona Lewis, *America's Stake in International Investments* (Washington, D.C.: Brookings Institution, 1938), pp. 654–55.
a. In descending order of financial importance in 1929: Greece, Bulgaria, Rumania, Luxemburg, Ireland, Estonia, Danzig, and Lithuania.

regimes made them especially interested in European economic reconstruction and political harmony. The major international bankers, then, wanted a more internationalist foreign policy for the United States, lower tariffs, and American aid for a European settlement.

The financiers acted on their beliefs, and the postwar period saw the construction of formal and informal institutions and networks that have ever since been at the center of the American foreign policy establishment. The Council on Foreign Relations was formed right after the war: John W. Davis, Morgan's chief counsel and later a Democratic candidate for president, was the council's first president; Alexander Hemphill, chairman of the Guaranty Trust Co., headed the council's finance committee. Thomas W. Lamont of J. P. Morgan and Co. played an active role in the council and brought the founding editor of the council's journal, *Foreign Affairs,* to the job (he was editor of Lamont's *New York Evening Post*). Otto Kahn and Paul Warburg of the investment bank Kuhn, Loeb were founding directors, as was Paul Cravath, the firm's lawyer. Norman H. Davis, another founding director, was a Wall Street banker who served as assistant secretary of the treasury and undersecretary of state under Wilson; he worked closely with Lamont and financier Bernard Baruch in defining the postwar economic settlement in Europe.[17]

The council was the most important such organization, but the internationalist segment of the American business community, headed by the international bankers, also worked with other similar groups. The Foreign Policy Association, the Carnegie Endowment for International Peace (founded 1908), the League of Nations Association, and many others brought scholars, bankers, journalists, politicians, and government officials together in the pursuit of internationalism. In addition to consultation, coordination, and research, the internationalist network aimed to convince average Americans, in the words of the chairman of the Foreign Policy Association, "that their stake in the restauration of normal economic conditions in Europe is in reality as direct and vital as that of the international banker."[18]

More direct was the initiation during World War I of a system of close cooperation between foreign policymakers, especially those concerned with foreign economic policy, and America's international bankers. It was common for important figures in American international financial circles to serve on policy advisory bodies and sometimes to rotate through positions in

17. Lawrence H. Shoup and William Minter, *Imperial Brain Trust: The Council on Foreign Relations and United States Foreign Policy* (New York: Monthly Review, 1977), pp. 11–28.

18. Cited in Frank Costigliola, "United States–European Relations and the Effort to Shape American Public Opinion, 1921–1933," in Schmidt, ed., *Konstellationen Internationaler Politik,* p. 43. See also Costigliola, *Awkward Dominion,* pp. 56–75 and 140–66, and Robert A. Divine, *Second Chance: The Triumph of Internationalism in America During World War II* (New York: Atheneum, 1972), pp. 6–23.

government, usually at the State Department and the Federal Reserve Bank of New York. Indeed, during and after the war, the State Department and the Federal Reserve Bank of New York established durable working relations with the New York bankers. On every significant foreign policy initiative of the 1920s—from the Versailles Treaty itself, to war debts and reparations, to the tariff issue, to the Dawes and Young Plans, to the boom in foreign borrowing and the establishment of the Bank for International Settlements—the international bankers worked together with the like-minded internationalists of the State Department and the Federal Reserve Bank of New York in the evolution of policy.

The financial and other internationalists faced the opposition of extremely powerful forces of economic nationalism in the United States. Senior Morgan partner Thomas Lamont decried "the failure of the American people to understand that the United States of America held a new position in the world," and later reflected on the unfortunate fact that "America entered upon the new decade of the 1920s in full panoply of wealth and power, but possessing little ambition to realize her vast potentialities for strengthening the world in stability and peace."[19]

The stumblingblock was the existence of a considerable anti-internationalist political bloc with support from business people who had little interest in foreign affairs, worried about foreign competition, and opposed the export of American capital. The Commerce Department of Herbert Hoover, the prime mover of U.S. economic policy in the 1920s, was closely linked and deeply committed to American domestic industry. In foreign economic affairs, its principal concern was thus to promote industrial exports and primary imports, not overseas lending and manufacturing investment. America's domestic industrialists could, like Hoover, agree on some things with the bankers. They all favored expanding American exports, and some kinds of imports. Yet there was little sympathy in domestically oriented industry for freer trade insofar as it meant manufactured imports. Domestic industrialists were also unhappy with American bank loans to foreign competitors, and some of them were wary of capital exports in general. As Hoover put it, "a billion dollars spent upon American railways will give more employment to our people, more advance to our industry, more assistance to our farmers, than twice that sum expended outside the frontiers of the United States."[20]

The United States faced a bewildering array of foreign policy problems in the 1920s, and in virtually every case the tension between internationalists and nationalists defined the discussion and outcome. There is no need to

19. Thomas W. Lamont, *Across World Frontiers* (New York: Harcourt, Brace, 1951), pp. 215, 217–18.

20. Jacob Viner, "Political Aspects of International Finance," *Journal of Business of the University of Chicago* 1 (April 1928), p. 146.

describe these debates at length, for there is an ample literature on them.[21] Three broad problems—European reconstruction, trade policy and capital exports—were of special importance, and later I shall summarize the major issues involved in these debates and note the common pattern. In virtually every case, internationalist financiers and their allies in the State Department and the Federal Reserve faced the opposition of nationalist forces in Congress and other segments of the executive. The internationalists were almost always defeated, forced to compromise, or forced to adopt some form of semi-official arrangement that kept the process out of the public eye.

European reconstruction and war debts

The general desire of the United States international bankers was for the rapid reconstruction of Europe. Private funds might be used for this purpose but the financial shakiness of the potential borrowers (especially in Central Europe) made U.S. government involvement preferable. Inasmuch as the debts owed the U.S. government by the Allies were an obstacle to European reconstruction, especially since they encouraged the French to demand larger reparations payments from the Germans, the American financiers favored partial or total cancellation of official war debts.[22] All of this required American leadership: the United States government should help the Europeans back onto the gold standard, arrange for a government-backed bankers' consortium to restore Europe's shattered currencies, regularize and encourage American private capital exports to Europe, force the Europeans to negotiate a reduction of Germany's reparations burden in return for war debts leniency, and combat economic nationalism on the Continent.

This leadership was not forthcoming. Talk of war debt cancellation was quashed by economic nationalists in the Cabinet and in Congress, for whom war-debt forgiveness represented a levy on American taxpayers who would be called upon to make up the Treasury's loss, in favor of the country's European competitors. Although some refunding and reduction did occur, the bankers were forced to retreat. Government-backed loans to the Europeans were also vetoed, as was any official American involvement in the

---

21. See, in addition to works cited above, Paul P. Abrahams, *The Foreign Expansion of American Finance and its Relationship to the Foreign Economic Policies of the United States, 1907–1921* (New York: Arno, 1976); Herbert Feis, *The Diplomacy of the Dollar: First Era 1919–1932* (Baltimore: Johns Hopkins University Press, 1950); Joan Hoff Wilson, *American Business and Foreign Policy, 1920–1933* (Lexington: University Press of Kentucky, 1971); Frank Costigliola, "The United States and the Reconstruction of Germany in the 1920s," *Business History Review* 50 (Winter 1976), pp. 477–502; and Frank Costigliola, "Anglo-American Financial Rivalry in the 1920s," *Journal of Economic History* 38 (December 1977), pp. 911–34. Because the issues are so widely treated, citations will only be given where necessary to confirm a specific fact, controversial interpretation, or direct quotation.
22. On these issues, see the articles by Thomas Lamont, James Sheldon, and Arthur J. Rosenthal in *Annals of the American Academy of Political and Social Science* 88 (March 1920), pp. 114–38.

reparations tangle. Only in monetary matters, where the bankers' house organ, the Federal Reserve Bank of New York, was given fairly free rein, was limited progress made.[23]

Opposition to the bankers' plans solidified under President Warren Harding in the early 1920s. Congress and much of the executive branch were intransigent on the war debts and reparations issues. Herbert Hoover's Commerce Department was not generally favorable to financial schemes that might strengthen overseas competitors of American industry or that might allow foreign raw materials producers to raise prices to American manufacturers.[24] Morgan partner Thomas Lamont bitterly blasted "ill-advised steps for the collection of that debt, every penny, principal and interest," while Lamont's *New York Evening Post* editorialized: "We cannot emphasize too often the mischief for the European situation to-day wrought by Herbert Hoover's assertion that 95 percent of America's claims on the continent are good."[25]

It was not for lack of trying that the bankers were unable to secure government involvement. Benjamin Strong at the Federal Reserve Bank of New York played a major role in European reconstruction planning and implementation. As he said when proposing central-bank cooperation for exchange stabilization to an October 1921 meeting of the Board of Governors of the Federal Reserve System, "whether we want to or not we are going to take some part in this situation abroad. We probably won't do it politically, but we have to do it financially and economically." The governors, far more sympathetic to the desperate straits of European finances than the administration, were strongly in favor, as Governor Norris of Philadelphia indicated:

> I think the three great opportunities that we have had to accomplish the stabilization of foreign exchange were, first, to go into the League of Nations; second, to make a readjustment of our tariff . . . and the third was to empower the Secretary of the Treasury to deal in an intelligent way with the refunding of foreign obligations. . . . But because we have lost those three it does not follow, of course, that we ought to throw aside and discard all others . . . [and] it seems to me that the proposition you have suggested is one that undoubtedly has merit and may reasonably be expected to accomplish some results.[26]

23. See especially Abrahams, *Foreign Expansion of American Finance*; and Costigliola, "Anglo-American Financial Rivalry," pp. 914–20. For an interesting view of one aspect of the war debts tangle, see Roberta A. Dayer, "The British War Debts to the United States and the Anglo-Japanese Alliance, 1920–1923," *Pacific Historical Review* 45 (November 1976), pp. 569–95.

24. Joseph Brandes, *Herbert Hoover and Economic Diplomacy* (Pittsburgh: University of Pittsburgh Press, 1962), pp. 170–96; and Melvyn Leffler, "The Origins of Republican War Debt Policy, 1921–1923," *Journal of American History* 59 (December 1972), pp. 585–601.

25. Cited in Silverman, *Reconstructing Europe,* pp. 157 and 189.

26. Cited in U.S. Congress, House of Representatives, Committee on Banking and Currency, Subcommittee on Domestic Finance, *Federal Reserve Structure and the Development of*

Yet a month later, the executive branch refused to allow a central bank conference that Strong and Montagu Norman of the Bank of England had proposed. Strong wrote to Norman at the time, "between the lines I read that there would in fact be no objection if the matter were undertaken privately and without government support or responsibility." Thus when the League of Nations' Financial Committee was supervising an Austrian stabilization program in 1922–23, the New York bankers were regularly consulted to ensure that the program would meet with the approval of U.S. financial markets—which it did when the U.S. portion of the stabilization loan was floated in June 1923.[27]

Nevertheless, for all intents and purposes the bankers' plans for an American-supervised economic settlement in Europe were foiled. As the Central European economies collapsed in 1923 and 1924, the administration attempted to balance the financiers' insistence on American involvement against equally insistent nationalist demands that the United States stay out of Europe. The State Department, anxious to use American influence and finance to stabilize Europe, began the process that would lead to the Dawes Plan in April 1924. The arrangement worked out was ingenious: negotiations were entrusted to an unofficial delegation of American business people, headed by internationally minded Chicago banker Charles G. Dawes and Owen D. Young, chairman of the board of General Electric. The prominent internationalist bankers and business people at the center of the negotiations consulted closely, if surreptitiously, with the State Department and the Federal Reserve Bank of New York.[28]

The Dawes Plan called for foreign supervision of German public finances, with reparations payments overseen by an American with discreet ties to Morgan's. The German currency was stabilized and investor confidence in Germany restored with a $200 million bond flotation, of which J. P. Morgan and Co. managed $110 million in New York.[29] All things considered, the plan was a reasonable compromise: it used American financial supremacy to settle (at least temporarily) a major European wrangle without committing the U.S. government directly. The only open government involvement was an encouragement to American investors to subscribe to the Dawes loan, and indeed Morgan received over a billion dollars in applications, ten times

Monetary Policy, 1915–1935: Staff Report (Washington, D.C.: GPO, 1971), p. 62. I am grateful to Jane D'Arista for bringing these and other documents to my attention.

27. Hogan, *Informal Entente*, pp. 62–66.

28. See, for example, Stephen V. O. Clarke, *Central Bank Cooperation 1924–1931* (New York: Federal Reserve Bank of New York, 1967), pp. 46–57, and Charles G. Dawes, *A Journal of Reparations* (London: Macmillan, 1939), pp. 262–64, for evidence of just how central the bankers were.

29. The agent-general, S. Parker Gilbert, was a close associate of Morgan partner Russell Leffingwell. Costigliola, "The United States and the Reconstruction of Germany," pp. 485–94; Feis, *Diplomacy of the Dollar*, pp. 40–43; Leffler, *Elusive Quest*, pp. 90–112; Nearing and Freeman, *Dollar Diplomacy*, pp. 221–32; Nicolson, *Dwight Morrow*, pp. 272–78; Schuker, *French Predominance in Europe*, pp. 284–89.

the amount of the loan. The settlement satisfied most internationalists and most nationalists in the United States temporarily, and even this was quite a feat.[30]

Free trade and the tariff

Fundamental domestic differences over U.S. trade policy were harder to paper over. Indeed, the future of America's traditional protectionism was perhaps the most contentious issue in American politics in the 1920s. During World War I, the administration had apparently committed itself to low and flexible tariffs, in line with the bankers' preferences. When the United States became a major lender, foreign borrowers had to be permitted freer access to the U.S. market or loans could not be serviced. Tariff barriers, argued the bankers, were a cause of useless trade rivalries and war. As Morgan partner Dwight Morrow put it, "leadership in world trade is not a thing to be sought by any nation to the exclusion of all others."[31]

But in Congress, those American economic actors who demanded protection from foreign imports had the upper hand. In 1921, Congress passed a restrictive Emergency Tariff Act that was followed in 1922 by the Fordney–McCumber tariff.[32] This act had provisions that attempted to satisfy both protectionist industrialists and farmers and, less successfully, internationalist bankers, investors, and traders. The compromise was generally unsatisfactory to both factions, and controversy on the tariff raged throughout the 1920s. Few doubted that traditional American protectionism had returned, and the French Finance Ministry called Fordney–McCumber "the first heavy blow directed against any hope of effectively restoring a world trading system."[33]

Such financiers as Otto Kahn looked with dismay on the continued strength of protectionist sentiment:

> Having become a creditor nation, we have got now to fit ourselves into the role of a creditor nation. We shall have to make up our minds to be more hospitable to imports. We shall have to outgrow gradually certain inherited and no longer applicable views and preconceptions and adapt our economic policies to the changed positions which have resulted from the late war.[34]

30. For Lamont's optimism, see *Proceedings of the Academy of Political Science* 11 (January 1925), pp. 325–32.

31. Nicolson, *Dwight Morrow*, pp. 191–92.

32. Wilson, *American Business*, pp. 70–75.

33. Cited in Silverman, *Reconstructing Europe*, p. 239.

34. Mary Jane Maltz, *The Many Lives of Otto Kahn* (New York: Macmillan, 1963), pp. 204–5. For the similar views of Norman H. Davis, see *Proceedings of the Academy of Political Science* 12 (January 1928), pp. 867–74. See also Wilson, *American Business*, pp. 65–100.

Supervision of foreign loans

In the early 1920s, opposition to the export of American capital mounted. Domestic industrial interests were concerned that the loans were strengthening foreign competitors, especially in Germany, and reducing the capital available to domestic producers. They were also concerned that loans to raw-materials producers might be used to organize producers' cartels that would raise prices charged to U.S. industry. Hoover and Treasury Secretary Andrew Mellon thus wanted to make new loans contingent on the use of at least part of them for the purchase of American goods, or to a commitment by the borrowers to allow American suppliers to bid on ensuing contracts; they also opposed lending to nations disinclined to service their war debts to the U.S. government and lending that might reinforce the position of suppliers to or competitors with American industry. The bankers, of course, along with Benjamin Strong of the Federal Reserve Bank of New York, opposed any government controls; Secretary of State Charles E. Hughes leaned towards their position.

In 1921, President Harding, Hoover, Hughes, and Mellon met with the leading New York bankers and reached an agreement that the banks would notify the Department of State of all foreign loans and give the department the opportunity to object. Formalized in 1922, the policy was applied as sparingly as possible by a State Department that supported the bankers. Even so, in a number of instances Hoover was able to override the bankers; two prominent successes were blocked loans to a French–German potash cartel and to Brazilian coffee-growers. The commerce secretary warned "the American banking community" that "the commissions which might be collected on floating such loans would be no compensation" for the "justifiable criticism . . . from the American potash and coffee consumers when [they] become aware that American capital was being placed at the disposal of these agencies through which prices were being held against our own people." Hoover also threatened to form a pool to break a British rubber cartel, complained about Amerian lending to the German steel trust, and he and Mellon succeeded in stopping several loans for reasons related to war debts or other foreign policy objectives.[35]

Here, again, the conflict between the international interests of financiers and the national concerns of many American business people and politicians clashed. Once more, the outcome was indecisive; the State Department

---

35. Hoover is cited in Joseph Brandes, "Product Diplomacy: Herbert Hoover's Anti-Monopoly Campaign at Home and Abroad," in Ellis Hawley, ed., *Herbert Hoover as Secretary of Commerce* (Iowa City: University of Iowa Press, 1981), p. 193. See also H. B. Elliston, "State Department Supervision of Foreign Loans," in Charles P. Howland, ed., *Survey of American Foreign Relations 1928* (New Haven, Conn.: Yale University Press for the Council on Foreign Relations, 1928) pp. 183–201; John Foster Dulles, "Our Foreign Loan Policy," *Foreign Affairs* 5 (October 1926), pp. 33–48; Brandes, *Herbert Hoover*, pp. 151–96; Feis, *Diplomacy of the Dollar*, pp. 7–17; Leffler, *Elusive Quest*, pp. 58–64.

succeeded in blunting most of Hoover's attacks on foreign lending he regarded as excessive, yet pressure never let up.

The deadlock between internationalism and nationalism that formed in the early 1920s remained in place throughout the Coolidge and Hoover administrations. Foreign economic policy retained much of its ambiguity, with government departments and the international bankers cooperating and colliding, depending on the issue and the department involved. Internationalist bankers and business people complained bitterly of the Commerce Department's attempts to restrict their activities and to penalize their overseas clients. As Owen Young wrote to Hoover in 1926, "I am sincerely troubled by our national program, which is demanding amounts from our debtors up to the breaking point, and at the same time excluding their goods from our American markets, except for those few raw materials which we must have.[36]

Although a wide range of issues in American foreign economic policy remained unsolved, the financiers fought continually to implement some form of European economic reconstruction. After the Dawes Plan gave Germany, and by implication other Central European borrowers, the stamp of approval of international finance, loans to Europe exploded. Between 1925 and 1930, Americans lent a total of $5.3 billion to foreigners; $1.3 billion went to Canada, $1.6 billion to Latin America, and $305 million to Japan. Virtually all of the rest—$2.6 billion—went to Europe, as follows: Germany $1.2 billion (47 percent of the European total), Italy $345 million (13 percent), Eastern and Southeastern Europe $386 million (15 percent), and Scandinavia $385 million (15 percent); the remainder was scattered across a number of lesser borrowers.[37]

The United States had become the world's leading capital exporter, its bankers often acting as leaders in international financial consortia. By far the most important borrower was Germany; by 1929, American portfolio investment there had gone from nearly nothing to over a billion dollars (see Table 4). Germany and Central European prosperity, deemed essential to the political and economic stabilization of Europe, depended largely on injections of United States capital. Between 1925 and 1928, foreigners provided 39 percent of all long-term borrowing by the German public sector, and 70 percent of all long-term private borrowing; half of the foreign lending was from America.[38]

Yet it was clear to the financiers that European economic expansion was precarious, and the fundamental division of American foreign economic policy made it more so. The bankers and their allies in the State Department

36. David Burner, *Herbert Hoover: A Public Life* (New York: Alfred A. Knopf, 1979), p. 186.
37. These are recalculated from Lewis, *America's Stake*, pp. 619–29; her aggregate figures are inexplicably inconsistent.
38. McNeil, *American Money*, p. 282.

and the Federal Reserve System did what they could to solidify their tenuous attempts at international economic leadership. The curious and often awkward *modus vivendi* that evolved was illustrated by the financial stabilization programs arranged in a series of European nations between late 1926 and late 1928. In Belgium, Poland, Italy, and Rumania, cooperative central-bank credits—generally put together by the Bank of England and the Federal Reserve Bank of New York—were extended in conjunction with longer-term private loans, of which American banks typically provided at least half. The private bankers were closely involved in the negotiations leading up to the stabilization agreements.[39]

In early 1929, the international bankers who had put together the Dawes Plan—including many who had participated in the financial stabilization programs of the late 1920s—came together again to attempt a further regularization of international financial matters. The United States was represented (unofficially, of course, as at the Dawes Conference) by Owen Young and J. P. Morgan; Thomas Lamont was Morgan's alternate. After dealing with German issues, the conference established the Bank for International Settlements (BIS) to accept continuing German reparations (renamed "annuities") payments and, more broadly, to manage the international financial system. The BIS, which was the product of the American financiers, was to promote financial stability and take finance out of the hands of unreliable politicians. Indeed, it was founded in such a way as to make congressional approval unnecessary and congressional oversight impossible.[40]

The BIS, however, was powerless to counter the effects of the Great Depression. In May 1931, the Kreditanstalt failure triggered panic throughout Central Europe. President Hoover recognized the inevitable and, in late June 1931, declared a moratorium on the payment of war debts in an attempt to stave off, in Treasury Undersecretary Ogden Mills's words, "a major catastrophe of incalculable consequences to the credit structure of the world and to the economic future of all nations."[41] Nevertheless, in 1932, defaults began in Hungary, Greece, Bulgaria, Austria, Yugoslavia, Sweden, and

39. See Richard H. Meyer, *Banker's Diplomacy* (New York: Columbia University Press, 1970).

40. Frank Costigliola, "The Other Side of Isolationism: The Establishment of the First World Bank, 1929–1930," *Journal of American History* 59 (December 1972), and Harold James, *The Reichsbank and Public Finance in Germany 1924–1933* (Frankfurt: Knapp, 1985), pp. 57–94. On BIS attempts at international financial cooperation from 1930 to 1931, see William A. Brown, Jr., *The International Gold Standard Reinterpreted, 1914–1934*, vol. 2 (New York: National Bureau of Economic Research, 1940), pp. 1035–47. For the views of New York bankers see the articles by Shepard Morgan of Chase and Jackson Reynolds of the First National Bank of New York in *Proceedings of the Academy of Political Science* 14 (January 1931), pp. 215–34, and Shepard Morgan, "Constructive Functions of the International Bank," *Foreign Affairs* 9 (July 1931), pp. 580–91. For an excellent overview of this period, see Clarke, *Central Bank Cooperation*.

41. Cited in Leffler, *Elusive Quest*, p. 238. On German–American financial relations after 1930, see Harold James, *The German Slump: Politics and Economics 1924–1936* (Oxford: Clarendon Press, 1986), pp. 398–413.

Denmark; in 1933, Germany and Rumania joined the list. By the end of 1934, over 40 percent of American loans to Europe were in default.[42] In the interim, of course, the United States substantially raised tariffs, even though, as Morgan's Thomas Lamont recalled, "I almost went down on my knees to beg Herbert Hoover to veto the asinine Hawley–Smoot Tariff."[43]

The contradictory nature of American foreign economic policy in the 1920s was much noted by financiers and scholars at the time. On the one hand, there was a massive outflow of private capital to Europe while, on the other, European exports to the United States, necessary to debt service, were severely restricted. To top it off, the Harding–Coolidge–Hoover administrations insisted on considering the Allies' war debts to the U.S. government as binding commercial obligations, which further restricted Europe's capacity to service American commercial debts.[44] The reason for this vacillation was that two powerful sets of interests, economic nationalists and economic internationalists, were fighting for power within the United States, and the battle raged through the 1920s and into the 1930s.

The degree to which the contradictions of U.S. foreign economic policy were recognized by the general public is indicated in Franklin Delano Roosevelt's August 1932 campaign-speech explanation of American foreign lending in *Alice in Wonderland* style:

> A puzzled, somewhat skeptical Alice asked the Republican leadership some simple questions:
> "Will not the printing and selling of more stocks and bonds, the building of new plants and the increase of efficiency produce more goods than we can buy?"
> "No," shouted Humpty Dumpty. "The more we produce the more we can buy."
> "What if we produce a surplus?"
> "Oh, we can sell it to foreign consumers."
> "How can the foreigners pay for it?"
> "Why, we will lend them money."
> "I see," said little Alice, "they will buy our surplus with our money. Of course these foreigners will pay us back by selling us their goods?"
> "Oh, not at all," said Humpty Dumpty. "We set up a high wall called the tariff."
> "And," said Alice at last, "how will the foreigners pay off these loans?"

42. Lewis, *America's Stake*, pp. 400–1; Foreign Bondholders Protective Council, *Annual Report for 1934* (New York: FBPC, 1934), pp. 218–24.

43. Burner, *Herbert Hoover*, p. 298.

44. M. E. Falkus, "United States Economic Policy and the 'Dollar Gap' in the 1920s," *Economic History Review* 24 (November 1972), pp. 599–623, argues that America's enormous balance of trade surplus in the 1920s was due more to the structure and composition of U.S. industry and trade than to trade barriers. Whether this is true or not, the fact remains, as Falkus recognizes, that contemporaries on both sides of the tariff wall *perceived* U.S. tariffs to be of major significance in limiting European exports.

"That is easy," said Humpty Dumpty, "did you ever hear of a moratorium?"

And so, at last, my friends, we have reached the heart of the magic formula of 1928.[45]

From 1914 on, major overseas investors, led by the international banks, rapidly extended their influence abroad and at home. Yet the battle for control of the state was undecided; instead of a unitary foreign policymaking apparatus with a coherent strategy, the United States had a foreign economic policy in the 1920s and early 1930s that was dualistic and irrational, in the sense that its various parts were in direct conflict with one another.[46] The political ambiguity of American foreign policy left American financial and other internationalists alone with their grandiose plans in a devastated world, determined that they would not again be defeated by forces that did not share their world vision.

The rise of American economic internationalism, 1933–1940

Just as the shock of World War I dramatically accelerated the extension of American international economic interests, the shock of the 1930s accelerated the demise of America's economic nationalists. During the first two Roosevelt administrations, economic internationalism gradually and haltingly came to dominate U.S. foreign policy, even as policymaking became ever more protected from the economic nationalists who continued to dominate the legislature. Faced with international and domestic economic crises of unprecedented depth and scope, the Roosevelt administration, after a brief attempt to rebuild international economic cooperation, retreated into domestic New Deal reforms, then slowly reemerged in the mid and late 1930s with a series of international economic initiatives that foreshadowed the postwar Bretton Woods system.

The Depression, indeed, had a devastating impact on the traditional economic and political base of the economic nationalists. Industrial production did not regain its 1929 peak until World War II, and in the interim few regarded industry as the dynamo it had been. Agriculture was even more

45. Feis, *Diplomacy of the Dollar*, p. 14.
46. These conclusions about American foreign policy in the 1920s differ a bit from those of some of the historians upon whose work my analysis is based. Leffler and Costigliola, especially, stress what they see as the unity of American policy, although both emphasize the importance of domestic constraints on this policy. In my view both scholars, despite their innovations, are too wedded to a modified Open-Door interpretation that overstates the unity and purposiveness of U.S. economic interests, and this methodological overlay colors their conclusions. I believe that the evidence, even as presented by them, warrants my analytical conclusions.

devastated. The banking system, of course, was also hard-hit, but most of the failures were of smaller banks. The big internationally oriented banks remained active both at home and abroad, although their economic and political influence was reduced both by the Depression itself and by Depression-era banking reforms. Table 1 demonstrates the continuing importance of international economic interests. Foreign direct investment, as a percentage of total corporate and agricultural invested capital, climbed through the 1930s, largely due to domestic deflation. Foreign bondholdings, of course, dropped because of defaults; this certainly harmed the bondholders but had little effect on the big investment and commercial banks themselves. In any case, holdings of foreign bonds remained substantial, and international bankers continued to hope that pre-1930 levels of lending could be restored.

When Roosevelt took office in March 1933, he hoped to reconcile two major goals: to stabilize international economic relations, and to resolve the country's pressing domestic economic problems. Britain had gone off the gold standard in 1931 to devalue the pound and improve Britain's trade position; it had also moved towards trade protection within the empire. By 1933 international monetary, financial, and trade relations were in shambles. At the same time, the United States was in the midst of a serious banking crisis, and the agricultural depression that had begun in the late 1920s was deepening. Roosevelt made no secret of the fact that his first priority was domestic, not international, stability.

The administration went into the international economic conference, which began in London in June 1933, willing to discuss some form of monetary cooperation with the British and French, but determined that these discussions should not interfere with domestic economic measures. As it turned out, the participants in the London conference were unable to reconcile national economic priorities with internationalism. Early in July, Roosevelt effectively wrecked the conference and any hopes for international currency stabilization, saying that "what is to be the value of the dollar in terms of foreign currencies is and cannot be our immediate concern."[47]

With the collapse of international cooperative efforts, Roosevelt turned his attention to the domestic economy. In October, U.S. began devaluing the dollar's gold value from $20.67 to $35 an ounce. Although the devaluation was not quite the success its proponents had expected, it did mark the administration's disenchantment with internationally negotiated attempts at stabilization.[48]

47. Stephen V. O. Clarke, *The Reconstruction of the International Monetary System: The Attempts of 1922 and 1933*, Princeton Studies in International Finance No. 33 (Princeton, N.J.: International Finance Section, Department of Economics, 1973), pp. 19–39; James R. Moore, "Sources of New Deal Economic Policy: The International Dimension," *Journal of American History* 61 (December 1974), pp. 728–44.

48. See especially John Morton Blum, *Roosevelt and Morgenthau* (Boston: Houghton Mifflin, 1970), pp. 45–53, and Ferguson, "Normalcy to New Deal," pp. 82–85. For a sympa-

Many international bankers approved of Roosevelt's domestic banking decisions and of the dollar devaluation. Yet as 1933 wore on, they were alarmed by his more unorthodox positions. Hostility between the administration and the financiers continued despite the attempts of Roosevelt and some of the bankers to call a truce, and in late 1933 and 1934, a number of financiers and policymakers close to the financial community left the administration or denounced it.[49]

The first two years of the Roosevelt administation were, in fact, characterized by divisions within the administration and the banking community, as well as a great deal of policy experimentation. Within the administration, a running battle was waged between Wilsonian Democrat Cordell Hull as secretary of state, Assistant Secretary Francis Sayre (an international lawyer and Wilson's son-in-law) and other free-trade internationalists on the one hand, and such economic nationalists as Presidential Foreign Trade Advisor and first President of the Export-Import Bank George Peek on the other.[50] To add to the confusion, Treasury Secretary Henry Morgenthau, Roosevelt's closest adviser on economic affairs, was both fascinated by and ignorant of international financial matters.

The nearly desperate economic crisis made the early Roosevelt administration willing to consider politically and ideologically unorthodox policies.[51] Indeed, much of the bankers' distrust of FDR in 1933–34 stemmed from the belief that he was embracing the notion of national self-sufficiency—economic nationalism with feeling—that was becoming so popular at the time and was often laced with semi-fascist ideology. For his part, Roosevelt was seriously concerned with the Depression's effect on the nation's social fabric, and was convinced that the British and French were insurmountable obstacles to a stabilization agreement that would allow for American economic recovery. Alarmed by the domestic political situation and thoroughly disenchanted with the British and French, Roosevelt enacted emergency measures to stabilize the system. Some financiers approved; most did not.

After the first frenzied phase of crisis management, however, the administration did indeed begin to move in a cautiously internationalist direction. In June 1934, Congress passed Hull's Reciprocal Trade Agreements Act, which

---

thetic European view of Roosevelt's policy, see Paul Einzig, *Bankers, Statesmen and Economists* (London: Macmillan, 1935), pp. 121–57.

49. See Blum, *Roosevelt and Morgenthau*, pp. 40–42, and, for an interesting example, Irving S. Mitchelman, "A Banker in the New Deal: James P. Warburg," *International Review of the History of Banking* 8 (1974), pp. 35–59. For an excellent survey of the period, see Albert Romasco, *The Politics of Recovery: Roosevelt's New Deal* (New York: Oxford University Press, 1983).

50. For details of the Hull–Peek controversy, see Frederick C. Adams, *Economic Diplomacy: The Export-Import Bank and American Foreign Policy 1934–1939* (Columbia: University of Missouri Press, 1976), pp. 81–93 and Robert Dallek, *Franklin D. Roosevelt and American Foreign Policy 1932–1945* (New York: Oxford University Press, 1979), pp. 84–85, 91–93.

51. For a discussion of the impact of crisis on ideologies and institutions, see Judith Goldstein, "Ideas, Institutions and American Trade Policy," this volume.

was broadly understood as a move towards freer trade. By 1934, too, the value of the dollar had been essentially fixed at $35 an ounce, indicating a renewed commitment to currency stability. In spring 1935, Roosevelt began cooperating with the French (over British objections) to stabilize the franc and pushed for English, American, and French collaboration for exchange-rate stability.[52] In late 1935, George Peek resigned in disgust over Roosevelt's drift to internationalism.

The financiers responded optimistically, if cautiously, to the administration's international initiatives. Early in 1936, Leon Fraser of the First National Bank of New York expressed his general approval of administration policy and his wish that this policy might become wholehearted:

> . . . [A]fter a period of painful trial and harmful error, the authorities have seemingly reached three conclusions, each vital to monetary stabilization at home and abroad. First, they have in fact, but in silence, rejected the proposed elastic dollar and have relinked the dollar to gold instead of to some commodity index. Second, they have been, and are, practising the gold standard internationally, subject to certain qualifications deemed to be necessary because of the present chaos. Third, as the logical next step, they stand ready to participate with other countries in the restoration of foreign exchange stabilization . . . Excellent—but a more affirmative stand will become necessary, a more explicit recognition of the responsibility which the advocacy of stabilization implies, and some assurances of a readiness to discharge these responsibilities in order to maintain the reestablished order.[53]

The commitment Fraser sought was indeed forthcoming. Through the summer of 1936 the Administration, the British, and the French moved slowly towards a "gentlemen's agreement" to restore their currencies' convertibility to gold and commit themselves to mutual consultations and intervention to avoid exchange-rate fluctuations. On 25 September 1936, the three governments agreed on a scheme embodying these commitments, with a dollar effectively linked to gold. The Tripartite Agreement—soon joined by Belgium, Switzerland, and the Netherlands—was a step towards rebuilding international economic cooperation. As one scholar has noted, "the Tripartite system may be seen as the beginning of an historical evolution that would issue after World War II in a global dollar standard."[54] For

52. Blum, *Roosevelt and Morgenthau*, pp. 64–67; Stephen V. O. Clarke, *Exchange-Rate Stabilization in the Mid-1930s: Negotiating the Tripartite Agreement*, Princeton Studies in International Finance No. 41 (Princeton, N.J.: International Finance Section, Department of Economics, 1977), pp. 8–21.

53. *Proceedings of the Academy of Political Science* 17 (May 1936), p. 107.

54. Harold van B. Cleveland, "The International Monetary System in the Inter-War Period," in Benjamin Rowland, ed., *Balance of Power or Hegemony: The Interwar Monetary System* (New York: NYU Press, 1976), p. 51. For a lengthier explanation of the ways in which the Tripartite Agreement marked the turning point in the evolution of U.S. economic internationalism, see Charles Kindleberger, *The World in Depression 1929–1939* (Berkeley: University of California Press, 1973), pp. 257–61. See also Blum, *Roosevelt and Morgenthau*, pp. 76–88; and Clarke, *Exchange-Rate Stabilization*, pp. 25–58.

the first time, the United States participated openly and prominently in leading the way towards international monetary cooperation, and the symbolic importance was more significant than any real accomplishments of the agreement.

By 1937, one prominent banker was able to name three developments that had given hope to those whose greatest fear was economic nationalism:

> First, the tripartite monetary agreement of last September was a challenge to the application of economic nationalism in monetary affairs. Second, our bilateral trade negotiations are a challenge to economic nationalism in trade affairs. . . . Third, some progress is being made in the direction of the re-creation of a normal international capital market in the Western hemisphere by the recent and current negotiations with South America.[55]

Yet the developing internationalism was hardly the same as the bankers' gold-standard liberal orthodoxy. The new system compromised more with domestic countercyclical demand management and with the imperatives of the embryonic "welfare state."[56] Many of the financiers indeed realized that a return to the classical gold standard was unthinkable and, with Leon Fraser in 1936, looked forward merely to "a union of what was best in the old gold standard, corrected on the basis of experience to date, and of what seems practicable in some of the doctrines of 'managed currencies'."[57] Yet during the late New Deal, the foreign exchange cooperation of the Trilateral Agreement, the tentative attempts at trade liberalization (by 1939 the reciprocal trade agreements covered 30 percent of American exports and 60 percent of imports[58]) and newfound moderation towards errant debtors all indicated a less ambiguous internationalist course than at any time since Wilson.

The episode considered

Economic nationalism reigned supreme in the U.S. political economy from 1860 until World War I, while since World War II, economic internationalism has dominated; the period considered here marks the transition from a

55. Robert B. Warren, "The International Movement of Capital," *Proceedings of the Academy of Political Science* 17 (May 1937), p. 71.

56. John G. Ruggie, "International Regimes, Transactions, and Change: Embedded Liberalism in the Postwar Economic Order," *International Organization* 36 (Spring 1982), pp. 379–415, discusses the order that emerged.

57. *Proceedings of the Academy of Political Science* 17 (May 1936), p. 113.

58. Herbert Feis, *The Changing Pattern of International Economic Affairs* (New York: Harper, 1940), p. 95. Stephen Schuker has, in personal communication, insisted that it was not until 1942 or 1943 that Roosevelt moved away from extreme economic nationalism. He marshals important evidence and convincing arguments to this effect, but the account presented here reflects current scholarly consensus. If, as he has done in the past, Schuker can disprove the conventional wisdom, this analysis of U.S. foreign economic policy in the late 1930s would, of course, need to be revised in the light of new data.

protected home market to full participation in and leadership of world investment and trade. As such, it is of great interest to those who would draw more general conclusions about the origins of state policy in the international arena. The era involved open conflict over the levers of foreign economic policy. In the midst of this conflict, the state was unable to derive and implement a unitary foreign economic policy; faced with a fundamentally divided set of domestic economic interests in foreign economic policy, the state and its policies were also divided. Each grouping of economic interests concentrated its forces where it was strongest: economic internationalists built ties with the State Department and the Federal Reserve System, while economic nationalists concentrated their efforts on Congress and a congenial Commerce Department. As socioeconomic interests were split, so too were policymakers and foreign economic policy itself.

The Depression and eventually World War II weakened the economic nationalists and allowed the state to reshape both policies and policy networks. By the late 1930s, economic nationalists were isolated or ignored, and most relevant decisions were placed within the purview of relatively internationalist bureaucracies. As economic internationalism was consolidated, the foreign-policy bureaucracy came to reflect this tendency—even as, in pre-World War I days, the apparatus had been unshakably nationalist in economic affairs.

The evidence examined here provides little support for theories that regard nation-states as rational, unitary actors in the international system. The most serious challenge of the interwar period is to "statist" assertions that foreign policymakers represent a national interest that they are able to define and defend.[59] By extension, interwar American foreign policymaking calls into question systemic-level approaches that attempt to derive national foreign policies solely from the position of the nation-state in the international structure.[60]

The national interest is not a blank slate upon which the international system writes at will; it is internally determined by the socioeconomic evolution of the nation in question. Some nations aim primarily to expand their primary exports, others to restrict manufactured imports, still others to protect their overseas investments. These goals are set by the constraints and opportunities that various domestic economic interests face in the world arena, and by the underlying strength of the various socioeconomic groups. The ability to pursue these "national interests" successfully, and the best strategy to do so, may similarly be determined by international conditions, but the interests themselves are domestically derived and expressed within the domestic political economy. A nation dominated by agro-exporters may

59. See, for example, Stephen D. Krasner, *Defending the National Interest* (Princeton, N.J.: Princeton University Press, 1978).

60. As, for example, David A. Lake, "International Economic Structures and American Foreign Policy, 1887–1934," *World Politics* 35 (July 1983), pp. 517–43.

respond to a world depression with redoubled efforts to expand exports, while a nation dominated by domestically oriented industry may respond to the same events with a spurt of industrial protectionism.

Nonetheless, underlying socioeconomic interests are mediated through a set of political institutions that can alter their relative influence. Although the relative importance of American overseas investment to the U.S. economy was roughly equal in the 1920s and 1970s, the institutional setting in the first period was far less suited to the concerns of overseas investors than it was in the second period. By the same token, policymakers can, at times, take the initiative in reformulating the institutional setting and the policies it has produced, as the Roosevelt administration did in the 1930s.

Indeed, one of the questions this survey of interwar American policy raises is the role of major crises in precipitating changes in political institutions, and in policymakers' room to maneuver. The Depression and World War II removed many of the institutional, coalitional, and ideological ties that had bound policymakers in the 1920s. In the United States, the result was the defeat of economic nationalism, but of course the crisis had very different effects elsewhere. It would be comforting to regard the victory of economic internationalism in the United States in the 1930s and 1940s as predetermined by the country's previous evolution and experiences, but this is far too facile a solution to a complex problem. A fuller explanation of the forces underlying American foreign policymaking in the 1930s and 1940s is clearly needed, and indeed it is the logical next step for the historians who have added so much to our understanding of the 1919–33 period, or for their followers.

More generally, the interwar period in American foreign economic policy is a fascinating and extreme case of a broader problem, the conflict between domestic and international interests in modern political economies. Virtually all nations have some economic actors for whom the international economy represents primarily opportunities, and others for whom it is mostly threats. This tension is especially evident in major capital exporters, since the needs of holders of overseas assets may well conflict with the desires of domestic groups. The twentieth century is full of examples in which the international–domestic divide has been central to political developments in advanced industrial societies: Britain and Germany in the interwar years are perhaps the best-known examples.[61] The American interwar experience is thus an important example of conflict between internationally oriented and domestically based interests. The conditions under which such interaction leads to major sociopolitical clashes or is overcome, and under which the foreign-

61. For a survey of each, see Frank Longstreth, "The City, Industry and the State," in Colin Crouch, ed., *State and Economy in Contemporary Capitalism* (London: Croom Helm, 1979), and David Abraham, *The Collapse of the Weimar Republic* (Princeton, N.J.: Princeton University Press, 1981). On a related issue, see Paul Kennedy, "Strategy *versus* Finance, in Twentieth-Century Britain," in his *Strategy and Diplomacy 1870–1945* (London: Allen & Unwin, 1983).

policy outcome is aggressively nationalistic or internationally cooperative, or some mix of the two, are obviously of great interest to analysts of international politics.

Conclusion

This essay has used the evolution of U.S. foreign economic policy from 1914 to 1940 as a benchmark against which to examine the role of international and domestic determinants in the making of foreign economic policy. We have argued that the foreign economic policy of the United States in the interwar period was the result of domestic political struggle between domestic economic actors with conflicting interests in the international economy, and thus different foreign economic policy preferences. After World War I, many U.S. banks and corporations saw great opportunities for overseas expansion, and fought for U.S. foreign economic policy to be assertively "internationalist." Other U.S. corporations saw the world economy primarily as a competitive threat and fought for protection and "isolationism." The evolution of the international political and economic environment, the reaction of domestic actors to this evolution, and the unfolding of domestic political struggle combined to determine U.S. foreign economic policy. This essay's effort to specify the interplay of international and domestic forces in the making of foreign policy, raises real questions about approaches that ignore domestic determinants of foreign policy. Between 1914 and 1940 at least, the foreign economic policy of the United States simply cannot be understood without a careful analysis of conflict among the disparate socio-economic and political forces at work inside the United States itself. Such domestic forces deserve careful, rigorous, and systematic study.

The institutional foundations of hegemony: explaining the Reciprocal Trade Agreements Act of 1934 Stephan Haggard

In 1930, Congress approved the highly restrictive Smoot–Hawley tariff, the textbook case of pressure group politics run amok. Four years later, Congress passed the Reciprocal Trade Agreements Act (RTAA), surrendering much of its tariff-making authority to a policy process in which internationalists had increasing influence. While the United States had used reciprocity to expand exports before, the stick of discriminatory treatment took precedence over the carrot of liberalizing concessions. With the transfer of tariff-making authority to the executive, the United States could make credible commitments and thus exploit its market power to liberalize international trade. Despite later modifications, the RTAA set the fundamental institutional framework for trade politics.

This study examines this watershed in U.S. trade policy. In doing so, it makes two sets of arguments that are broadly in line with a "statist" or "institutionalist" approach. The first challenges "weak state" and societal explanations of policy change by showing how executive officials molded the agenda and policy process to their own ideological, bureaucratic, and above all international interests. The second suggests how institutional setting affects the incentives of groups to organize, the balance of power among them, and even the discourse in which groups must frame their efforts to exercise influence.

I am greatly indebted to Jeff Frieden, Barbara Geddes, Judith Goldstein, Joanne Gowa, Joe Grieco, Cynthia Hody, John Ikenberry, Peter Katzenstein, David Lake, Mark Levy, Michael Mastanduno, Helen Milner, Andy Moravcsik, Timothy McKeown, Doug Nelson, John Odell, Mark Peterson, Beth Simmons, Sven Steinmo, Ray Vernon, and two anonymous reviewers for their advice and assistance.

International Organization 42, 1, Winter 1988

1. The problem: the RTAA as institutional change

The concrete achievements of the RTAA are the subject of some controversy; some people doubt that it constituted a "watershed" at all. A number of devices limited both the product and geographical range of liberalization. Francis B. Sayre, an architect of the RTAA, admitted that the "whole program was based upon finding places in the tariff wall where reductions could be made without substantial injury to American producers," including through product reclassification.[1] The promise of liberalizing concessions to trading partners conflicted directly with restrictive trade provisions written into other New Deal legislation. Apparent levels of protection on dutiable goods dropped from 53.6 percent in 1933 to 25.5 percent in 1946, but this was only marginally better than pre-Smoot–Hawley levels.[2]

Canada and Britain signed significant agreements, but most of the reciprocal agreements were with small countries. They were restricted in scope by the "principal supplier" provision that limited the range of goods over which the executive could negotiate. The provision that concessions would not be extended to countries that discriminated against the United States and sector-specific restrictions, such as those against Japanese textiles, diluted unconditional most-favored-nation status. To defend the achievements of the RTAA, even the Tariff Commission could produce only weak evidence that trade with countries signing reciprocal agreements expanded more than trade with non-signatories.[3]

While early studies of the trade agreements program touted it as an exercise in altruistic international leadership,[4] revisionist interpretations have been more restrained. Lloyd Gardner and Joan Hoff Wilson both interpret it as a continuation of previous Open Door efforts to secure markets for American exports.[5] John Conybeare argues that the trade agreements reflected

1. Francis Bowes Sayre, *Glad Adventure* (New York: MacMillan, 1957), p. 170.
2. This result can be partly attributed to price increases over the 1930s and early 1940s. Apparent protection is the ratio of total duties collected to total value of dutiable imports. By 1945, 60% of dutiable imports were entered under specific rates; ad valorem equivalents of specific duties thus varied inversely with prices. Since concessions were greater on raw materials than on manufactures, effective protection on some manufactures probably increased over the 1930s.
3. United States Tariff Commission, *Operation of the Trade Agreements Program, July 1934 to April 1948* (Washington, D.C.: GPO, 1948), Part 1, p. 84.
4. See Henry J. Tasca, *The Reciprocal Trade Policy of the United States* (Philadelphia: University of Pennsylvania Press, 1938), chaps. 4–8; Francis Bowes Sayre, *The Way Forward: The American Trade Agreements Program* (New York: Macmillan, 1939).
5. Lloyd Gardner, *Economic Aspects of New Deal Diplomacy* (Boston: Beacon, 1964), pp. 40–42, 45; Joan Hoff Wilson, *American Business and Foreign Policy, 1920–1933* (Lexington: University Press of Kentucky, 1971), pp. 98–100.

"hegemonic predation": the use of monopsonistic power by the United States to impose optimal trade restrictions.[6]

To assess the RTAA solely in terms of its immediate success in lowering trade barriers is to miss more lasting *institutional* changes in U.S. trade politics.[7] These were of two sorts: First, by delegating its authority, the Congress allowed new organizational interests and centers of expertise to develop within the executive. Giving the State Department a central role in trade policy introduced broader international economic and political considerations onto the policy agenda while providing a strong institutional base for free-traders. Executive influence over trade policy was obviously strengthened.

Second, the structure of business-government relations in the trade issue-area also changed. Prior to the RTAA, direct constituent pressures, coupled with institutional norms of reciprocity, increased the incentives for members of Congress to engage in protectionist logrolling. As Lowi points out in a classic article, the RTAA began the redefinition of the trade issue from a distributive to a regulatory one.[8] But what was key for future trade policy outcomes was the new *institutional setting* in which conflicts among interests were waged. Since gaining concessions in trade negotiations also requires making some, the trade-off between export- and import-competing interests was more clearly exposed. Moving decision-making towards the executive resulted in a relative decline in the influence of protectionist forces. The new structure also created new channels through which export-oriented industries could influence policy, and therefore new incentives for them to organize.

Protectionist forces were not, of course, wholly defeated. New channels of business representation could be bent to protectionist ends, and Congress retained powers of oversight. But industries seeking protection confronted a new institutional "filter" of liberal trade policy experts, a more technocratic decision-making process, and contending export interests. Previous chan-

---

6. John Conybeare, "Trade Wars: A Comparative Study of Anglo-Hanse, Franco-Italian and Hawley-Smoot Conflicts," *World Politics* 38 (October 1985).

7. These are hinted in Theodore Lowi's classic piece, "American Business, Public Policy, Case Studies, and Political Theory," *World Politics* 16 (July 1964), though, as will become clear, Lowi's interpretation of the change in trade policy from a "distributive" to a "regulatory" issue is only partly correct. Robert Pastor takes an explicitly institutional approach to trade policy in *Congress and the Politics of U.S. Foreign Economic Policy* (Berkeley: University of California Press, 1980); see pp. 84–93 for his interpretation of the RTAA. See also the excellent study by Steven Robert Brenner, "Economic Interests and the Trade Agreements Program, 1937–1940: A Study of Institutions and Political Influence," unpublished Ph.D. dissertation, Stanford University, 1977, which influences my interpretation; I. M. Destler, *American Trade Politics: System Under Stress* (Washington, D.C.: Institute for International Economics, 1986), chap. 2.

8. Lowi, "American Business, Public Policy," pp. 699–701; E. E. Schattschneider, *Politics, Pressure and the Tariff* (New York: Prentice-Hall, 1955).

nels of influence and modes of argument were devalued; the nature of issue-relevant power had changed.

2. Contra "weak state" and societal explanations

Told in brief, this story seems to contradict a dominant model of U.S. foreign economic policymaking, according to which the United States is externally strong, but internally "weak."[9] This characterization is not limited to academic studies. From proponents of industrial policy to those advocating stronger leadership in international economic affairs, the incoherence and inconsistency of U.S. foreign economic policy has been traced to unique features of the American system of governance.

Some "weak state" arguments border on the tautologous. When certain outcomes, such as the ability to change private behavior or the social structure, are used to define weakness and strength, it is difficult to use "strength" as an explanatory variable.[10] Also, a number of embarrassing definitional issues continue to plague the strong–weak state distinction, including the failure to differentiate among "the state"—that is, an enduring set of institutions, roles, and procedures—particular parts or branches of the state, a particular government, and individual office-holders.

The weak state argument has emerged primarily in efforts to place American foreign economic policy in a comparative perspective.[11] Viewed comparatively, proponents argue, institutional features of the American state differ from other advanced industrial democracies and affect the nature of public policy outcomes. Each of these institutional features may be viewed as an analytic dimension of state strength, on which the U.S. score is low. First, the policy process is particularly *fragmented,* with Congress and the executive sharing overlapping powers and jurisdictions. Second, all branches, but particularly Congress, are *highly accessible to interest*

9. For examples of "weak state" arguments, see Peter Katzenstein, "Conclusion: Domestic Structures and Strategies of Foreign Economic Policy," and Stephen Krasner, "United States Commercial and Monetary Policy: Unravelling the Paradox of External Strength and Internal Weakness," in Katzenstein, ed., *Between Power and Plenty* (Madison: University of Wisconsin Press, 1978); Raymond Vernon, *Two Hungry Giants: The United States and Japan in the Quest for Oil and Ores* (Cambridge: Harvard University Press, 1983), chap. 4; John Zysman and Laura Tyson, "American Industry in International Competition," in Zysman and Tyson, eds., *American Industry in International Competition* (Ithaca, N.Y.: Cornell University Press, 1983).

10. This problem is visible in Stephen Krasner, *Defending the National Interest* (Princeton, N.J.: Princeton University Press, 1978), pp. 56–57.

11. For some of the problems with this literature, see John Ikenberry, "The State and Oil Shocks," *International Organization* 40 (Winter 1986); Helen Milner, "Resisting the Protectionist Temptation: Industry and the Making of Trade Policy in France and the U.S. in the 1970s," paper delivered to the annual meeting of the American Political Science Association, August 1986; and David Lake, "The State and American Trade Policy in the Pre-Hegemonic Era," in this volume. My arguments are very similar to Lake's, which are developed for an earlier period.

groups, who also gain by having multiple channels through which they can seek to exercise influence. In contrast to countries in which the channels of interest group contact with the state are limited or controlled, the policy-making process in the U.S. is poorly insulated from, or even captured by, societal interests. Third, the consistency of policy is further undermined by the *lack of expertise and cohesion within the bureaucracy.* Turnover at the top of the bureaucracy is rapid, with no high-level bureaucratic cadre to guarantee continuity. While intra-bureaucratic politics is hardly peculiar to the United States, the potential for conflict is increased by the overlapping authority exercised by Congress and the president. Finally, the state is weak in that it *lacks the policy instruments other states possess.* A narrower range of policy instruments naturally limits the government's *ability* to act, but it may also influence the range of issues on which the government deems it *appropriate* to act.

An analysis of the politics of the RTAA suggests that these claims can be misleading. Even for broad comparative purposes, the weak state argument is overly static and ahistorical. It wrongly suggests a constancy in "state strength"—indeed, in the nature of American politics—over time. Rather, the "strength" of the state on any of these four dimensions varies over time and by issue-area. The RTAA resulted in a decrease in the fragmentation of the policy process, a decline in the access enjoyed by at least some interest groups and an increase in the cohesion of the trade-policy bureaucracy. While the bulk of the literature on U.S. trade policy has been devoted to explaining discrete policy outcomes—the level and incidence of protection—much less has been given to examining changes in the institutional context of trade policy.

Second, the weak state argument has explanatory limitations that stem from its affinity with societal models of policy whether pluralist, Marxist, or rational choice in nature. If the state is a relatively passive register of demands, the policy changes are best explained by the interests, organization and power of societal coalitions, working through their representatives in government. Testing such coalitional models is difficult, however. Since the relevant coalition is hard to identify, particularly during crises when interests are somewhat fluid, and the number of possible winning coalitions is often large, the temptation to post hoc analysis is particularly high. Coalitional arguments suffer from a further theoretical weakness, however: they are ill-suited to explain *institutional* change. Theorists of public goods have offered a reason: As Douglass North points out, "institutional innovation will come from rulers rather than constituents since the latter would always face the free rider problem."[12] While interest groups will try to ensure that

---

12. Douglass North, *Structure and Change in Economic History* (New York: Norton, 1981), p. 32. See also Joanne Gowa, "Public Goods and Political Institutions: Trade and Monetary Policy Processes in the United States," in this volume.

the new structure is vulnerable to pressure, explaining the institutional innovations themselves demands attention to the initiatives, interests, and motivations of state actors (who are, for the purposes of this analysis, the
political and administrative officials of the executive branch).

I develop a number of hypotheses consistent with such an intentional
"state-as-actor" approach.[13] Before turning to them in more detail, I attempt
to show that, in 1933, neither the Democratic majority in Congress, the
attitude of the president, the outlook of his closest advisors, nor sectoral
interests pointed unambiguously towards trade policy reform.[14]

The Democratic party in Congress

Of course, a tractable and Democratic Congress, with large numerical
majorities in both houses, gave FDR wide legislative leeway in trade policy,
just as it did on other issues.[15] But the very expansion of the Democratic
coalition, which ensured its electoral success, had also subtly altered the
party's stand on the tariff. In his 1928 campaign, Al Smith made significant
concessions to protectionist sentiment. Formal voting on Smoot–Hawley
broke on partisan lines, but Democratic statements on the tariff in 1930 were
"nothing but a weak echo of Republican views."[16] Hull and older Wilso-
nians struggled to steer the party away from the Smith faction precisely
because of their protectionist views. Hull's ties with Southern Democrats
were an asset in this fight and again in 1934. But Congressional Democrats
were not the source of trade policy initiatives; in fact, FDR feared the
political forces that might be unleashed if trade legislation were put forward.[17] In addition, institutional interests pulled against the State Department's interest in the centralization of trade policy. Smoot–Hawley had
demonstrated the problems of congressional tariff-making even to the legislators themselves, but the resistance to a broad delegation of authority to the
executive cut across party lines.

13. On the logic of this approach, see Ikenberry, "The State and Oil Shocks," and Theda
Skocpol, "Bringing the State Back In: Strategies of Analysis in Current Research," in Peter
Evans, Dietrich Rueschemeyer, and Theda Skocpol, eds., *Bringing the State Back In* (New
York: Cambridge University Press, 1985).
14. On the limits of coalitional analysis, see Margaret Weir and Theda Skocpol, "State
Structures and the Possibilities for 'Keynesian' Responses to the Great Depression in Sweden,
Britain and the United States," in Evans, Rueschemeyer, and Skocpol, eds., *Bringing the State
Back In,* p. 115.
15. James T. Patterson, *Congressional Conservatism and the New Deal* (Lexington: University of Kentucky Press, 1967), chap. 1.
16. Frank Whitson Fetter, "Congressional Tariff Theory," *American Economic Review* 23
(September 1933), p. 416.
17. On 9 June 1933, FDR noted in a press conference that "Congress would never give me
complete authority to write tariff schedules"; a reporter responded, "Well, they have given you
everything else." *Complete Presidential Press Conferences of Franklin D. Roosevelt* (New
York: Da Capo, 1972), vol. 1, p. 368; also press conference 25 May 1933, pp. 324–25.

Roosevelt as internationalist

Roosevelt is held by most historians to be an internationalist.[18] Yet coalitional considerations pulled him *away* from tariff revision during the campaign. Roosevelt sacrificed the issue to other domestic legislation in 1933 and wavered on it up to the last minute in 1934. In his inaugural address, he stated bluntly that

> . . . our international trade relations, though vastly important, are in point of time and necessity secondary to the establishment of a sound national economy . . . I shall spare no effort to restore world trade by international economic readjustment, but the emergency at home cannot wait on that accomplishment.[19]

Roosevelt was not active in the debate over the RTAA, and even after it was passed, admitted privately that he thought its importance was exaggerated.[20]

The brains trust

The outlook of Roosevelt's closest political advisors—the central policy coalition within the government—did not appear at all sympathetic to trade policy reform, either. Members of Roosevelt's "brains trust" recognized the contradiction between the nationalism of New Deal policies and the making of trade concessions.[21] In addition, there were important differences on trade *strategy*. George Peek thought exports critical for U.S. recovery, but was hostile to the unconditional granting of most-favored-nation status favored by Hull. Not until after the passage of the RTAA was his more mercantilist conception of reciprocity decisively defeated.

Sectoral interests and trade policy

Seeking the explanation of trade policy change in shifting sectoral interests is a more plausible approach, and helps identify the beneficiaries of the

---

18. Historians credit Roosevelt with internationalist preferences, even where he was forced to modify them in reaction to circumstance. See Frank Freidel, *Franklin D. Roosevelt: Launching the New Deal* (Boston: Little, Brown, 1973); chap. 7; Robert Dallek, *Franklin D. Roosevelt and American Foreign Policy 1932–1945* (New York: Oxford University Press, 1979); William E. Leuchtenberg, *Franklin D. Roosevelt and the New Deal* (New York: Harper & Row, 1963); Arthur M. Schlesinger, Jr., *The Coming of the New Deal* (Boston: Houghton Mifflin, 1958), section 3. Schlesinger's qualifications are discussed later.

19. From the 1933 inaugural address, in Franklin Delano Roosevelt, *Public Papers and Addresses,* compiled by S. I. Rosenman (New York: Random House, 1938–1950), vol. 2 (1933), p. 14.

20. In 1935, FDR noted that "the amount involved in the special trade agreements is so small in dollars and cents and so small in relation to our total commerce that it is captious of George Peek to try to make this an issue." FDR to Jesse Jones, 18 July 1935, President's Secretary's File (PSF) 73, FDR Library, Hyde Park, New York.

21. See the excellent study by Elliott A. Rosen, *Hoover, Roosevelt and the Brains Trust: From Depression to New Deal* (New York: Columbia University Press, 1977).

new course. Thomas Ferguson and Helen Milner have suggested that an industry's international competitive position, trade, and foreign investment linkages condition preferences for protection.[22] According to Ferguson, a block of internationally competitive, capital-intensive industries had captured the Democratic party, at least by 1936, marking the "triumph of multinational liberalism."[23] Aside from the problem of timing and the mistaken emphasis given to the Democratic party as a source of policy initiatives, Ferguson confuses an argument explaining industry *preferences* for one explaining policy *outcomes*. By focusing on the interests of some industries at the expense of others, he underestimates the continuing ambivalence towards freer trade and virtually ignores the role of state actors in forging a new course.

Export-oriented manufacturers, commercial interests, and the internationalized financial community of New York strongly favored reciprocal trade agreements; a network of interlocking foreign trade associations were active in lobbying the State Department towards that end.[24] Those American banks and underwriters with large foreign portfolios were hurt by the declining capacity of their clients to service their debts through exports. The United States exported over 30 percent of total production of cotton, tobacco, and rice; these interests, concentrated particularly in the South, were well represented in Congress. The export dependence of the manufacturing sector was much less. Industrial machinery, automobiles, and some chemical products showed a small increase in export dependence over the 1920s, but from a low base. These industries were nonetheless hurt by the sharp contraction of U.S. exports, whose value declined 68 percent between 1929 and 1933.[25]

The State Department officials designing the trade legislation understood the link between the international trade and financial systems. They sought to trade concessions in industries in which the United States was less competitive for expanded market access for agricultural products and the new, internationally competitive mass-production industries.[26]

22. Thomas Ferguson, "From Normalcy to New Deal; Industrial Structure, Party Competition and American Public Policy in the Great Depression," *International Organization* 38 (Winter 1984); Helen Milner, "Resisting the Protectionist Temptation," Ph.D. diss., Harvard University, 1986. This explanation also mirrors revisionist interpretations that emphasize export interests. See Gardner, *Economic Aspects*; Wilson, *American Business*.

23. Ferguson, "From Normalcy to New Deal," p. 93.

24. On the interest groups organized around the trade issue, see memo, Office of the Special Assistant on Foreign Trade (SAFT), 7 May 1934, "List of Foreign Trade Associations and their Inter-Relationshps," General Records of the SAFT (Record Group 20), National Archives. Jeff Frieden has argued most convincingly about the influence of financial interests on American foreign policy during this period. See "Sectoral Conflict in U.S. Foreign Economic Policy, 1914–1940," this volume.

25. Department of Commerce, *Foreign Trade of the United States: Calendar Year 1933* (Washington D.C.: GPO, 1934), pp. 12–14.

26. Wilson, *American Business*, pp. 73–74 and chap. 3, passim; "Report of the Executive Committee on Commercial Policy," enclosed in Phillips to FDR, 23 December 1933, Presi-

Only four short years before, however, Congress had been swamped by industry representatives clamoring for protection. The inward-looking perspective of uncompetitive business, the changing views associated with industrialization in the South, and the severity of the Depression pulled strongly in a protectionist direction.[27] The "nationalists" were not limited to small firms, but included in their ranks concentrated sectors such as chemicals, steel, and rubber and well-organized industries, such as textiles and shoes.[28] Even export-oriented industries were ambivalent about making trade concessions. A hundred and fifty large and medium-sized firms telegraphed Roosevelt to voice their support for the reciprocal trade agreements in 1933, but noted at the same time that they "believed thoroughly in the protective principle."[29] Despite its export orientation, agriculture took a similar stance, and played a crucial role in Roosevelt's ambivalence towards trade policy during the campaign and after.

How do we know, without reference to the outcome, that a sectoral coalition favoring freer trade was "dominant"? In fact, Ferguson's hypothesis of the emergence of a "hegemonic bloc" would lead one to expect a more open trade policy than the United States adopted. Nor should it be forgotten that, in 1933, when trade policy was being rethought, the political standing and influence of business had reached an all-time low. Without allies in industry and agriculture who were capable of benefiting from a new trade policy, the administration could not have acted. But executive initiatives and interests were crucial in defining the trade policy agenda, and even in shaping the "dominant coalition."

3. The state as actor

I have argued that congressional majorities and the interests of export-oriented industry and agriculture were necessary, but not sufficient, conditions for the policy and institutional changes associated with the RTAA. An explanation emphasizing executive initiatives raises two further puzzles, however, First, if coalitional interests are ruled out, why would elites in the executive want to innovate? If a statist approach is to avoid purely voluntarist explanations, it must tackle the issue of where state interests come from.

dent's Official File (OF) 614A (cited hereafter as *Executive Committee Report*), FDR Library, Hyde Park, New York.

27. This point is made by Fetter, "Congressional Tariff Making," and by Wilson, *American Business,* chap. 3.

28. Ferguson, "From Normalcy to New Deal"; Wilson, *American Business,* chap. 3.

29. See two telegrams, D. S. Ingelhart (President, W. R. Grace and Co.) to FDR, 8 June 1933, OF 61, FDR Library. The first, signed by thirty-nine large manufacturers, supported the negotiation of reciprocal trade agreements, citing growing bilateralism and systems of imperial preference as the principal reason. The second telegram reports a poll of "upwards of 150 important manufacturers" and found almost unanimous support for the reciprocal trade program. Two days later, however, FDR announced that he was not seeking trade legislation!

One approach focuses on ideology. Cordell Hull's fanatical devotion to free trade is well known. While Hull was particularly single-minded in his concern, the core group of economic advisers most influential on the trade issue shared his Wilsonian outlook, which resonated with the internationalist outlook of the State Department as a whole.[30] An alternative approach focuses on bureaucratic interests and conflicts. To achieve their ideological ends, the State Department needed to consolidate its power vis-à-vis Congress and other agencies; the Department's interest in the reform of trade policy was therefore linked to particular institutional interests. New Deal legislation had fragmented trade policy among a number of competing agencies. Each dealt independently with foreign governments, making the conduct of economic diplomacy more complex. The State Department criticized the incoherence of policy, using historical precedent to justify a recentralization of trade policy.[31]

Ideological and bureaucratic motivations thus had some role in the reform process. But both were linked to more fundamental *international political interests* and a concern with American influence. Hull's liberalism represented a broad world-view that was concerned primarily with international order and American power. Hull recognized clearly that the exercise of U.S. power rested on a particular domestic institutional foundation. The broad move within the international trading system towards bilateralism and the creation of preference schemes that accompanied the Depression put a premium on executive ability to negotiate credibly and flexibly.[32] It was not the international *structure* that changed during the interwar period; if anything, the international structure was less conducive to liberalization attempts. Rather, it was the international *processes* and *rules* governing world trade that had changed.[33] Testifying before the House Ways and Means Commit-

30. On the "internationalist" outlook, see Frieden, "Sectoral Conflict," this volume.

31. On the problem of the fragmentation of trade policy, see "The Urgent Necessity of Working Out an Adequate and Co-ordinated Method for Dealing with Commercial Policy," Memo for the President, enclosed in Hull to FDR, 27 October 1933, OF 614 A; *Executive Committee Report.*

32. On the changes in the processes that governed trade in the 1930s, see Richard Snyder, "Commercial Policy as Reflected in Treaties from 1931 to 1939," *American Economic Review* 30 (December 1940); Joseph M. Jones, Jr., *Tariff Retaliation: Repercussions of the Smoot-Hawley Bill* (Philadelphia: University of Pennsylvania Press, 1934); Margaret Gordon, *Barriers to World Trade: A Study of Recent Commercial Policy* (New York: MacMillan, 1941). The Tariff Commission began investigating reciprocal negotiations in early 1933 at the request of Congress. United States Tariff Commission, *Tariff Bargaining Under Most-Favored-Nation Treaties,* Report to the United States Senate (Tariff Commission Report #62, 2d Series, GPO, 1934).

33. Examples of a structuralist view are Charles P. Kindleberger, *The World in Depression, 1929–39* (Berkeley: University of California Press, 1973); Stephen Krasner, "State Power and the Structure of International Trade," *World Politics* 28 (April 1976); and David Lake's sophisticated synthesis in "Beneath the Commerce of Nations: A Theory of International Economic Structures," *International Studies Quarterly* 28 (June 1984). Lake defines structural position in

tee, Hull spelled out the implications:

> . . . it is manifest that unless the Executive is given the authority to deal with the existing great emergency somewhat on a parity with that exercised by the executive departments of so many other governments for purposes of negotiating and carrying into effect trade agreements, it will not be practicable or possible for the United States to pursue with any degree of success the proposed policy of restoring our lost international trade."[34]

The "state as actor" approach raises a second set of problems, however. Even if we concede that executive interests and initiatives are important, there is still the question of why some innovations succeed while others fail. From the passage of the Corn Laws to the present, even modest liberalization attempts have sparked political controversy. We need to specify the political conditions under which state initiatives are likely to succeed.

The RTAA case suggests two hypotheses and one more idiosyncratic factor. The first is the existence of a manifest crisis. Economic crisis was not important simply because of the export-oriented interests it served to mobilize; the Depression also served to mobilize countervailing nationalist forces. "Crisis" was important for more purely political reasons. Reformers used crisis conditions to justify an "extraordinary" delegation of power to the executive. Crises break the normal incremental mode of decision-making, generate demands for centralization and leadership, and thus strengthen the flexibility of the executive.

The second condition for successful reform is the partial compensation of opponents. The construction of winning coalitions, whether congressional or sectoral, demands compromise. The process of compensation helps explain several enduring features of U.S. trade policy, since *some of the compromises were themselves institutional in nature.*

The RTAA did not usher in "free trade," but instead what John Ruggie has called the "compromise of embedded liberalism."[35] This historic com-

---

terms of both relative size and relative productivity—the first variable explaining the capacity to act as leader, the second the interest in doing so. Yet Frieden has pointed out that while relative productivity was higher than that of any other advanced industrial state in 1929, U.S. share of world trade was only 13.9%. Yet in 1960, the highpoint of American hegemony, U.S. share of world trade was 15.3%. Frieden, "The Internationalization of American Banking and the Transformation of American Foreign Policy, 1890–1940," paper delivered to the annual meeting of the American Political Science Association, Washington, D.C., 1–3 September 1984. In addition, between 1929 and 1938, U.S. share of world trade went *down,* while its relative productivity remained constant.

The idea of a "process" level of the international system separate from the structural level is articulated in Robert O. Keohane and Joseph Nye, *Power and Interdependence* (Boston: Little, Brown, 1977).

34. House of Representatives, Reciprocal Trade Agreements. Hearings before the Committee on Ways and Means, 73d Congress, 2d session, pp. 5–6.

35. John Ruggie, "International Regimes, Transactions and Change: Embedded Liberalism in the Post-war Economic Order," *International Organization* (Spring 1982). See also Judith Goldstein, "The Political Economy of Trade: the Institutions of Protection," *American Political Science Review* 80 (March 1986), pp. 161–84.

promise sought to accommodate the benefits of liberalism to growing social pressures, in part by expanding the role of government in the management of economic life. Uncertain of its passage in 1933, Roosevelt put off the tariff issue until 1934, when domestic legislation was passed that shielded business and agriculture from external threat and extended new guarantees to labor. Roosevelt also forged institutional compromises that set the basic nature of executive-congressional relations on trade policy ever since.[36] While the executive clearly gained, the final success of the legislation hinged on allowing some congressional oversight and granting trade-affected industries circumscribed access to trade policymaking. The "escape clause" provisions, which permit the protection of industries injured by liberalizing concessions, represents the clearest example of the institutional "compromise of embedded liberalism" in the trade area. First written into reciprocal trade agreements during the war, the escape clause muted the confrontation between internationalist and nationalist industries, and thus the potential for conflict between the executive and Congress as well.

A final, more idiosyncratic aspect of the policy setting was a series of distinctly uncooperative actions that were taken on the international monetary policy. Though a "liberal" international order is usually seen to consist of mutually interdependent and reinforcing monetary and commercial regimes, FDR's internationalism was hardly of a piece. The RTAA was not introduced until *after* Roosevelt, in the name of national policy autonomy, had crushed any meager hopes the London economic summit might have offered for international cooperation. The dollar's steady descent over the second half of 1933 naturally improved the situation of American exporters and effectively raised the level of protection to domestic industry. Hoover had sought to shelter American industry behind high tariffs while surrendering American finance to the workings of the international gold standard; the New Deal reversed that policy. It "aimed at securing national control over finance while at the same time it sought to unfetter and increase world trade."[37] In fact, an autonomous monetary policy provided strong arguments to those in the administration who defended trade liberalization.

My argument may now be summarized. I draw a distinction between discrete changes in policy—such as a lowering of tariffs—and those reforms that change the policy *process*. I suggest that institutional innovations in the trade issue-area in the 1930s "strengthened" the state in a number of enduring ways. Moving trade policy authority towards the executive, establishing new centers of policy expertise, and insulating the policy process from interest group pressures facilitated a gradual move towards a more liberal trade policy. On both empirical and theoretical grounds, it is difficult to explain

36. Pastor, *U.S. Foreign Economic Policy,* pp. 84–93.
37. Arthur M. Schlesinger, *The Coming of the New Deal,* p. 260; see also Ken Oye, "The Sterling-Dollar-Franc Triangle: Monetary Diplomacy 1929–1937," *World Politics* 38 (October 1985).

such changes by reference to societal interests alone. I focus on the initiatives and interests of state actors, particularly in the State Department, who sought reform to expand American power. The reform process benefited from crisis, from compensatory procedural and institutional compromises, and from monetary policies that offset the political costs of trade policy reform.

I organize this case historically. Section 4 identifies the political forces that surrounded Roosevelt prior to his election. I show that these forces were by no means conducive to trade policy reform. Section 5 traces the initial focus of Roosevelt's economic policy, stressing the domestic compromises that set the stage for trade policy reform in 1934. Section 6 shows the resurgence of State Department interest in trade policy reform in late 1933, its strategy towards restructuring the trade policy machinery, the conflicts between the internationalists, and George Peek's more mercantilist conception of reciprocity. In Section 7, I suggest how the new institutional structure partially insulated trade policy from protectionist pressures and consolidated a "liberal machinery." The conclusion makes some theoretical observations on systemic theory and the utility of the state–society distinction in explaining public policy.

4. The political foundations of Democratic nationalism: trade policy through March 1933

The constellation of political forces in the Democratic party in 1932 was hardly propitious for tariff reform. Over the course of the campaign, Roosevelt gradually abandoned his internationalism for a program that stressed domestic autonomy. In addition to their immediate political desire to cement a winning coalition by placating farmers' protectionist impulses, FDR's advisers were beginning to formulate plans for an interventionist state role in agriculture and industry to meet the crisis of the Great Depression. This program dictated a softening commitment to freer trade.

Since the first decade of the century, progressives had recognized the importance of moving tariff-making out of a Congress habituated to logrolling. Their advocacy of a "scientific tariff" entailed both a shift in arena towards a non-partisan, independent investigatory body and the elaboration of principles on which the Tariff Commission would make investigations. But depressed agricultural prices and the demand for protection from industries which developed during World War I conspired against a consistent low-tariff stance on the part of the Democrats.[38]

The return of the Republicans to political power demonstrated the under-

38. See William B. Kelly, Jr., "Antecedents of Present Commercial Policy, 1922–1934," in Kelly, ed., *Studies in United States Commercial Policy* (Chapel Hill, N.C.: University of North Carolina Press, 1963).

lying idealism of the progressive design. With only limited advisory powers in the first place, the now-Republican Tariff Commission was subject to significant political pressures. Moreover, the commission was expected to "equalize" costs of production between the U.S. and its trading partners. This equalization guaranteed that "flexibility" would be exercised to raise, rather than lower, tariffs; logically, the principle of "flexibility" denied the principle of comparative advantage altogether.[39]

By 1932, political forces within the Democratic party tugged in four directions. In one corner, the Democratic millionaire John J. Raskob, with close ties to the DuPont empire, wanted to stick with the conservative strategy of 1928 by committing the party more openly to protection. Al Smith had concurred, in part to lure agriculture and Eastern labor, but more importantly because of his deference to business.[40] For Wilsonian Democrats, the second important group, these policies seemed a betrayal. Cordell Hull supported Smith in 1928, but thereafter launched a campaign to get the party out of the hands of the Smith–Raskob faction; he was motivated primarily by the importance he placed on a free trade policy.[41]

Understanding the intellectual motivations behind Hull's liberalism is crucial to assess his interest in reform.[42] As a Wilsonian, Hull argued against the unequal and monopolistic benefits conferred by tariffs. Hull saw imports as largely noncompetitive with domestic industry, however, and he showed little understanding of the principle of comparative advantage. Hull relentlessly attacked the assumption that the United States could export without importing, pointed to the contradictions between U.S. trade and financial policies, and staunchly defended the most-favored-nation (MFN) principle as a way of reducing discrimination abroad. More important to Hull, however, were international leadership and the connection he drew between protectionism, nationalism, and international conflict. For Hull, free trade was a universal political solvent that would dissolve underlying international conflicts.

Hull recognized an important source of opposition to a liberal trade pro-

---

39. Wilson, *American Business,* pp. 67–71. For a commissioner's view of the problems of the flexible provision, see John Lee Coulter, "The Tariff Commission and the Flexible Clause," *Proceedings of the American Academy of Political Science* 15 (June 1933).

40. In choosing Raskob to chair the National Committee, Smith wished "to let the businessmen of this country know that one of the great industrial leaders of modern times had confidence in the Democratic Party and its platform." Cited in Mathew and Hannah Josephson, *Al Smith: Hero of the Cities* (Boston: Houghton Mifflin, 1969), p. 371. Smith's views are included in his acceptance address, Albany, 22 August 1928 and his Louisville speech, 13 October 1928, *Campaign Addresses of Gov. Alfred E. Smith* (Washington, D.C.: Democratic National Committee, 1929), pp. 7, 165–67.

41. See Cordell Hull, *Memoirs,* vol. 1, pp. 142, 146; Rosen, *From Depression to New Deal,* chap. 2.

42. The most careful analysis of Hull's thinking on the issue is William R. Allen, "The International Trade Philosophy of Cordell Hull, 1907–1933," *American Economic Review* 63 (March 1953).

gram in a third group, the intellectuals around Roosevelt.[43] Roosevelt's nomination meant a defeat of the Smith group, and it also increased the stature of the "brains trust": Raymond Moley, Rexford Tugwell, and Adolf Berle, Jr. According to Moley, the brains trust "proceeded on the assumption that the causes of our ills were domestic, internal, and that the remedies would have to be internal too."[44] This line of thinking contradicted Hoover's claim that the causes of the Depression were international, but also clashed with Hull's liberalism and the "financial internationalists" who tried to steer Roosevelt towards multilateralism.[45] Tugwell and Moley recognized the contradictory nature of the Republican policy of high tariffs, and they sought a gradual return to a more open commercial system—but both believed that this policy would have to await recovery.[46]

The reasons had to do less with manufacturing than with agriculture, a fourth political force and one that proved decisive in Roosevelt's campaign stance on trade.[47] During the 1920s, agricultural production was high worldwide and prices correspondingly low. Tariffs might raise the prices of imported commodities, but for exporters, world market conditions set domestic prices. While many farmers did support the tariff—irrationally, Democratic free-traders argued—increasing attention was turned to the problem of the "exportable surplus."

George Peek was responsible for devising a solution to the agricultural depression, in which trade policy played an important role. Peek developed a two-price system that would offer the farmer a "tariff equivalent": a high domestic price that would bear the same ratio towards other commodities that it had borne before 1914; and a low foreign price, which implied that agricultural surpluses would be dumped abroad. An Agricultural Export Corporation would be authorized to buy on the American market at the "ratio price" and sell abroad. To cover the losses, farmers would be assessed an "equalization fee," on the assumption that the fees would be less than the benefits of higher domestic prices. Legislation introduced by Senator Charles L. McNary of Oregon and Representative Gilbert N.

43. Hull, *Memoirs,* vol. 1, p. 352.

44. He continued, "How unorthodox this was at the time may be judged by the amount of bitterness with which we were called nationalists by older economists." Raymond Moley, *After Seven Years* (Lincoln: University of Nebraska Press, 1971), p. 23.

45. See Elliot Rosen, "Intranationalism vs. Internationalism: The Interregnum Struggle for the Sanctity of the New Deal," *Political Science Quarterly* 81 (June 1966).

46. As Tugwell argued, "We were convinced that in order to work out our problems of recovery and reform we would have to be insulated from European interference." Rexford Tugwell, *The Brains Trust* (New York: Viking, 1968), p. 475; Rexford Tugwell Diary, vol. 5, "June 1933 to March 1934," pp. 9–14; Tugwell Papers, FDR Library, Hyde Park, N.Y.

47. The following draws on John D. Hicks, *Republican Ascendancy, 1921–1933* (New York: Harper & Row, 1960), pp. 195–202; Gilbert C. Fite, *George N. Peek and the Fight for Farm Parity* (Norman, Okla.: University of Oklahoma Press, 1954); Rosen, *From Depresion to New Deal,* pp. 188–89. FDR's first mention of the tariff issue in the campaign was in a speech before the New York Grange; Roosevelt, *Public Papers and Addresses,* vol. 1, pp. 155–57.

Haugen of Iowa in 1924 embodied these ideas, and Smith gave the legislation his half-hearted support in the 1928 campaign. Despite a sharp presidential veto, McNary–Haugenism held considerable popular appeal during the 1920s.

More important were the ideas on agriculture that were brewing within the brains trust itself. Tugwell's domestic allotment system drew ideas from agricultural economist M. L. Wilson, who was a strong proponent of planning; the system first became a campaign issue over the summer. Henry A. Wallace, later to become secretary of agriculture, was particularly torn between his commitment to domestic planning and internationalism; he tried to seek a middle way between the two, but the eventual move towards a focus on planning by Moley and Tugwell forced them to openly abandon their internationalism.[48]

Reconciling the Wilsonian internationalists with the political imperative of wooing the Midwest was one of the most divisive issues of the campaign.[49] Early in September, Roosevelt was given draft speeches that reflected Hull's proposal for a unilateral 10 percent tariff cut and a compromise that called for negotiated tariff reductions. Roosevelt left Ray Moley "speechless" by telling him to weave the two contradictory drafts together.[50] M. L. Wilson argued that advocating a unilateral reduction, as Hull urged, would be politically suicidal, particularly as Hoover was planning to launch a vigorous defense of the tariff in an effort to hold the corn and wheat belts. These electoral considerations proved decisive. Roosevelt's Sioux City speech on agriculture and tariffs was a hodge-podge of compromises.[51] Denouncing the excesses of Smoot–Hawley, Roosevelt supported the cost-equalization formula and confessed that his doctrine was "not widely different from that preached by Republican statesmen and politicians."[52]

Despite these concessions, two important departures remained intact. The first was the commitment to international negotiation as the means of lowering tariff rates, which guaranteed greater executive involvement in trade policy. Second, Roosevelt recognized the importance of limiting congres-

48. As Rosen argues, "their conflict with Hull . . . was rooted in the requirement for a self-contained economy and an artificial internal price structure." *From Depression to New Deal,* p. 180ff. For Wallace's views, see his *New Frontiers* (New York: Harcourt Brace, 1934), and the critique by Alonzo E. Taylor, *The New Deal and Foreign Trade* (New York: MacMillan, 1935). For an analysis of state intervention in agriculture, see Theda Skocpol and Kenneth Finegold, "State Capacity and Economic Intervention in the Early New Deal," *Political Science Quarterly* 97 (Summer 1982).

49. Tugwell saw the fight as one between the brains trust and certain Westerners, including Senators Walsh and Pittman, against Hull, traditional Democrats, and "others in Wall Street who sold foreign securities to American investors . . . and wanted to speculate as they liked and therefore objected to national economic fences." *The Brains Trust,* p. 476.

50. Moley, *After Seven Years,* p. 47.

51. The speech was drafted by protectionist Senators Pittman and Walsh. Hull's representative, Charles Taussig, was pushed to the side. Ibid., p. 50; Tugwell, *The Brains Trust,* pp. 478–90.

52. Roosevelt, *Public Papers and Addresses,* vol. 1, pp. 766, 767.

sional logrolling by supporting restrictions on the ability of Congress to amend Tariff Commission recommendations. With this innovation, "each particular tariff rate proposed would be judged on its merits alone."[53]

Following his Sioux City speech, hundreds of telegrams from farmers and processors asked whether his reference to "outrageously excessive" rates under Smoot–Hawley referred to specific commodities. In October, Roosevelt relented altogether on the lowering of agricultural duties. Immediately, the barrage from the East and Northeast began. Did Roosevelt mean to suggest that tariffs on manufactured articles were too high? In the very last days of the campaign, Roosevelt announced that he favored "continuous protection for American agriculture as well as American industry."[54] Roosevelt wavered briefly towards a multilateral approach during December and early January, but Moley and Tugwell held the line against what they characterized as the "Wall Street view."[55]

5. The triumph of domestic priorities

The administration's nationalism had two components. First, sectoral policies that were formulated to launch industrial and agricultural recovery rested on the assumption of an insulated domestic market. Second, the United States went off gold and pursued an independent monetary policy. These policies put in place certain guarantees to industry, agriculture, and labor that ultimately strengthened the administration's political position in moving towards trade policy reform in 1934.

The conflict between the domestic priorities of the brains trusters and Cordell Hull's internationalilsm was first revealed in the administration's handling of the London Economic Conference.[56] In April, Roosevelt had announced his intention to seek trade legislation. The State Department drafted a bill for submission to Congress that authorized the executive to negotiate reciprocal trade agreements on an MFN basis. Hull describes the bill repeatedly in terms of its importance for U.S. leadership:

53. This idea had already been put forward in the Collier trade bill of 1932, which contained many innovations in trade policy, but was vetoed by Hoover. Roosevelt, *Public Papers and Addresses*, vol. 1, p. 769.

54. Moley, *After Seven Years*, p. 51; Roosevelt, *Public Papers and Addresses*, vol. 1, p. 853.

55. Rosen traces Norman Davis's effort to push a multilateral view in "Intranationalism vs. Internationalism," p. 285.

56. The best overview of the London economic conference is Kindelberger, *World in Depression*, chap. 9. The most thorough discussion of the commercial aspects of the conference are in Richard N. Kottman, *Reciprocity and the North Atlantic Triangle, 1932–1938* (Ithaca, N.Y.: Cornell University Press, 1968), chap. 2. For the views of the principles, see Herbert Feis, *Characters in Crisis 1933* (Boston: Little, Brown, 1966) chaps. 14–20; Raymond Moley, *The First New Deal* (New York: Harcourt Brace, 1966), chaps. 33–38; and Hull, *Memoirs*, vol. 1, chaps. 18 and 19. Norman Davis raised hopes through successful negotiation of a limited tariff truce in May, but the many reservations expressed by its adherents called the value of the agreement into question.

I expected to be able to show this to other delegations in London and to use it to prove to them we were sincere in our efforts to reduce tariffs and also that I had the power to do so.[57]

Yet on the same day that Hull set sail for London, Roosevelt was announcing to a press conference, off the record, that the bill was too complex and that he still feared congressional resistance.[58] On 10 June, in the middle of his journey, Hull found out that Roosevelt was not going to submit the trade bill to Congress, citing the priority of other legislation.[59] Roosevelt claimed somewhat disingenuously that Hull already had the authority to negotiate commercial treaties. The State Department and Tariff Commission had begun investigating the prospects of negotiating reciprocal agreements. But for Hull, the State Department's authority suffered from a crucial defect: tariff treaties demanded approval by two-thirds of the Senate. As Hull knew, "no American Senate had ever approved a trade treaty negotiated by the Executive which materially reduced tariffs."[60] Hull's legislation, by contrast, enhanced American bargaining power because of its novel institutional arrangements. Under the proposed bill, negotiated agreements could be overturned only by congressional veto within sixty days. Hull's *Memoirs* stress again and again the lack of American credibility:

> When I arrived in London, I found that delegations of other countries were well aware of the severely handicapped situation in which the American delegation was thus left . . . I had represented to Washington that the hands of the delegation would be virtually tied . . . and they were tied indeed.[61]

In fact, Hull's expectations for the conference were optimistic, if not fanciful.[62] By the time of the conference, the "hundred days" were just coming to a close, and the new direction in U.S. economic policy was unambiguous. The negotiation of industry codes under the National Industrial Recovery Act (NIRA) was the prime New Deal task in the summer of 1933.[63] The philosophy of both the NIRA and the Agricultural Adjustment Act (AAA) was to raise prices. Increased prices could leave code signatories vulnerable to imports. To correct this anomaly, the NIRA gave the president virtually unlimited powers to restrict imports. Turf battles between the

57. Hull, *Memoirs,* vol. 1, p. 250. For the draft bill see Record Group 59, 611.0031/428, National Archives.
58. Roosevelt, *Press Conferences,* 31 May 1933, vol. 1, pp. 324–25.
59. See Frank Freidel, *Launching the New Deal,* pp. 439–40, 450; Feis, *Characters in Crisis 1933,* p. 174; Hull, *Memoirs,* vol. 1, p. 251; Moley, *The First New Deal,* pp. 420–22.
60. Hull, *Memoirs,* vol. 1, p. 252.
61. Ibid.
62. Feis calls Hull's laments on the fate of the conference "histrionic." Feis, *Characters in Crisis 1933,* p. 175.
63. William E. Leuchtenberg, *Franklin D. Roosevelt,* p. 64.

National Recovery Administration (NRA) and the State Department revealed the ascendence of domestic priorities. In July, Undersecretary of State William Phillips brought the problems that the codes created for American trade to the attention of the NRA. Phillips asked that the codes not contain clauses that would negatively affect imports and exports, and also asked that State Department officials be allowed to help regulate the codes. The NRA refused.[64]

In October, an executive order established the procedures to administer the NRA's trade provisions.[65] This order created a channel for industry grievances that was similar to the one later adopted under the RTAA. The NRA was empowered to make a preliminary investigation based on industry or labor organization complaints. The president was then empowered to either dismiss the complaint or direct the Tariff Commission to launch a full investigation.[66]

Monetary policy constituted the second pillar of Roosevelt's nationalism.[67] As with the NIRA and the AAA, the goal of monetary policies over 1933 was to raise prices in the questionable belief that price increases were a precondition for recovery. Roosevelt was fiscally orthodox, however, as shown by his draconian Economy Act, and he was also opposed to outright money creation. His monetary policy unfolded in three stages. Beginning in April 1933, Roosevelt came under strong congressional pressure for inflation. The Thomas amendment to the Farm Relief bill gave the president discretionary power to create paper money. This necessarily entailed going off gold; that decision came on 20 April, triggering a steady descent of the dollar. Depreciation was accelerated in July by Roosevelt's famous "bombshell" to the London Economic Conference in which he rejected international cooperation aimed at stabilization. Finally, in mid-July, after intervention to break the dollar's decline had produced drops in the stock and commodity markets, a sharp debate broke out within the administration over whether further monetary measures were required. On one side stood

64. State's relations with Henry Wallace and the AAA were less strained, but in agriculture the principle problem was promoting exports. Section 15(e) of the AAA empowered the president to levy an equal compensating tax on agricultural goods, subject to processing taxes. On the turf fights, see Dick Steward, *Trade and Hemisphere, the Good Neighbor Policy and Reciprocal Trade* (Columbia: University of Missouri Press, 1975), pp. 15–16.

65. *New York Times*, 25 October and 5 November 1933.

66. *New York Times*, 5 November 1933. The NRA could also initiate its own investigations. Herbert Feis argues that the trade provisions were used only to prevent codes from toppling, although the United States did place import quotas on liquor, lumber, tobacco, potatoes, cotton, and sugar. Feis, *Characters in Crisis 1933*, p. 262; Steward, *Trade and Hemisphere,* p. 15ff.

67. This paragraph draws on Kindleberger, *World in Depression*, chap. 9; Oye, "The Sterling-Dollar-Franc Triangle"; Elmus Wicker, "Roosevelt's 1933 Monetary Experiment," *The Journal of American History* 57 (March 1971); James R. Moore, "Sources of New Deal Economic Policy: The International Dimension," *Journal of American History* 61 (December 1974); Jeanette Nicholas, "Roosevelt's Monetary Diplomacy in 1933." *American Historical Review* 56 (January 1951).

officials in the Treasury, the Federal Reserve, and the budget bureau, on the other, Henry Morgenthau, at that time head of the Farm Credit Administration, and a Cornell professor named George F. Warren. Warren managed to convince Morgenthau and Roosevelt that by simply increasing the purchase price of gold, the price level would automatically rise. On 8 September, Roosevelt raised the gold price sharply. While the economic effects of the gold purchase policy are questionable, it was a political success. By January, Roosevelt was in a position to support stabilization and a refixing of the price of gold.

The changed competitive position of American industry that resulted from the devaluation of the dollar gave the administration an important set of arguments for a new trade policy. Between February and December 1933, American exports doubled. In his congressional testimony on the 1934 bill, Secretary of Commerce Daniel C. Roper argued that the devaluation amounted to "an additional all-around tariff protection or handicap on imports which has been in only small measure offset by increased costs of production . . . resulting from the NRA or other recovery measures." Similarly, "the pick-up in exports . . . reflects the new advantage which American exporters now have . . . because of the depreciated exchange value of the dollar." As a result, "this dollar devaluation has put the American tariff on such a heightened level that the United States is now in a better position than it has been for a long time to make partial reductions in duties . . . without inducing destructive competition through enlarged imports."[68]

6. Towards the RTAA

The array of New Deal initiatives had as its corollary an increasing fragmentation of authority over trade policy. Undersecretary of State Phillips worried that "various departments and more especially the new Government agencies, such as the N.R.A., the R.F.C. [Reconstruction Finance Corporation], et cetera, are dealing with these matters independently as they see fit without cooperating with the State Department."[69] "Driven to distraction," Herbert Feis noted, "we in the State Department strove to inaugurate some plan of unified control."[70] Four times between August and October 1933, Hull took State Department recommendations for a reorganization to Cabinet meetings, but with little effect. Finally, in early November, Hull convinced Roosevelt to create an interdepartmental Executive Committee on Commercial Policy to be chaired by the State Department. Two circumstances were cited as compelling reasons for the moves: the fragmentation of

68. House of Representatives, *Hearings,* pp. 65–66. Feis also recognized the importance of devaluation for trade policy in his *Characters in Crisis 1933,* p. 264.
69. William Phillips Diary, 8 December 1933, Houghton Library, Harvard University.
70. Feis, *Characters in Crisis,* p. 262.

trade policymaking, and the move to greater state intervention in trade on the part of other governments.

The new group was chaired by Harvard economist Sayre. Sayre, a Wilsonian, defined the task of the committee as enlarging American export markets through the negotiation of reciprocal trade agreements on an unconditional MFN basis. Sayre recognized that this required a shift of tariff-making authority from Congress to the president.[71] The reasons were outlined by Feis after a crucial meeting with Roosevelt on 28 December:

> The President clearly recognized the fact that if we are to sustain or develop foreign trade we must find a way of deciding that industries should *not* be protected. It was agreed that the type of commercial policy envisaged in the memorandum [of the executive committee] could only be carried out if the President were given certain tariff-making powers.[72]

Bargaining demanded the ability to make trade-offs. The committee developed a complex—and secret—scheme to classify all American industries. At one end of the spectrum were those export industries, mainly agricultural staples and mass-produced manufactures, that depended on exports and in which the United States had a comparative advantage. The underlying objective of trade policy would be to gain concessions for these industries by opening the market for other products, at least where necessary. Some of these goods would be commodities that were not competitive with American manufactures, but the committee recognized that the protection granted some inefficient industries might have to be relaxed.[73]

Even though reciprocal trade agreements would necessarily require extended negotiations, the legislative strategy of the administration was to exploit the opportunity presented by crisis conditions. The increase in executive authority was justified as a temporary and emergency measure. Before the Senate, Hull argued that "there should, I repeat, be no misunderstanding as to the nature or the purpose of this measure . . . Its support is only urged as an emergency measure to deal with a dangerous and threatening emergency situation."[74] In his 2 March message to Congress that introduced the legislation, FDR emphasized two factors to justify this extraordinary grant of authority: the economic crisis and the resultant decline in U.S. exports; and the move on the part of the other governments towards reciprocal bargaining.[75]

71. Sayre, *The Way Forward*, p. 56; Hull, *Memoirs*, vol. 1, p. 354.

72. Feis, *Characters in Crisis 1933*, p. 264.

73. It was widely recognized that the negotiation of reciprocal agreements would require lifting protection from some industries. See *Executive Committee Report*, supplement 1, which offers a detailed classification scheme; Tariff Commission, "Draft Statement on Reducible Tariff Rates," 13 February 1934, OF 60; and Willard Thorp's observations on the thinking in the Department of Commerce in Katie Louchheim, ed., *The Making of the New Deal: The Insiders Speak* (Cambridge: Harvard University Press, 1983), pp. 275–76.

74. Senate Finance Committee, *Hearings*, p. 5.

75. *Public Papers and Addresses*, vol. 3, pp. 113–16.

The individual components of the legislation were not new, but grouping them together into a single piece of legislation was.[76] Given the drift to bilateralism, the choice of reciprocal bargaining as the means of lowering tariffs was hardly surprising, and had its roots in earlier reciprocity efforts. Even Hull, who in 1932 had suggested a 10 percent unilateral, across-the-board reduction in tariffs and preferred multilateral action, recognized that neither were politically viable.[77] Once reciprocity was favored over either unilateral action or multilateralism, tariff-cutting clearly would be selective rather than horizontal. Though the inclusion of the unconditional MFN clause in reciprocal agreements was to become one of the more controversial elements of the new trade program, American adoption of unconditional MFN treatment dated to 1923. Even the delegation of tariff-making authority to the executive had its precedent in the "flexible" tariff provisions.[78]

Despite these precedents, the administration's trade legislation provoked a heated debate, particularly on the floor of the Senate. In contrast to 1930, however, when interest groups were the main protagonists and specific tariff rates the issue, the most important issues at stake in 1934 were institutional, centering on the transfer of authority from Congress to the executive. Critics argued on two grounds that the delegation of tariff-making authority was unconstitutional. First, since the trade agreements were in fact treaties, they required two-thirds Senate approval. Second, the power delegated to the executive under the RTAA was unconstitutionally broad and discretionary, threatening to cut both Congress and industry out of the trade policy process. Senator Arthur Vandenburg complained that the bill would entitle "Washington bureaucrats" to "identify so called 'inefficient industries' and to put them out of business by their fiat."[79] Congress was being forced to give advance approval for any agreements into which the president might enter. Rejecting the Democratic theory that linked Smoot–Hawley and the Depression, Senator Walcott even defended the tradition of tariff logrolling, arguing that it at least gave representatives some voice in trade policy.[80]

In the course of debate within the Senate Finance Committee, the administration accepted two important institutional compromises. These mollified congressional concerns and established the delicate balance between congressional and presidential authority that has characterized trade politics ever since.[81] First, the authority for the president to negotiate trade agreements was limited to three years. This allowed protectionist groups to hold the renewal of broad negotiating authority hostage to particular compro-

76. I am thankful to David Lake for this point. See Kelly, "Antecedents."

77. Hull, *Memoirs,* vol. 1, p. 356.

78. On the growth of executive power over the tariff, see John Day Larkin, *The President's Control of the Tariff* (Cambridge: Harvard University Press, 1936).

79. "Minority Views," in *Congressional Record,* 27 March 1934, pp. 5532–33; Vandenburg, *Congressional Record,* 18 May 1934, pp. 9081–82. For an overview of the constitutional issues see Sayre, *The Way Forward,* chap. 7.

80. *Congressional Record,* 25 May 1934, p. 9567.

81. This balance is the main theme of Pastor, *U.S. Foreign Economic Policy.*

mise, and made specific negotiations more sensitive to political pressures. Of thirty-one bilateral agreements signed between 1934 and 1945, only two unimportant ones were signed between January and June of the year in which authority had to be renewed.[82]

Second, a machinery was established by which industries could express their concerns over pending negotiations. The administration had opposed this move because it would reintroduce the very type of politics that the RTAA was designed to limit.[83] Many amendments seeking exemptions for particular products were defeated on the floor of the Senate, however, with solid support from the Southern Democrats.

7. Aftermath: the Peek–Hull controversy and the consolidation of liberal machinery

Even before the passage of the RTAA, Roosevelt created difficulties for the liberal program by appointing George Peek to act as a special adviser on foreign trade issues in December 1933.[84] Peek reflected a very different conception of reciprocity than that favored by the State Department.[85] Roosevelt was ambivalent, if not simply ignorant, of the details at stake, and was willing to grant Peek wide leeway. Peek operated at a considerable institutional disadvantage, however, To succeed, he would have to force centralization of all trade policy in an independent Foreign Trade Board outside the control of the State Department.[86] Peek's efforts to this end were a losing battle. The passage of the RTAA allowed the State Department to control the trade policy agenda and to design a new policy machinery that was not only centralized, but at least somewhat more insulated from industry pressures than what had gone before.

The story of the Hull–Peek controversy can be summarized briefly.[87] In December 1933, Peek was given a position as presidential adviser on trade

82. Kelly, "Antecedents," p. 81; Pastor, *U.S. Foreign Economic Policy*, pp. 179–85. On the renewals of 1937 and 1940, see Steven Robert Brenner, "Economic Interests and the Trade Agreements Program, 1937–1940."

83. For the administration's objections to public hearings, see Senate Finance Committee, *Hearings*, pp. 15, 29, 80–81, 130.

84. See Phillips Diary, 11 December 1933.

85. Peek's views also reflected more immediately the interests of the food and textile industries. Steward, *Trade and Hemisphere*, p. 32.

86. A 70-page draft of Peek's plan for a Foreign Trade Board is enclosed with Peek to FDR, 16 July 1935. See also FDR to Peek, 17 July 1935, both in President's Secretary's File 73, FDR Library; Phillips Diary, 2 January 1934.

87. On the Peek–Hull controversy, see George Fite, *George N. Peek*, chaps. 16–17; Steward, *Trade and Hemisphere*, chap. 2; George N. Peek and Samuel Crowther, *Why Quit Our Own?* (New York: Van Nostrand, 1936). The correspondence between Peek, FDR, and Hull, and Peek's objections are set out in "Report of the Special Adviser on Foreign Trade," enclosed with Peek to FDR, 31 December 1934; OF 614A, cited hereafter as *Report of the Special Adviser*, and in a series of six articles in the *Saturday Evening Post*, 16 May–20 June 1936.

questions. When the Export–Import Banks were established in early 1934, Peek was made their president, giving him a base from which to widen his ties with industry.[88] In March, just as the RTAA was going to Congress, Roosevelt created the Office of the Special Adviser on Foreign Trade for Peek, an appointment that could not have stunned Hull more "if Mr. Roosevelt had hit me between the eyes with a sledge hammer . . ."[89] At first there was some confusion over the fate of the Executive Committee on Commercial Policy, which had become the meeting point for liberals in the State, Agriculture, and Commerce Departments and had been responsible for drafting the trade legislation. Only with a second executive order did Roosevelt signal his intention of keeping that body in place, creating a system of "dual power" in trade policy.

After the passage of the RTAA, the new institutional machinery for implementing the legislation began to take shape. Peek had suggested the creation of an independent centralized body, a move bitterly opposed by the State Department.[90] Failing that, Peek sought to control the newly created interdepartmental Committee on Trade Agreements. A new Trade Agreements Division was also created within the State Department, and became the center of trade-policy expertise. It reviewed each proposed trade agreement, examined in detail the concessions recommended for inclusion, oversaw the activities of the country subcommittees responsible for drafting bilateral agreements, and incorporated the information provided by the Committee for Reciprocity Information, the body set up to hear industry concerns. The discussions of the Executive Committee were based largely on facts supplied by the professionals staffing the Committee on Trade Agreements. The interdepartmental nature of the two key committees allowed Peek's Office of the Special Adviser to air its views, but the new machinery was clearly rooted in an internationalist State Department.[91]

Nonetheless, the conflicts between Peek and the State Department were to drag on for over a year-and-a-half. Two substantive issues were at stake; both centered on the way the United States was to exercise leverage in gaining advantages with trading partners. The first concerned the emphasis to be given to exchange controls in the Trade Agreements Program. Peek argued, rightly in many cases, that exchange restrictions and competitive devaluations were a more damning limitation on trade than tariffs. The

88. On the establishment of the Ex-Im banks, see Frederick C. Adams, *Economic Diplomacy: the Export–Import Bank and American Foreign Policy 1934–1939* (Columbia: University of Missouri Press, 1976), chap. 3.

89. Hull, *Memoirs*, vol. 1, p. 370.

90. Francis Bowes Sayre, "Draft: Memorandum on Machinery for the Effectuating of a Foreign Trade Policy," attached to *Executive Committee Report;* Phillips Diary, 2 January, 27 February, 23 March 1934.

91. See Mary Trackett Reynolds, *Interdepartmental Committees in the National Administration* (New York: Columbia University Press, 1939), pp. 47–70; Sayre, *The Way Forward,* chap. 8; Rexford Tugwell Diary, vol. 5, pp. 13–14; Steward, *Trade and Hemisphere,* pp. 44–45.

United States should use the promise of trade agreements to eliminate these practices or to secure preferential treatment.

This argument was closely related to a second, more complex concern—Peek's contending vision of reciprocity and opposition to unconditional MFN. Peek raised five objections.[92] First and foremost, unconditional MFN led to free-riding. This took two forms: 1) countries not signing agreements would exploit U.S. concessions, leading to an uncontrollable flood of imports; and 2) equally important, Peek believed that committing the United States to unconditional MFN would constitute "unilateral economic disarmament," and discourage other states from negotiating.[93] Making MFN conditional allowed the United States to exploit its market power more effectively. Second, Peek pointed out that the principle supplier clause was inadequate to control free-riding, since many smaller countries, such as Haiti, were not the principle supplier of anything. Third, Peek noted that maintaining U.S. presence in third markets might rest on the ability to force smaller countries to establish quota systems that protected U.S. market share against lower cost producers, such as Japan. These agreements would violate our commitment to unconditional MFN. Fourth, on several occasions, Peek suggested that the State Department was poorly situated to consider trade issues because of its tendency to mix diplomatic and political concerns with purely commercial ones. Finally, Peek argued that the United States needed flexibility in its export promotion methods. While barter, subsidization, and dumping were perhaps inferior ways of conducting international trade over the long run, they could be important in disposing of surpluses, maintaining market share, and increasing bargaining power. It was, in fact, a barter deal with Germany involving the sale of American cotton that led to the most heated controversy between Peek and the State Department, a fight that Peek eventually lost after a concerted State Department effort to sway Roosevelt.[94]

In the meantime, a new institutional machinery for the conduct of trade policy was being consolidated under State Department auspices that insulated the government from protectionist pressures. The activities of the country committees responsible for drafting agreements were closely guarded, and even the identities of their members were held secret. Not until the process of gathering and analyzing data was fairly far advanced was an announcement made of the intention to negotiate. According to Sayre, "partisan or purely political considerations play no part throughout this long

---

92. The following passage draws on the *Report of the Special Adviser*.

93. See "Memorandum submitted by the Special Adviser . . . for consideration at its Meeting December 4 . . . ," enclosed with the *Report of the Special Adviser*.

94. On the German deal, see Steward, *Trade and Hemisphere*, pp. 52–53; Phillips Diary, 13 and 14 December 1934. For almost a year after that conflict, Roosevelt kept Peek around. Only after Peek had supplied the press with material critical of the reciprocal trade program, did Roosevelt finally lose his patience. FDR to Peek, 22 November 1935; Peek to FDR, 26 November 1935; FDR to Peek, 11 December 1935.

study."[95] The announcement of negotiations included only the name of the country in question, rather than a listing of particular products under consideration. Industries protested this arrangement, but the Stae Department held firm.[96] Industry could air its views through the Committee for Reciprocity Information, based on their calculations of which products were likely to be negotiated. But expressing concerns before a nonpartisan committee of trade policy experts was quite different than lobbying Congress. The setting of the agenda and the analysis of concessions to be sought and offered rested on independent economic criteria, and as a result, the information supplied by industry was heavily discounted.[97]

An interesting exchange of letters between Senator Frederick Steiwer and FDR over the efficacy of the Committee for Reciprocity Information shows a sense of industry frustration.[98] At the negotiation of the Canadian agreement, Steiwer pointed out that Canadian producers dealt directly with American negotiators, but American producers "present their cause through an information committee which at the most can act only as an intermediary." Steiwer argued that representatives of producer associations should be given access during the earlier stages of the formulation of the trade agreements. Somewhat disingenuously, FDR denied that the committee was only a "buffer agency," arguing that Steiwer's proposals would "so complicate and delay the negotiation of trade agreements as to hinder seriously the carrying out of the purposes of the act."

The Committee on Reciprocity Information exposed cross-cutting cleavages within industry, provided additional incentives for export-oriented interests to organize, and thus strengthened the hand of the liberals. In the case of smaller developing countries, the vast majority of petitioners sought concessions from the foreign country; industry signals were unambiguous and the committee became a means of collecting information from exporters. Negotiations with more advanced countries were quite different. After announcing the intent to negotiate an RTA with Belgium, for example, the committee received eighty-six communications. Forty-eight opposed granting concessions in particular products, twenty-one sought Belgian concessions while another eleven actually sought reductions in U.S. tariffs.[99] The

95. Sayre, *The Way Forward,* p. 94.

96. Typical of the numerous letters protesting this arrangement is Congressman Edward Eicher to Hull, 17 August 1934, which encloses a letter from the Iowa Manufacturers Association and R. Walter Moore (State Department) to Eicher, 1 September 1934, Record Group 59, 611.0031/1013, National Archives. See also Robert Lund, chairman of the board, National Association of Manufacturers to FDR, 23 April 1935, RG 59, 611.0031/1650.

97. Brenner, "Economic Interests," p. 108ff.

98. Steiwer to FDR, 4 April 1935; FDR to Steiwer, 8 April 1935; OF 614A.

99. Six of the communications asked that particular concessions not be sought from the Belgians. See "Belgium: Committee for Reciprocity Information: Record of Correspondence, Oct. 19–Oct. 25, 1934," RG 59, 611.0031/Committee for Reciprocity Information/75, National Archives.

Cotton Textile Institute went on record against U.S. concessions in textiles, while the National Council of American Importers and Traders sought them.

The negotiations themselves provided a second opportunity for industries to exert pressure, particularly since the president passed judgment on the agreement and thus had to weigh the political costs of concessions. The bargaining period itself posed the most difficulty to the State Department, because, according to Sayre, "high-powered lobbyists make their voices heard throughout the country using every device to prevent the giving of concessions . . . Pressure is brought against members of Congress; Washington is deluged with inspired letters and telegrams."[100] No doubt these last-minute pressures had some effect on limiting the range of concessions. But the very process of bargaining allowed, in fact, demanded, that negotiators build liberalizing coalitions. In the British negotiations, for example, Sayre explicitly recognized that "opposition in New England to the tariff relaxations on British textiles could be offset by support for the agreement and the administration from the Far West and agricultural regions."[101] The combination of negotiated tariffs and a new trade policy structure enhanced executive autonomy.

8. Conclusion

The RTAA marked an important institutional innovation in American trade policy. Expanding the executive presence in the trade area created new expertise and institutional interests in liberalization while broadening the context for formulating trade policy. The new structure also changed the relationship between business and government. Protectionist forces were by no means silenced. But congressional tariff-making had obscured the costs of particularism and made protectionist lobbying relatively cost-free. The new institutional structure exposed the trade-off between export expansion and protection, provided new incentives for internationally competitive industries to organize, and thus increased the costs of protectionist lobbying while decreasing the likelihood of success.

The dramatic fall in exports during the Depression stimulated agriculture and export-oriented manufacturers to support some trade-policy initiative. Yet, as Judith Goldstein has argued most cogently, conflicting norms were institutionalized.[102] Even as liberals sought to advance the cause of freer trade, the "compromise of embedded liberalism" guaranteed at least tacit political support from potentially affected industries. This compromise took two forms. The NRA, the AAA, and an independent monetary policy offered an additional layer of protection to the economy. The institutional compro-

100. Sayre, *The Way Forward*, p. 96.
101. Kottman, *Reciprocity and the North Atlantic Triangle*, p. 257.
102. Goldstein, "The Political Economy of Trade."

mises included congressional oversight and channels, albeit circumscribed, for industry to express its grievances.

The initiative for reforming the policy machinery came not from the private sector, nor from the White House, but from champions of freer trade in the State Department. The State Department had ideological and institutional interests in institutional reform, but these were largely tied to broader international interests. The State Department saw that the move to preferences and bilateralism in the international system demanded a more flexible and credible *domestic* bargaining structure. Negotiating tariff reductions required some insulation from protectionist pressures. This insulation was achieved in part by shifting authority towards the executive, and in part by expanding the government's expertise and capacity to independently gather and process information.

This study raises three larger theoretical issues: one concerns the utility of international structural explanations; the second concerns the contention that the United States has a "weak" state; the third concerns the controversy over "statist" and "societal" approaches to policymaking.

Attempts to construct international systemic explanations of trade policy have stumbled on the interwar years. Though the United States had achieved the stature of a hegemon by many objective indicators, it refused to play its assigned role. In his study, *World in Depression*, Charles Kindleberger summarizes the political as well as explanatory puzzle: the British *couldn't* supply international leadership in 1929 and the United States *wouldn't*.[103] Power to act as a stabilizer was not at issue, only "will." But what explains the change in will?

Beginning with structural explanations, Stephen Krasner and David Lake revert to domestic political factors to explain the "lag" in policy.[104] Oddly, they may abandon the international level of analysis too quickly. The weakness of their systemic argument stems from an overly narrow conception of international structure as the distribution of capabilities and from paying inadequate attention to how domestic actors actually perceived international constraints and opportunities. The international system comes into an explanation of the RTAA in two ways, but neither fit neatly into a Waltzian conception of structure. First, changes in the international political *processes* that governed trade demanded greater domestic flexibility, pushing State Department officials to seek a restructuring of the trade policy machinery. Second, a series of uncooperative actions, beginning with Smoot–Hawley and continuing through Roosevelt's monetary policy, ultimately facilitated a more forthcoming trade policy by compensating potential losers. Redundant levels of protection and an improvement in trade in

---

103. Charles P. Kindleberger, *World in Depression,* p. 292.
104. Krasner, "State Power." Contrast Lake, "Beneath the Commerce of Nations" and "The State and American Trade Policy in the Pre-hegemonic Era," this volume.

1933—both associated with an aggressive monetary policy—gave the administration arguments for moving ahead.[105]

This article casts some doubt on the value of a "weak state" approach to U.S. foreign economic policy. While it is perhaps useful for some broad comparative purposes, the approach is overly static, suggesting a constancy in "state strength" over time. In fact, the "strength" of the state, or more simply, the capability of the executive, can shift, particularly in response to crisis. If institutions matter in explaining policy outcomes, political scientists should spend more effort unravelling those historical conjunctures or "turning points" when the context of policymaking changes fundamentally. Second, the weak state argument overlooks the various ways that state actors can take the initiative to pursue their own organizational and ideological interests and to structure opportunities for new or latent social coalitions. In the trade case, the reforms that were associated with the RTAA made protectionist alliances more difficult by moving authority towards more insulated executive arenas, in which broader foreign policy calculations and technical expertise entered into decision-making. Gil Winham's insightful analysis of the Tokyo Round negotiations reaches a similar conclusion, showing how astute institutional engineering limited the ability of different sectors to veto executive initiatives.[106]

I have attempted to counter purely societal explanations of trade policy by examining the role of executive initiative and by showing that the very power of "societal" actors cannot be divorced from their institutional context. The distinction between "statist" and "societal" models seems, in the end, artificial.[107] Students of American politics have long observed that bureaucratic and business interests frequently converge, resulting in policy coalitions that span the state–society divide. They have also paid attention to the agenda-setting and coalition-building power of the executive.[108] The debate on the domestic determinants of American foreign economic policy should rotate less around whether state actors, societal actors, or international pressures are more important in particular instances, and more on how institutions differentially process external constraints and structure the access of groups to decision-making.

105. Oye makes a similar argument in "The Sterling-Dollar-Franc Triangle."
106. Pastor, *U.S. Foreign Economic Policy*; Gil Winham, "Robert Strauss, the MTN and the Control of Faction," *Journal of World Trade Law* 14 (September/October 1980). Pastor virtually ignores the role of the private sector.
107. For example, Stephen Krasner, *Defending the National Interest* (Princeton, N.J.: Princeton University Press, 1978).
108. Examples of recent work in American politics that gives weight to "state" actors would include the literature on agenda-setting; see John Kingdon, *Agendas, Alternatives and Public Policies* (Boston: Little, Brown, 1984); and on policy communities, Hugh Heclo, "Issue Networks and the Executive Branch," in Anthony King, ed., *The New American Political System* (Washington, D.C.: American Enterprise Institute, 1978).

Trade as a strategic weapon: American and alliance export control policy in the early postwar period Michael Mastanduno

The study of postwar American foreign economic policy recently has been informed by a dual conventional wisdom: that the American state[1] is relatively weak domestically, yet powerful internationally. Domestic weakness refers to the ability of private actors to penetrate and influence the state; to the institutional fragmentation and decentralization of the state apparatus; and to the difficulties state officials encounter in extracting resources from domestic society and in achieving their policy preferences in the face of domestic opposition. International strength, on the other hand, refers to the high degree of resources controlled by the United States relative to other nation-states, and to the ability of state officials to translate those resources into influence over international outcomes.[2] In the early postwar period,

An early version of this article was presented at the 1985 Meeting of the American Political Science Association. For comments and suggestions, I am grateful to Valerie Bunce, Beverly Crawford, Jeff Frieden, Joanna Gowa, Cynthia Hody, John Ikenberry, David Lake, Melanie Mastanduno, Timothy McKeown, John Odell, four anonymous reviewers for *IO* and the participants at the University of Chicago's Program on Interdependent Political Economy session on 29 April, 1987. I also acknowledge Hamilton College and the Institute for the Study of World Politics for financial support.

1. In this article the state is defined as the executive branch of the U.S. government. Unless otherwise noted, state officials refer to the president and his central foreign policy advisors. To minimize verbal monotony, I use "state officials," "U.S. officials," and "executive officials" interchangably. These definitions are similar to those employed by Stephen Krasner in *Defending the National Interest* (Princeton, N.J.: Princeton University Press, 1978).

2. For the characterization of the United States as a weak state, see Stephen Krasner, "United States Commercial and Monetary Policy: Unravelling the Paradox of External Strength and Internal Weakness," and Peter Katzenstein, "Conclusion: Domestic Structures and Strategies of Foreign Economic Policy," in Katzenstein, ed., *Between Power and Plenty* (Madison: University of Wisconsin Press, 1978), pp. 51–88, and 295–336. See also J. P. Nettl, who notes the low level of American "stateness," in "The State as a Conceptual Variable," *World Politics* 20 (July 1968), pp. 559–92.

Though it should be apparent as the argument develops, I should clarify that I use the terms "strength" and "weakness" to refer primarily to the ability of state officials to achieve their preferred political outcomes in the face of domestic or international opposition. On the domes-

International Organization 42, 1, Winter 1988

America's external strength more than compensated for its internal weakness, and enabled state officials to pursue effectively their primary foreign economic policy objective: the creation of a liberal international economic order, characterized by the free movement of goods and capital across borders and by stable exchange rates.[3]

The case of early postwar American East–West trade policy is distinctive because it contradicts both aspects of the conventional wisdom. Rather than economic openness, U.S. officials preferred a strategy of international economic closure in trade with the East during this period. They perceived it to be in America's national security interest to deny the benefits of international economic exchange to the Soviet Union, Eastern Europe and China, and organized a broad export embargo against them. State officials encountered few domestic constraints in pursuing this policy. They enjoyed the support of Congress, the acquiescence of the business community, and a lack of bureaucratic fragmentation within the executive branch. Moreover, they possessed a wide array of policy instruments that allowed them to implement comprehensive export denial. Because the United States had relatively little at stake economically, and East–West trade was perceived to be directly related to military security, the American state could be much stronger, domestically, than in other areas of foreign economic policy.

By itself, however, domestic strength was not enough to ensure the effectiveness of American East–West export control strategy. For economic warfare to be effective, state officials needed the cooperation of America's Western allies, who might act as alternative suppliers of strategic materials and equipment. Yet the allies were wary, for political and economic reasons, of participating in a broad embargo directed at the Soviet Union. What is most striking about the ensuing conflict is that the United States, despite possessing a preponderance of power resources and undertaking a sustained, high-level diplomatic effort, was ultimately unsuccessful in obtaining alliance support. Alliance policy on multilateral export controls reflected American preferences only for the relatively brief period 1950–1953; following that, the position of the allies became dominant and remained so for the duration of the cold war. Notwithstanding its power and prestige in the alliance, the United States was unable to maintain the East–West export

---

tic side, I examine the ability of state officials to pursue economic warfare as American strategy and avoid coercion in their efforts to coordinate that strategy internationally. On the international side, I assess the ability of state officials to gain alliance support for economic warfare. Since the latter task was by far the most difficult of the three, most of the analysis of this article is devoted to examining it.

3. Krasner makes this argument in "U.S. Commercial and Monetary Policy," note 2, pp. 52–53. See also Robert Gilpin, *U.S. Power and the Multinational Corporation* (New York: Basic Books, 1975); Charles Maier, "The Politics of Productivity: Foundations of American International Economic Policy After World War Two," in Katzenstein, ed., *Between Power and Plenty,* pp. 23–50; and Fred Block, *The Origins of International Economic Disorder* (Berkeley: University of California Press, 1977), for discussions of the use of American power to restructure the postwar world economy.

control regime it preferred. Moreover, state officials were prompted by the international outcome to reconsider and revise America's own East–West export control strategy. In the era of undisputed American hegemony, U.S. officials were not only unable to determine alliance policy, but found themselves adjusting American policy to the preferences of their allies.

Thus, to understand fully U.S. export control policy, we must understand alliance conflict and cooperation. The main analytic task of this article is to explain the evolution of alliance policy, and the role of U.S. officials in shaping it, during the period 1947–1954. More specifically, I focus on two critical outcomes: the decision of the Western allies to pursue economic warfare multilaterally in 1950, and their decision to abandon it in 1954.

The generally accepted explanation for this pattern of outcomes focuses on the utility of American coercive power. In 1950, the argument runs, the Western allies reluctantly participated in the broader embargo effort, in order to retain their access to much-needed U.S. economic assistance. By 1953, as the volume and significance of that aid declined, Western governments became free to follow their political and economic interests and trade more heavily with the East. Lacking aid as an instrument of coercion, U.S. officials could no longer keep the allies in line and thereby lost their ability to determine multilateral export control policy.

This article challenges the dominant interpretation, and provides an alternative. I argue that coercion was *not* an effective instrument of leverage; in fact, I demonstrate that executive officials consciously and effectively sought to delink aid from trade, despite congressional efforts to force such a linkage. Moreover, an emphasis on the utility (or lack thereof) of coercion leads to a misunderstanding of the broader interests of state officials, and of the constraints placed by those interests on the state in the East–West trade issue-area. Coercion, in particular the denial of American trade, or economic or military aid, to the North Atlantic Treaty Organization (NATO) allies threatened to undermine the multilateral economic and security regimes that provided the foundation for American national security in the postwar era. State officials, in effect, were trapped by their own commitments, and as a result, could not translate their formidable resources into influence in the alliance conflict over East–West trade.

With West European cooperation a necessity, and with American coercive instruments effectively neutralized, the ultimate determinants of alliance strategy were the preferences of West European leaders, particularly British and French. Their preferences, in turn, were shaped by their own conceptions of the relationship between East–West trade and national security. In 1950, the belief that military conflict was highly likely, and that it would take the form of a protracted conventional war, combined to make a broad embargo against the East a compelling strategy. By 1953, as the threat of war subsided and the emphasis of alliance defense planning shifted to nuclear deterrence, the strategy no longer justified the economic and political sacrifices it entailed. West European leaders thus demanded a revision of the multilateral control system; U.S. officials, still in possession of coercive instruments yet constrained in their ability to use them, were forced to acquiesce.

The manner in which the alliance conflict was handled created an ongoing domestic one, between the executive and members of Congress. The majority in Congress believed that aid denial should be used to force West European compliance with U.S. export control policy. Congressional pressure did exert some influence on executive officials in their negotiations with the allies. Ultimately, however, the executive prevailed, by exercising its discretionary power over export control policy and by enlisting the cooperation of the allies in a transnational bargain that was designed to frustrate the intent of congressional legislation. State officials may have been unable to determine alliance policy, but they did manage to use their relationship with the allies to help overcome domestic opposition.

This article has two broad objectives. First, it seeks to provide a reinterpretation of an important episode in early postwar American foreign economic policy that is sensitive both to the conflicting interests of U.S. state officials and to the link between East–West trade strategies and the national security concerns of Western states. Second, like other articles in this volume, it seeks to further our understanding of the role and efficacy of the American state in foreign economic policy. While many consider the state to be a significant actor, how and why it is so, across time and issue-area, is less apparent. The analysis of this case reminds us that state officials may derive and enjoy considerable domestic strength at times or in policy areas in which economic affairs are perceived to have national security significance. More imporantly, it suggests the need, when assessing the international influence of the United States, to take account of conflicts among the objectives of state officials that may inhibit the exercise of cross-issue linkage.

Finally, the argument carries with it certain policy implications. Notwithstanding its failure in the immediate postwar period, the United States recently attempted to gain alliance support for economic warfare, and may initiate further attempts in the future. The experience of the early 1950s is suggestive regarding the limits of U.S. influence, and the circumstances under which cooperation is likely to be obtained.

The next section of the article accounts for the strategic preferences of American state officials, and examines the constraints they faced. The following two sections consider, respectively, the alliance conflicts of 1950 and 1954, and the role of executive officials in shaping their outcome. The concluding section addresses the implications for students of American foreign economic policy.

State officials and export control policy: strategies and constraints

East–West trade deals with America's principal geopolitical competitor and potential military adversary. Consequently, throughout the postwar period state officials have treated it differently than they have trade with other destinations. The general thrust of U.S. commercial policy has been to minimize state intervention and remove barriers to the free flow of goods and services; in effect, to extricate the state from the market. In East–West trade, the pattern of state behavior has been reversed. Unwilling to leave such trade in private hands, state officials have sought actively to intervene in the market and manipulate transactions to serve political and national security objectives.

As I have argued elsewhere, three generic export control strategies are available to officials seeking to manage trade for national security purposes.[4] One such strategy, called tactical linkage, involves the conditioning of trade according to the behavior of a target government. Good behavior is rewarded by trade expansion, while bad behavior is punished by trade denial. Although U.S. officials contemplated the use of this strategy immediately following World War II, by early 1948 they had rejected it decisively because, in the words of George Kennan, the Soviet regime was "impervious to the logic of reason" and thus could not be influenced by U.S. economic inducements.[5] At the same time, U.S. officials had become increasingly apprehensive about the possible contribution of U.S. exports to Soviet military capabilities.

Two alternative strategies address this latter concern by relying on unconditional export denial. The distinction between them is critical for understanding the alliance conflict over East–West trade. A *strategic embargo* permits most exports, and prohibits only those exports that make a direct and significant contribution to an adversary's military capability. The criteria for inclusion under such an embargo may be military use (that is, whether or not an item will be employed directly for military purposes, in peacetime or wartime), or military use and significance (that is, whether an item will be used for military purposes *and* would give an adversary a capability beyond that which it could achieve indigenously in the short run). *Economic warfare,* on the other hand, involves more comprehensive export denial. In

---

4. See Michael Mastanduno, "Strategies of Economic Containment: U.S. Trade Relations with the Soviet Union," *World Politics* 37 (July 1985), pp. 503–31.

5. Kennan's comments are found in the infamous "long telegram" of 1946, reprinted in *Foreign Relations of the United States* (hereafter *FRUS*), vol. 6 (1946), pp. 696–709, citation at 706–7. For a discussion of the early postwar interest of state officials in "containment by integration," see John Lewis Gaddis, *Strategies of Containment: A Critical Appraisal of Postwar American National Security Policy* (New York: Oxford University Press, 1982), pp. 9–17.

addition to items of military use, this strategy also targets those exports likely to make a significant contribution to the economic growth and development of the target country. The logic is that since the military sector is one part of an integrated target economy, trade that strengthens the economy indirectly strengthens the military, either by providing additional resources for the military sector to draw from, or by enhancing the quality and sophistication of the industrial base which underlies modern military power. Thus, exports of raw materials, industrial equipment, or technology, even if not destined for the military sector, may be targeted for denial in the interest of national security.[6]

For any state, the choice between a strategic embargo and economic warfare is driven by a combination of economic and strategic factors. The more dependent a nation-state is on trade with the target, the more likely that state officials will opt for a strategic embargo, since that strategy affects a relatively more narrow range of traded goods. Less obvious, and crucial to the argument of this article, are strategic considerations, such as the perceived likelihood of war and the type of war likely to be fought. Economic warfare is most attractive when the target state is engaged in, or perceived to be mobilizing for, a long conventional war. In such circumstances, the military sector will be a heavy burden on the target economy, and thus the resources released by trade will likely contribute to the maintenance or improvement of target military capabilities. Such was the logic underlying the comprehensive trade embargoes employed by the belligerents during the two major wars of this century. On the other hand, when the target state is neither engaged in nor mobilizing for war, a strategic embargo becomes a more plausible option. In such circumstances, most of the resources released by trade are likely to be channeled into civilian consumption and investment, rather than military pursuits. State officials could thus afford, from the perspective of national security, to deny only those items in trade likely to be of direct military use to the target.

Faced with the choice between economic warfare and a strategic embargo, by 1948 American state officials clearly opted for the former. They believed that the United States would be locked in a long-term geopolitical struggle with the Soviet Union, which would require a full commitment of American resources.[7] Yet while the Soviet Union was a formidable adversary ideologically and militarily, it was also significantly weaker than the United States economically. Free trade, particularly in industrial equipment and technology, would provide greater benefits to the Soviets than to the United States. Economic warfare thus presented a national security oppor-

6. A more detailed discussion of the logic of these two strategies is found in Mastanduno, "Strategies of Economic Containment," pp. 506–14.

7. This vision is most clearly articulated in Kennan's long telegram (see note 5) and in NSC 68: "Report to the National Security Council by the Executive Secretary" 14 April 1950, reprinted in *FRUS*, vol. 1 (1950), pp. 234–92.

tunity, since it could help perpetuate the backwardness of the Soviet economy, and thereby delay the expansion of Soviet military capabilities.

Three related perceptions, shared by state officials, provided the more specific rationale for economic warfare. First, by 1948 the American planners of export control policy were firmly convinced that the Soviet economy was a "war economy," completely subservient to the demands of military production. State officials emphasized that Soviet industrial potential was military potential, and that attempts to distinguish between the two were fruitless and dangerous. Export controls, they contended, "must be broad and deep enough to affect the entire production complex of the Soviet state."[8]

Second, U.S. policy was premised on the expectation that war with the Soviet Union was inevitable, either in the short or longer run.[9] Executive officials believed that if war were to break out imminently, it would be most important to have denied the Soviets items of direct military significance. However, if war were to come in five or ten years' time, it would at present be "more important to keep basic production equipment from the Soviets than to deprive them of strategic military equipment," since much of the latter would become obsolete over a ten-year span.[10] Since they intended to prepare simultaneously for both contingencies, state officials deemed it necessary to deny broad industrial as well as direct military items.

A third factor concerned the issue of Soviet vulnerability, which was treated in detailed reports by the State Department's Office of Intelligence Research and by the Central Intelligence Agency (CIA) in 1951.[11] Both reports recognized that the Soviet economy, especially when integrated with that of Eastern Europe, was relatively self-sufficient. Since bloc trade with the West was only 1 percent of GNP in 1950, a general embargo would only have limited effectiveness. However, what was demanded from the West consisted mainly of items "essential for military preparedness and the economic basis of military preparedness," including vital raw materials, ball bearings, and capital goods ranging across transportation, energy, and heavy industrial sectors. An effective embargo would impair current levels of production, future production capacities, and the ability of the Soviets to wage a

8. Telegram from the secretary of state to the U.S. embassy in the United Kingdom, 22 August 1950, reprinted in *FRUS*, vol. 4 (1950), pp. 174–76.

9. See the memorandum by the associate chief of the Economic Resources and Security Staff, undated, reprinted in *FRUS*, vol. 4 (1950), pp. 116–23, at 117–18.

10. Ibid., p. 117, and "Trade of the Free World with the Soviet Bloc," report prepared by the Economic Cooperation Administration, February 1951, reprinted in *FRUS*, vol. 1 (1951), pp. 1042–45.

11. "Vulnerability of the Soviet Bloc to Existing and Tightened Western Export Controls," report prepared by the Office of Intelligence Research of the Department of State, 20 January 1951, and "Vulnerability of the Soviet Bloc to Economic Warfare," National Intelligence Estimate No. 22, prepared by the CIA, 19 February 1951, reprinted in *FRUS*, vol. 1 (1951), pp. 1026–45.

protracted war. Importantly, both reports recognized that to carry out an effective embargo would require the full support of the Western allies.

Just as the devastating experience of the 1930s influenced America's pursuit of a liberal world economy in the postwar era, the experience of World War II helped to shape the economic strategy directed at the East. The economic "lesson" of the war was that an implacable adversary in pursuit of global domination was best confronted by economic, as well as military, containment. For U.S. officials, the Soviet Union was potentially a similar threat in the postwar era, to be met by similar economic methods, to that posed by Nazi Germany during the war. The perceived success of economic warfare against Germany enhanced its attractiveness to U.S. officials, and furthered their willingness to adapt it to peacetime, or in the circumstances of cold war.[12]

The preferred export control strategy of executive officials was thus a function of America's geopolitical relationship with the Soviet Union. In pursuit of that strategy, they faced very few domestic constraints. In light of the close relationship between East–West trade and American security, this should not be surprising. Nevertheless, it is noteworthy when considered in the context of the prevailing conception of the United States as a weak state in the area of trade policy. None of the presumed characteristics of American state weakness—the effective penetration of the state by interest groups seeking to fulfill private, as opposed to national, objectives; the decentralization of governmental authority, in particular the deference of the executive to Congress, owing to the latter's Constitutional prerogative to regulate commerce; or the fragmentation of the executive itself along organizational or institutional lines[13]—posed a significant problem for executive officials in the articulation or pursuit of their export control preferences.

First, notwithstanding their natural inclination to increase market shares, American firms provided little opposition to economic warfare. Their political acquiescence occurred partly because U.S. firms, unlike their West European counterparts, previously had not developed a significant stake in Eastern markets. Corporate officials also tended to share a concern for the risks, and a healthy skepticism about the potential benefits, of commerce with a state-trading nation.[14] Perhaps the most important inhibiting factor in

---

12. See, for example, W. M. Medlicott, *The Economic Blockade,* vol. 2 (London: HMSO, 1959), pp. 660–61.

13. In addition to Krasner, "External Strength and Internal Weakness," studies that highlight the primacy of interest groups and Congress in trade policy include the classic by E. E. Schattschneider, *Politics, Pressure and the Tariff* (Englewood Cliffs, N.J.: Prentice-Hall, 1935) and more recently, James Cassing, et al., "The Political Economy of the Tariff Cycle," *American Political Science Review* 80 (September 1986), pp. 843–62. An alternative, statist approach is taken in this volume by David Lake.

14. This point is well described by Bruce W. Jentleson, "From Consensus to Conflict: The Domestic Political Economy of East–West Energy Trade Policy," *International Organization* 38 (Autumn 1984), pp. 625–60, at 635–36.

the early postwar era, however, concerned the general political climate in the United States. Extreme anti-communism exposed any firm that expressed even a passing interest in East–West commerce to the charge of trading with the enemy. Such a reputation, whether deserved or not, could greatly harm a firm's position in domestic markets. Thus, U.S. firms tended to avoid Eastern trade, even trade that state officials did not consider strategic, and when corporate officials spoke publicly on the subject, they generally expressed their opposition to it.[15]

The great majority in the U.S. Congress similarly supported the executive in favoring the broad denial of American trade with the Communist world. Given the prevailing anti-communist sentiment in American society, to take a strong negative stand on trade with the East was attractive politically. As early as 1948, seven of ten Americans surveyed believed that East–West trade should be discontinued; the public generally tended to view it as an evil to be eliminated.[16]

Congress not only supported the executive's economic warfare strategy; more significantly, it delegated remarkably powerful policy instruments to the executive so that it could implement that strategy. Prior to the early cold war period, the executive could restrict U.S. exports only in times of war or special emergencies. With the passage of the Export Control Act of 1949, however, Congress gave the executive the right to exercise that authority routinely in peacetime. In the words of law professors Harold J. Berman and John R. Garson, "probably no single piece of legislation gives more power to the President to control American commerce."[17] The vagueness of its directives left considerable discretion in the hands of executive officials to fix the extent to which trade should be regulated. In practice, they constructed export control lists, and prior to exporting an item on the list, private firms or individuals had to acquire formal permission from the Commerce Department, in the form of a validated license. By early 1950, the executive's lists of items of primary and secondary strategic significance contained approximately 500 categories.[18]

Equally important, the act gave executive officials the authority to control exports not only to the East, but to all destinations. The danger that U.S. goods or technology might be transshipped to the East through third coun-

---

15. See, for example, the statements of corporate officials in U.S. Congress, Senate, Committee on Governmental Operations, Permanent Subcommittee on Investigations, *East–West Trade,* hearings, 84th Congress, 2d session, 15–17 February and 6 March 1956.

16. See Gunnar Adler-Karlsson, *Western Economic Warfare, 1947–1967* (Stockholm: Almqvist & Wiksell, 1968), p. 33.

17. Harold J. Berman and John R. Garson, "United States Export Controls—Past, Present and Future," *Columbia Law Review* 67 (May 1967), pp. 791–890, citation at 792. Also cited by Jentleson, "From Consensus to Conflict," p. 635.

18. On the initial U.S. control lists, see Report of the Ad Hoc Subcommittee to the Secretary of Commerce, 4 May 1948, reprinted in *FRUS,* vol. 4 (1948), pp. 536–42, and the telegram from the secretary of state to certain diplomatic offices, 26 April 1950, reprinted in *FRUS,* vol. 4 (1950), pp. 87–93.

tries, or the possibility that an inflow of American goods might allow a country to export similar, domestically produced goods to the East made it imperative for state officials to monitor and possibly restrict U.S. exports even to America's closest allies. Thus in the circumstances of the cold war, the U.S. executive, while committing the United States and other nation-states to the creation of a liberal world economy marked by minimal government intervention, simultaneously was empowered by Congress to interfere drastically with global trade, in the interest of national security. For American firms, what had traditionally been a right to export suddenly became a privilege, even in peacetime, to be granted by the state.

Finally, in contrast to the interagency struggles that generally characterize American foreign economic policy, the existence of a bureaucratic consensus within the executive branch was an additional source of state strength. The three major agencies involved—the State, Defense, and Commerce Departments—all supported economic warfare unambiguously.[19] While that strategy was consistent with the institutional concerns of the Defense Department, one might have expected the State Department to prefer that trade be used conditionally to influence Soviet policy, and the Commerce Department to prefer a trade promotion strategy. As suggested above, however, in the immediate postwar period, State Department officials were unconvinced that the Soviet regime could be influenced by economic inducements, and thus were willing to support economic warfare and also to take the diplomatic initiative to secure alliance cooperation. Private industry's lack of a strong interest in commerce, combined with the Commerce Department's inherited responsibility for the administration of export controls (a legacy of World War II), rendered trade denial an acceptable, even desirable, strategy. Indeed, high officials in the Commerce Department were frequently more forceful than those in the Defense Department in pushing for severe restrictions on East–West trade.[20]

Overall, the distinctive features of export control policy created an environment in which executive officials could dominate domestically. The lack of a strong private commitment to Eastern markets enabled state officials to pursue a restrictive export strategy free from significant societal contraints. The perception of a clear link between East–West trade and American military security, at a time of heightened security concern, prompted Congress

19. While all three agencies agreed about American strategy, occasionally differences surfaced over how to deal with Western Europe's trade with the East. During the early part of 1950, commerce and defense officials, for example, were frustrated over the reluctance of the allies to cooperate fully in CoCom and suggested the use of coercion if negotiations at the highest levels of government proved futile. See, for example, the memo from the secretary of commerce to the NSC, 25 April 1950, reprinted in *FRUS*, vol. 4 (1950), pp. 84–85. As this discussion shall indicate, the position of the State Department—that coercion should not be employed—ultimately defined U.S. policy.

20. See, for example, the comments of Commerce Secretary Sinclair Weeks in the memorandum of discussion at the 197th meeting of the National Security Council, 13 May 1954, reprinted in *FRUS*, vol. 1 (1952–54), pp. 1159–66.

to delegate broad authority and powerful policy instruments to the executive. Agreement within the executive about an overall approach to the Soviet Union (that is, containment and confrontation) helped to create an interagency consensus on the appropriate economic strategy to complement it.

While domestic constraints were minimized, those in the international arena were far more significant. The effective implementation of U.S. strategy was contingent upon state officials' ability for sustained international cooperation. Yet, as of 1949, the major U.S. allies were clearly reluctant to participate in a broad denial strategy. To the extent they were willing to accept restrictions on trade with the East, they preferred a more modest strategic embargo.[21]

The aversion of West European states to economic warfare was motivated in part by economic considerations (see Table 1). Unlike the United States, those states had a traditional commitment to trade with the East and anticipated the restoration of it following the war. Their need for essential Eastern European imports—coal, timber, and grains—was particularly acute in the immediate postwar period. In exchange, the Soviet bloc expected to acquire Western European raw materials, machinery, and technology, much of which was considered strategic under the criteria of economic warfare. For West European officials, the need to obtain essential imports from the East, especially since there were limits to what could be acquired from the U.S. in light of dollar shortages, clearly outweighed any effort to restrict trade to retard Soviet bloc *economic* development.[22]

Though often overlooked, strategic considerations were also significant. Many West European officials believed economic warfare to be inevitably and inextricably linked to military conflict, as it had been during World War II. Engaging in economic warfare, or even its appearance, significantly increased the possibilities of East–West military confrontation. In the immediate postwar period, West Europeans were especially wary of provoking their powerful Eastern neighbor, given the inadequacy of their own defenses, and the uncertainty of the U.S. commitment to assist them.[23] A

21. West European preferences are discussed in a telegram from the U.S. ambassador in France to the acting secretary of state, 19 January 1949, reprinted in *FRUS*, vol. 5 (1949), p. 69, and in Economic Cooperation Administration, "Trade of the Free World," p. 1043.

22. U.S. officials did recognize the importance of maintaining some degree of East–West trade in Europe, in the interest of European recovery. They estimated that during the European Recovery Program, Western Europe would need to import $5–6 billion from Eastern Europe, and export a commensurate amount to the East. See Report of the Ad Hoc Subcommittee of the Advisory Committee of the Secretary of Commerce, 4 May 1948, reprinted in *FRUS*, vol. 4 (1948), pp. 536–42, citation at 537. See also William Diebold, "East–West Trade and the Marshall Plan," *Foreign Affairs* 26 (July 1948), pp. 709–22.

23. Those states—Norway, Denmark, and Belgium, in particular—that were directly exposed to Soviet aggression and had been overrun by the Germans only a short time earlier were especially wary of the strategic risks of economic warfare. See Economic Cooperation Administration, "Trade of the Free World," p. 1043.

TABLE 1. *Trade with Eastern Europe as percentage of total trade*

	1948 Exports/imports	1952 Exports/imports	1956 Exports/imports
Denmark	6.6/10.6	4.1/4.6	2.6/3.7
Belgium	3.5/3.9	2.4/1.4	2.5/2.0
Italy	4.0/3.0	4.0/3.6	3.2/2.3
Norway	10.0/8.0	5.0/3.7	6.0/4.6
Netherlands	4.5/4.1	1.8/2.5	1.6/2.5
France	1.6/1.9	1.0/1.2	2.4/2.1
United Kingdom	1.3/2.5	0.6/2.1	1.3/2.5
United States	1.1/1.7	0.0/0.4	0.6/0.5

Source. Gunnar Adler-Karlsson, *Western Economic Warfare, 1947–1967* (Stockholm: Almqvist & Wiksell, 1968), pp. 48–49.

strategy that, to U.S. officials, appeared to promise national security benefits, to West European officials carried with it serious risks.

Economic warfare as alliance strategy: coercion or congruent interests?

American efforts to gain West European cooperation in export restrictions began in 1948. By then, U.S. officials had divided their own controls into "List 1A," containing items of primary strategic significance and constructed according to the criteria of a strategic embargo, and "List 1B," consisting of items of secondary strategic significance and reflecting the concerns of economic warfare.[24] Many of the West European states had developed control lists of their own, yet they were far less restrictive than the U.S. lists. After protracted negotiations, the allies agreed to coordinate their export controls in November 1949, and formed the multilateral organization that has come to be known as CoCom. At its inception, CoCom members agreed to restrict most of the items on U.S. List 1A.[25]

There were, however, important conditions attached to West European participation in CoCom. While accepting 1A, West European governments were reluctant even to discuss List 1B, since it moved beyond a strategic embargo and into the realm of economic warfare. Moreover, to minimize the appearance of participating in a peacetime economic blockade, West European governments demanded that CoCom's deliberations and decisions be

24. List 1A contained items of direct military utility and those which contained advanced technology. List 1B contained items of general industrial significance. As of early 1950, there were 167 items on the former list, and about 300 on the latter. See the sources cited in note 18.

25. On the origins of CoCom, see the telegram from the special representative in Europe for the Economic Cooperation Administration (ECA) (Harriman) to the administrator of the ECA (Hoffman), 15 October 1949, reprinted in *FRUS,* vol. 5 (1949), pp. 150–53, citation at 150; and the telegram from the secretary of state to certain diplomatic offices, 26 April 1950, reprinted in *FRUS,* vol. 4 (1950), pp. 87–93.

kept secret and informal. Executive officials in France, the Netherlands, and elsewhere made clear that if CoCom's existence, and their participation in it, were acknowledged publicly, domestic debate and pressure might force them to withdraw.[26] Thus, the agreement was not granted treaty status, and CoCom decisions were to have no binding authority. Compliance was voluntary, yet essential if the organization were to survive. Finally, the West Europeans insisted that CoCom be dissociated from NATO, reasoning that the newly formed defensive alliance should not be "tainted" by the embargo, since linkage might suggest an offensive posture.[27]

U.S. officials compromised, and accepted the ground rules of confidentiality and informality. Within that framework, however, they continued to press for an expansion of the CoCom list to cover U.S. 1B items. In March 1950, amid much controversy, CoCom members agreed at least to consider the 1B list. By January 1951, a substantial portion of that list had been accepted for control by CoCom. A further round of U.S. initiatives was made in the middle of that year, leading to even more extensive multilateral controls. By early 1952, the difference between U.S. 1A and 1B and their counterparts, CoCom Lists I and II, was relatively insignificant. Alliance strategy had become the one preferred by the United States—economic warfare.

Given their serious reservations, what accounts for the willingness of the West European states to cooperate in economic warfare? The dominant explanation has been offered in Gunnar Adler-Karlsson's classic study, which focuses on the ability of the United States to use its economic resources as weapons of *coercion* against the allies. Adler-Karlsson writes:

> In spite of all the West European reluctance, its governments did cooperate in the embargo policy. Thus we must also ask why the West European nations did cooperate as much as they did. *The answer is clearly to be found in the American threats to cut off aid in cases of noncompliance.*[28]

Adler-Karlsson's interpretation has been overwhelmingly accepted by students of East–West trade policy. Klaus Knorr, for example, argues that in the late 1940s, "the United States used its economic power to impose the policy on its reluctant allies by threatening to cut off economic and military aid to them at a time when American economic aid to the West European countries was several times larger than the total turnover of their trade with the Communist states of Eastern Europe."[29] The Office of Technology As-

---

26. Telegram from the secretary of state to certain diplomatic offices, 15 February 1950, reprinted in *FRUS*, vol. 4 (1950), pp. 81–82.

27. The relationship between CoCom and NATO is discussed in a telegram from the U.S. embassy in the United Kingdom to the secretary of state, 8 March 1951, reprinted in *FRUS*, vol. 1 (1951), pp. 1056–58.

28. Adler-Karlsson, *Western Economic Warfare*, p. 45, italics added.

29. Klaus Knorr, *The Power of Nations* (New York: Basic Books, 1975), p. 142.

sessment, in its authoritative background study on East–West trade prepared for the U.S. Congress, makes a similar point and cites Adler-Karlsson.[30] In their recent studies, Stephen Woolcock and Gary Bertsch also emphasize the importance of U.S. aid as a coercive instrument.[31] Other analysts, while qualifying the argument somewhat, nevertheless accept the basic validity of the trade–aid link as the key explanatory factor.[32]

The argument for coercion rests on the fact that in 1950 and 1951, Congress passed successive pieces of legislation that explicitly linked the continuation of U.S. aid to full West European acceptance of U.S. export controls. Riders to the Supplemental Appropriations bills of 1950 and 1951, known as the Cannon and Kem Amendments, required the executive to deny economic aid to uncooperative states, during any time that the armed forces of the United States were actively engaged in hostilities.[33] In October 1951, more permanent legislation, in the form of the Mutual Defense Assistance Control Act of 1951,[34] replaced the Cannon and Kem Amendments. The so-called Battle Act linked the provision of both economic and military aid to compliance with U.S. export controls, and was to be applied in peacetime as well as wartime. It directed the executive to terminate assistance to any nation that exported primary strategic materials (U.S. List 1A), or "other materials" (in effect, U.S. List 1B), to the Soviet bloc, unless the president determined, in exceptional cases, that it was in the national interest not to do so.

The Battle Act and the amendments that preceded it thus provided the executive with a legislative obligation to coerce allies who refused to cooperate fully with U.S. controls. Because U.S. economic assistance in the 1950–53 period was far more valuable to Western Europe than East–West trade (see Table 2), Adler-Karlsson's argument runs that the allies buckled under U.S. pressure and reluctantly agreed, despite their own preferences, to join the United States in its economic warfare.

Despite the legislation and West European dependence on U.S. assistance, there are strong reasons to doubt that the threat of aid denial coerced the West Europeans into America's economic warfare. First, the legislation

30. U.S. Congress, Office of Technology Assessment, *Technology and East-West Trade* (Washington, D.C.: GPO, 1979), pp. 114, 154.

31. Stephen Woolcock, *Western Policies on East–West Trade* (London: Royal Institute for International Affairs, 1982), p. 8; and Gary Bertsch, *East–West Strategic Trade, CoCom and the Atlantic Alliance* (Paris: Atlantic Institute for International Affairs, 1983), p. 10.

32. See Richard J. Ellings, *Embargoes and World Power* (Boulder: Westview, 1985), pp. 80–84; Beverly Crawford and Stephanie Lenway, "Decision Modes and International Regime Change: Western Collaboration on East–West Trade," *World Politics* 37 (April 1985), pp. 375–402, citation at 388, and Bruce W. Jentleson, *Pipeline Politics* (Ithaca, N.Y.: Cornell University Press, 1986), pp. 71–72.

33. The amendments are reprinted in Adler-Karlsson, *Western Economic Warfare*, pp. 26–27, and 200.

34. The text of Public Law 213, 82d Congress, is reprinted in Mutual Defense Assistance Control Act of 1951, *Reports to the Congress,* hereafter *Battle Act Reports*, No. 1, 15 October 1952, Appendix A.

TABLE 2. *U.S. assistance to Western Europe, compared to East-West Trade (in millions of U.S. dollars)*

	1949	1950	1951	1952	1953	1954	1955
Western Europe							
U.S. economic aid	6276	3819	2268	1349	1265	637	466
U.S. military aid	—	37	605	1014	2867	2226	1541
Total exports to Eastern Europe	832	653	746	743	791	974	1100
Total imports from Eastern Europe	1012	813	1010	995	909	1039	1358
Total aid	6726	3856	2873	2363	4132	2863	2007
Total East–West trade	1844	1466	1756	1738	1700	2013	2458
England							
U.S. economic aid	1614	955	266	350	410	200	35
U.S. military aid	—	3	22	38	155	171	107
Total exports to Eastern Europe	109	72	45	43	43	70	103
Total imports from Eastern Europe	149	177	266	235	207	207	294
Total aid	1614	958	288	388	565	371	142
Total East–West trade	258	249	311	278	250	277	397
France							
U.S. economic aid	1313	701	435	263	397	86	3
U.S. military aid	—	16	346	486	1108	684	499
Total exports to Eastern Europe	65	35	39	39	51	74	126
Total imports from Eastern Europe	72	34	54	58	41	63	84
Total aid	1313	717	781	749	1505	770	502
Total East–West trade	137	69	93	97	92	137	210

Source. Gunnar Adler-Karlsson, *Western Economic Warfare, 1947–1967* (Stockholm: Almqvist & Wiksell, 1968), p. 46.

itself was a matter of serious dispute between Congress, which initiated and passed it, and the executive officials who were directed to implement it. Both the State Department, which conducted the export control negotiations, and the Economic Cooperation Administration, which was responsible for implementing the aid program, had profound reservations about coercion.[35] Officials in those agencies believed that linking U.S. aid to West

35. See the telegram to the administrator of the ECA, 12 May 1949, reprinted in *FRUS*, vol. 5 (1949), pp. 113–14, and the telegram from the secretary of state to the embassy in France, 13 April 1950, reprinted in *FRUS*, vol. 4 (1950), pp. 81–82.

European compliance in CoCom would cause controls to be implemented less effectively, and more importantly, might jeopardize the willingness of the allies to cooperate in CoCom altogether. As Dean Acheson argued:

> There is no intention of using the threat of withholding ECA aid to force the acquiescence of European governments in U.S. policies on export control, for U.S. policy in the long run will be infinitely more effective if based on the spirit and principle of cooperation and a common recognition of the dangers in developing the military potential of the Soviet Union and [its] satellites.[36]

Acheson also expressed the fear that West European governments, faced with the choice between American aid and East–West trade, might refuse the aid in the interest of asserting their sovereignty, and thereby bring about the destruction of the Mutual Security Program.[37] Thus, while state officials were willing to expend considerable diplomatic resources to convince the allies of the desirability of economic warfare, they explicitly rejected cross-issue linkage. If the allies could not be persuaded, executive officials were prepared to tolerate a differential in the scope of U.S. and CoCom controls.

The majority in Congress took a different view. As reflected in the Battle Act, the prevailing attitude was that no differential was tolerable; those allies unwilling to replicate U.S. controls fully were unworthy of U.S. aid. Congress was more conservative than the executive on this matter for two reasons. First, the secrecy of CoCom left many in Congress unaware of the extent to which West European governments had already participated in an export control program by mid-1950. Executive officials were placed in the unenviable position of having to convince Congress that the allies were cooperating, yet being unable to provide detailed, public evidence for it.[38] Not surprisingly, executive reassurances frequently met with skepticism, in light of routine press reports that "war materials" were making their way to the East from Western Europe.

More importantly, congressional sentiment reflected a larger discontent with the substance and process of U.S. foreign policy. Some of the most vocal proponents of coercive legislation (for example, Senators James Kem and Kenneth Wherry) were isolationists, still uncomfortable by the late 1940s with the multilateral thrust of U.S. policy. While skeptical in any case of the military and economic aid programs, they believed that, at the very least, the beneficiaries should display their gratitude by giving full support to U.S. policy.[39] In their eyes, for the U.S. to expect the allies' full cooperation

36. Ibid., pp. 81–82.
37. See the letter from Acheson to the chairman of the Senate Foreign Relations Committee, 9 June 1952, reprinted in *FRUS*, vol. 1 (1952–54), pp. 847–49.
38. For a discussion of the role of CoCom secrecy in the interbranch dispute, see the letter from Representative Laurie C. Battle to the director of Mutual Security, 29 September 1952, reprinted in *FRUS*, vol. 1 (1952–54), pp. 896–901.
39. For the Senate debate over the Battle Act, see *Congressional Record* (Senate), 27 August 1951, pp. 10661–78, an 10700–15.

in denying strategic goods to the East, particularly in light of armed conflict in Korea, was clearly not asking too much.

The Battle Act was also symptomatic of a larger struggle between executive and Congress over the control of foreign policy. By 1950 members of Congress, reacting to Truman's unilateral dispatch of U.S. forces to Korea and his decision to commit the United States to the defense of Europe through the North Atlantic Treaty, grew increasingly concerned over what they perceived as the dangerous usurpation of foreign policy power by the executive.[40] In East–West trade, the executive again was exercising unilateral control over policy, while keeping Congress at bay. Even for those in Congress who did not consider this issue all that significant, the Battle bill represented a way for Congress to reestablish its rightful position in the foreign policy process.

The divergent perspectives of the executive and Congress heighten the significance of the fact that the executive ultimately possessed responsibility for implementing the coercive legislation. And, although the West Europeans were in continual violation, executive officials never withdrew aid in accordance with its provisions. Both the Cannon and Kem Amendments allowed for some discretion in their implementation, and the Truman administration took full advantage. After the passage of the Cannon rider, the National Security Council (NSC) granted a blanket exception, determining that to stop aid to any foreign country would contravene U.S. security interests. The NSC argued that "national security should be interpreted broadly enough to permit situations where an assistance program might properly be continued even though trade with the Soviet Bloc in security items continues."[41] Immediately following the passage of the Kem Amendment, the NSC again approved a general interim exception for all countries, pending a case-by-case examination of each situation. After its review, and despite the protests of Senator Kem and others, the NSC granted country exceptions to each NATO member, and to Japan.[42]

Under the terms of the Battle Act, aid could only be continued to countries that exported U.S. List 1A items if "unusual circumstances" dictated that an aid cut-off would be detrimental to U.S. security interests.[43] Appar-

40. A good discussion is found in Ted Carpenter, *America and the Transformation of NATO: The Great Debate of 1950 and 1951* (unpublished manuscript, 1986), especially chaps. 5 and 6.

41. See "N.S.C. Determinations Under Public Law 843, Section 1304: The Cannon Amendment," Statement of Policy by the National Security Council, undated, included in a note from the executive secretary of the NSC to the NSC and reprinted in *FRUS*, vol. 4 (1950), pp. 249–55. The quotation is at p. 254.

42. A list of the countries granted exceptions, with supporting arguments, is found in Report by the N.S.C. Regarding a Review of its Determination under Section 1302 of the Third Supplemental Appropriations Act, 1951, 23 October 1951, reprinted in *FRUS*, vol. 1 (1951), pp. 1203–10.

43. The exception clause is found in Mutual Defense Assistance Control Act of 1951 (Public Law 213, 82d Congress), Section 103. Senator John Sparkman, a key member of the Foreign Relations Committee who was sympathetic to the need for some executive flexibility, was pivotal in swinging the Senate behind the Battle Bill and away from a more hardline proposal by

ently the circumstances were perpetually "unusual," since aid was never withdrawn, despite repeated violations, and exceptions were granted in every year, from the act's inception in 1952 through the end of the decade. For example, exceptions were granted in 1952 to Denmark for tankers; to Italy for grinding machines; to the Netherlands for oil drilling equipment; and to Britain and France for various machine tools, ball bearings, and chemical and electrical equipment. In 1953, West Germany, France, Norway, and Britain were permitted to sell ball bearings, aluminum, and locomotive equipment to the East.[44]

Finally, evidence suggests that America's European allies were not only aware of the conflict between executive and Congress, but also actively assisted the executive in evading the intent of congressional legislation. How to deal with the problems posed by the Battle Act was the subject of extensive discussion in CoCom. With the imminent passage of the bill in mid-1951, State Department officials proposed a new round of control negotiations in CoCom, along with the introduction of an "exceptions" procedure that would allow any member state to export a given item on the CoCom embargo list, so long as no other member state objected to the sale in that particular instance. U.S. officials proposed that list additions be made, with the understanding that the United States would grant exceptions when necessary—even for primary strategic goods—so that the allies could fulfill their existing contracts with the East. State Department cables indicate that U.S. officials presented these proposals as a "package" with regard to the U.S. legislative situation, and that West European officials were aware of the executive's "problem" and were willing to help resolve it.[45]

By early 1952, the bargain had been struck. West European officials accepted most of the CoCom list additions proposed by the United States and executive officials, keeping their side of the bargain, subsequently granted the noted exceptions to West European exporters. These were reported publicly to Congress, with executive officials paying careful attention to the timing and wording of their reports to minimize their domestic political impact. Prior to submitting reports to Congress, state officials actually circulated them in draft form to West European governments—the perpetrators of the "crime"—for revision and comment.[46]

To summarize, it is difficult to accept that the threat of aid denial was a

---

Senators Kem, Wherry and Malone, which would have removed all executive discretion. See the Senate debate, *Congressional Record* (note 39).

44. See *Battle Act Reports,* No. 1, 15 October 1952, pp. 47–57; No. 2, 16 January 1953, pp. 77–86; and No. 3, 27 September 1953, pp. 73–77.

45. Telegram from the U.S. ambassador in Britain to the secretary of state, 16 July 1951, reprinted in *FRUS,* vol. 1 (1951), pp. 1148–49, and from the U.S. ambassador in France to the secretary of state, 20 July 1951, reprinted in ibid., pp. 1157–58.

46. Memorandum to the executive secretary of the NSC, 22 September 1952, reprinted in *FRUS,* vol. 1 (1952–54), p. 882; and memorandum to the executive secretary of the NSC, 19 January 1953, reprinted in ibid., p. 937.

credible and effective instrument of coercion, given executive officials' obvious distaste for coercion, their failure to impose sanctions despite blatant violations, and the explicit collaboration of the allies in avoiding sanctions. While the Battle Act received great publicity, and created considerable political resentment in Western Europe, ultimately it had little to do with the shift in alliance policy to economic warfare.

Moreover, to emphasize coercion as the primary explanatory factor leads one to obscure the fundamental national security objectives of American executive officials. The concept that best captures those objectives in the early postwar period is that of multilateralism.[47] The export control program was part of a larger multilateral security effort, directed against the Soviet Union and global communism; its cornerstones were the creation of a stable transatlantic economy and the maintenance of an adequate NATO defense effort.[48] The threat of aid denial would jeopardize the political solidarity and cohesion of the nascent Atlantic Alliance, while actual denial would harm both West European economic recovery and the development of NATO at critical points in their infancy. For American state officials, this was simply too high a price to pay. Forced to choose between their preferred export control regime and the maintenance of alliance solidarity, they would opt for the latter. As discussed below, they had the luxury of avoiding that choice in 1950, but not in 1954.

Rather than as a consequence of effective coercion, the adoption of economic warfare as alliance policy is more adequately explained by a shift in the East–West trade preferences of the West European states, which took place during 1950. Prior to the middle of 1950, persistent efforts by U.S. officials to convince the allies of the need for economic warfare, on the grounds that the Soviet Union was an aggressive state whose economy primarily served as a mobilization base for the military sector, were unsuccessful. The crucial turning point, however, was the outbreak of the Korean War.

The North Korean invasion of the South generated a profound (albeit short-lived) security crisis in Western Europe. It led West European officials to reassess the nature of the Soviet threat, and how best to meet it. Prior to Korea, the dominant belief of West European (and American) officials was that the Soviet Union would attempt to expand its influence peacefully, that is, by subversion. The Korean attack signaled an alarming shift to overt aggression.[49] That, in turn, suggested to West European leaders the possibil-

---

47. A good recent discussion that emphasizes multilateralism as the dominant theme in U.S. national security policy is Robert Pollard, *Economic Security and the Origins of the Cold War, 1945–1950* (New York: Columbia University Press, 1985).

48. See, for example, statement of policy by the National Security Council on Economic Defense (NSC 152/2), 31 July 1953, reprinted in *FRUS*, vol. 1 (1952–54), pp. 1009–14, citation at 1010.

49. See Robert Osgood, *NATO: The Entangling Alliance* (Chicago: University of Chicago

ity of their worst security fear: a massive conventional Soviet attack, for which they were largely unprepared.[50] Many alliance officials even viewed the Korean attack as a deliberate Soviet ploy, designed to draw U.S. forces to the East and clear the way for a Soviet thrust against the far more attractive target of Western Europe.[51] In the wake of Korea, neither the European Recovery Program, which had been the primary defense against Soviet subversion, nor the relatively modest U.S. nuclear deterrent appeared adequate to provide for the security of Western Europe.

The primary alliance response to the increased likelihood of direct military conflict with the Soviet Union was rearmament. Prior to Korea, West European leaders resisted a defense build-up, arguing that economic recovery should be given priority, in the interest of sustaining domestic political stability. Korea provided the impetus for West European officials to accept that economic considerations had to be subordinated, at least in part, to defense needs.[52] Most West European governments adopted plans to increase defense spending and periods of military service. Multilaterally, NATO began its transformation from a "paper" alliance, designed to boost West European morale, to one that would make a serious effort to provide an adequate defense against Soviet attack. The provision of U.S. military aid (and troops) played a major role in that process, as tangible evidence of the American commitment to share the burden of rearmament.[53] Indeed, West European leaders viewed American aid as a precondition of the rearmament effort; in light of this, and the importance U.S. officials placed on getting the allies to rearm, the idea of cutting off aid in accordance with the Battle Act appears all the more implausible.

For West European officials, increased security fears and the consequent defense build-up enhanced the attractiveness of economic warfare in two

---

Press, 1962), p. 69. Osgood provides one of the best discussions of the impact of Korea on Western perceptions. The perceived shift in Soviet methods is also noted in "A Proposal for Strengthening Defense without Increasing Appropriations," 5 April 1950, enclosed in a memo from the undersecretary of the army to the secretary of state, 10 April 1950, reprinted in *FRUS*, vol. 3 (1950), pp. 43–48.

50. Osgood, *NATO: The Entangling Alliance*, pp. 37, 68–69. The fear of attack may not have been well founded, but as Osgood notes, "the estimate of a potential aggressor's intentions is peculiarly subject to sudden shifts from complacency to alarm" (p. 68).

51. See Bernard Brodie, *War and Politics* (New York: Macmillan, 1973), pp. 63–64; Carpenter, *America and the Transformation of NATO*, pp. i–ii; and "East–West Trade Controls in Relation to the Upcoming Foreign Ministers' Meeting," Guidance Paper for the Use of the U.S. Delegation to the Four Power Foreign Ministers' Meeting, Geneva, October 1955, dated 5 October 1955, annex 4, p. 2.

52. See the Agreed Minute of the United States, British, and French Foreign Ministers, 19 September 1950, reprinted in *FRUS*, vol. 4 (1950), pp. 187–88, and Osgood, *NATO: The Entangling Alliance*, pp. 65–68. U.S. officials had struggled, with little success, to get the allies to accept a reordering of priorities before Korea. See "Building Up the Defensive Strength of the West," 3 May 1950, paper presented in the Office of European Regional Affairs, as background for the May North Atlantic Council Meetings, reprinted in *FRUS*, vol. 3 (1950), pp. 85–90, relevant discussion at 86.

53. Osgood, *NATO: The Entangling Alliance*, pp. 40–41.

ways. First, the belief that the Soviets were preparing for an imminent conventional war lent credence to the view that the Soviet economy was a "war economy," devoted primarily to serving the needs of the defense sector. In peacetime, trade in industrial goods and raw materials would be expected to serve civilian needs; under the assumption of imminent military conflict, it was seen as contributing to defense mobilization. This argument, linking Soviet intentions, the Soviet economy, and industrial (that is, 1B) trade had been made by U.S. officials in CoCom since 1949; for West European officials, it gained credibility only in the atmosphere of heightened tension created by Korea.[54]

Second, by prompting West European leaders to allow security to outweigh economic considerations, the rearmament decision helped pave the way for the eventual adoption of economic warfare. As long as economic recovery was the overriding priority, West European leaders could (and did) resist economic warfare on the grounds that imports from the East made an important contribution to meeting recovery goals. (U.S. officials even had recognized and accepted this in 1948 and 1949.) Once the decision was made generally to grant priority to security concerns, it was a small step to allow the same ordering to apply to East–West trade policy. Economic warfare became a complement, in the economic realm, to a new approach to dealing with the Soviets—or, as Acheson reported to Truman, defense mobilization and the extension of export controls went "hand-in-hand as constructive responses" to the "unmistakable warning to the free world" sounded by the Korean invasion.[55]

The Western allies formally decided to adopt economic warfare in September 1950. As of May, U.S. officials had made little progress in gaining CoCom agreement on 1B items, largely because West European governments had not authorized their CoCom officials to accept the criteria of economic warfare. Agreement on criteria required acquiescence at the highest levels of government. At the September foreign ministers' meetings, Acheson, Bevin of Britain, and Schuman of France agreed that *"in the present world situation,"* the Western allies should employ effective export controls "to limit the short-term striking power of the Soviet bloc, and to retard the development of its war potential in the longer-term." This would entail new restrictions on exports "of selected items which are required in key industrial sectors that contribute substantially to war potential."[56] In addition to items

---

54. The impact of Korea on West European receptivity to economic warfare is discussed in "State Department Position with Respect to Export Controls and Security Policy," report by the executive secretary to the NSC, 21 August 1950, reprinted in *FRUS*, vol. 4 (1950), pp. 163–72, relevant discussion at 170.

55. "Report to the President on United States Policies and Programs in the Economic Field which May Affect the War Potential of the Soviet Bloc," enclosed in a letter from Acheson to Truman, 9 February 1951, reprinted in *FRUS*, vol. 1 (1951), pp. 1026–35, relevant discussion at 1027.

56. See the Agreed Minute of the Foreign Ministers (note 52), pp. 187–88, emphasis added.

of direct military application, the concept "war potential" covered "industrial sectors that served to support the basic economy of a country and which therefore support either a peacetime or wartime economy."[57]

Agreement at the ministerial level set the stage for reconsideration of the U.S. 1B list, which first took place among the three major powers and then in CoCom. In November, Britain and France agreed to add 175 items to the CoCom lists, and exchange information on 69 others. In January 1951, the remainder of the CoCom members accepted these tripartite recommendations.[58]

1954: preferences, power, and the demise of economic warfare

West European support for economic warfare was short-lived. By late 1953, America's CoCom partners, led by Great Britain, sought a dramatic liberalization of alliance export controls, and called for the expansion of East–West trade. Prime Minister Winston Churchill's frequently cited public statement of 25 February 1954 was a key catalyst. He stated, in part:

> The more trade there is between Great Britain and Soviet Russia and the satellites, the better still will be the chances of our living together in increasing comfort . . . the more the two great divisions of the world mingle in the healthy and fertile activities of commerce, the greater is the counterpoise to purely military calculations . . . I do not suggest that at the present there should be any traffic in military equipment, including certain machine tools, such as those capable only or mainly of making weapons, but a substantial relaxation of the regulations affecting manufactured goods, raw materials and shipping . . .[59]

In private, British officials proposed to their U.S. counterparts a 50 percent cut in the control list, and more importantly, a shift in the governing criteria to that of a strategic embargo.[60]

American state officials reacted with alarm. They contended that, although the Korean war had ended, the Soviet Union and China still posed a serious threat to Western security, and the risk of war was ever-present. They maintained that it would be imprudent to relax the control system, a valuable weapon for the West in the cold war. U.S. officials were willing to

---

57. The definition is found in the Guidance Paper (note 51), p. 4.

58. The results are reported in an editorial note, printed in *FRUS*, vol. 1 (1951), p. 1012.

59. Churchill is cited by Harold Stassen in U.S. Congress, Senate, Committee on Government Operations, Permanent Subcommittee on Investigations, *East–West Trade*, hearings, 84th Congress, 2d session, 15–17, 20 February and 6 March 1956, p. 450.

60. British proposals are discussed in the notes from the ambassador in the U.K. to the government of the U.K., 3 December 1953, and to the Department of State, 1 March 1954, both reprinted in *FRUS*, vol. 1 (1952–54), pp. 1062–64 and 1082–84.

accept some reductions in controls, but not the "wholesale downgrading" envisaged by the British. Moreover, in contrast to the British call for restrictions only on items of "military or near military character," they urged that the West "continue to control categories of items important to key sectors of the industrial base underlying the war potential of the Soviet bloc."[61]

The United States and other CoCom members (most of whom supported the British) attempted to settle their differences between March and August 1954, in a series of high-level talks involving American, British, and French officials, and subsequently in negotiations involving all members of CoCom. The outcome represented a clear victory for the British position. CoCom members agreed to slash the multilateral control list by nearly 50 percent, from 474 to 252 categories of items to be controlled.[62] Equally important, the reductions reflected a change in criteria to that of a strategic embargo. The allies formally abandoned their emphasis on Soviet bloc "war potential"— the control of items of major industrial as well as military significance—and instead agreed in the future to focus more narrowly on items used mainly or primarily in military production, or items whose impact would be felt in the Soviet defense, rather than civilian, sector.[63]

Thus, despite its dominant power and prestige in the alliance, the United States ultimately was unsuccessful in determining the direction of CoCom policy. For reasons discussed below, it was also forced, as a result of the 1954 revision, to adjust its national export control policy. Rather than alliance policy conforming to the dictates of the United States, American policy conformed to the preferences of its allies.

For the generally accepted explanation of this outcome, we again turn to Adler-Karlsson, whose analysis again emphasizes the relative utility of American coercive power. Adler-Karlsson depicts West European governments as facing a clear choice between American aid and East–West trade. In 1950, the value of aid outweighed that of trade, so the allies accepted economic warfare; by 1954, however, with aid declining and the potential for East–West trade expanding, they took an alternative approach. With the diminution of American coercive power, the allies could defy the United States, follow their political and economic instincts, and begin restoring trade with the East. Explaining the 1954 revision, Adler-Karlsson points out that "the economic pressure that the United States could bring to bear on

61. The U.S. position is described in the telegram from the Chief of Operations Mission in the U.K. to the Department of State, 10 November 1953, reprinted in *FRUS*, vol. 1 (1952–54), pp. 1039–49, and in the note from the U.S. ambassador to the government of the U.K. (note 60), pp. 1063–64.

62. CoCom List I was reduced from 270 to 167 items; List II from 80 to 23 items; and List III, the surveillance list, from 124 to 62 items. The final results are discussed in the memorandum of discussion at the 210th meeting of the National Security Council, 1 August 1954, and the Report to the N.S.C. by the Secretary of State and Director of Foreign Operations, 30 August 1954, both reprinted in *FRUS*, vol. 1, (1952–54), pp. 1235–55.

63. *Battle Act Reports*, No. 5, 23 November 1954, p. 43.

Western Europe lost its force and almost vanished with the disappearance of aid."[64] Table 2 shows the gradual decline of U.S. economic aid, which reflects the utilization and completion of the European Recovery Program.

Accepting Adler-Karlsson's argument for 1954 presupposes that one accepts his claim that aid was an effective coercive instrument prior to that date. Yet even leaving that problem aside, the argument for 1954 must acknowledge that the decline of *economic* aid did not leave U.S. officials devoid of potential coercive levers. As Table 2 indicates, American *military* assistance replaced economic aid in significance, and its volume outweighed Western Europe's total East–West trade turnover in 1953 and 1954, when the CoCom negotiations took place. The Battle Act, of course, empowered executive officials to cut off military aid, if they so desired. Moreover, they possessed other potentially coercive instruments. The broad delegation of authority contained in the Export Control Act allowed executive officials to deny American exports to Western states that traded the same or similar goods to the East. Even if one accepts that the denial of American aid was no longer a workable coercive instrument, the allies were likely to perceive American trade as more important than East–West trade during this period.

Such potential instruments of coercion were no more useful in 1954 than they had been in 1950. American state officials continued to be constrained by their own commitment to maintain the political cohesion, and economic and military strength, of the Western alliance. Military aid, for example, was as critical to the achievement of American and alliance defense objectives in 1954 as it had been during the initial rearmament effort of the Korean War. By 1954, the domestic economic strains and political discontent, which were generated by increased defense spending, placed considerable pressure on West European governments to reduce significantly their commitment to NATO's conventional forces. American aid, like U.S. troops, was a symbol of the United States' willingness to share the burden of Europe's defense, and had served since 1950 as a tacit *quid pro quo* for the allies to endure the economic sacrifice of defense spending. Without aid, West European governments would be tempted to rely even more fully on the American nuclear deterrent, allowing conventional forces to deteriorate further. To U.S. officials, the outcome would be strategically precarious; despite the shift to nuclear deterrence, they still believed that NATO required an adequate conventional capacity, in order to avoid recourse to nuclear weapons in the event of war.[65]

Similarly, employing the aid weapon would create profound resentment in Western Europe, and thus strain the political cohesion of the alliance. By 1954, U.S. officials recognized that the cold war was evolving largely into a

64. Adler-Karlsson, *Western Economic Warfare*, p. 47.
65. See Osgood, *NATO: The Entangling Alliance*, pp. 106–16, and 125. The nuclear strategy did not call for the replacement of conventional forces, but for the integration of tactical nuclear weapons into existing NATO units.

political struggle; for the United States to create a rift in the alliance by using threats and intimidation would result in a major propaganda victory for the Soviets. Defending the administration's decision not to deny aid before a hostile Congress, one executive official suggested that the result of denial might be "a successful operation, but the patient would be dead."[66] The theme of multilateral solidarity was particularly important to President Eisenhower, who continually lectured his more combative Cabinet aids that putting the allies first was "the best defense against Communism."[67]

Without military aid (and as discussed below, U.S. exports) as usable coercive instruments, the American state officials' ability to achieve their preferred East–West trade strategy again depended upon the preferences of other CoCom members. By 1954, the strategic, economic, and political conditions that had led West European governments to adopt economic warfare no longer obtained. Strategically, the circumstances surrounding the outbreak of the Korean War proved to be truly extraordinary, marking perhaps the only instance in the postwar era that West European governments actually feared an imminent Soviet conventional attack. With the death of Joseph Stalin, the armistice in Korea, and the beginning of a thaw in East–West relations, that fear subsided. NATO, in fact, decided officially in 1953 that "the tensions upon which its war plans were based should be regarded as of infinite duration."[68] Without the threat of an imminent war, the justification for denying the Soviets exports that contributed to their "war potential" was severely weakened. It permitted European CoCom members to argue, for example, that it was unnecessary to control the export of machinery and equipment that primarily served peaceful purposes, yet would be converted by the Soviets to military production *if* war broke out.[69]

More generally, if war were not inevitable, the idea that the Soviet economy was devoted overwhelmingly to war preparation could be challenged. Once it became arguable that the Soviet economy could serve "peaceful" or civilian needs, it became possible to justify the sale of items otherwise considered strategic, such as copper or petroleum. For these items, the allies argued during the 1954 review that Soviet domestic production was sufficient to meet military needs, and thus exports would serve civilian development. These arguments were assisted by the concurrent increase in Soviet demand for Western consumer goods, which enhanced the image that the Soviet economy was devoted to the pursuit of civilian needs.[70]

These strategic considerations took on greater significance in light of another major development by 1954, the beginning of West European eco-

66. Statement of John Barton, Department of Commerce, in *East–West Trade* (note 59), p. 356.
67. See the Memorandum of Discussion at the 197th Meeting of the National Security Council, 13 May 1954 (note 20), p. 1063.
68. "East–West Trade Controls" (note 51), annex 4, p. 2.
69. *Battle Act Reports,* No. 5, 23 November 1954, p. 11.
70. On copper and petroleum, see *East–West Trade* (note 59), pp. 240 and 420.

nomic recovery. Recovery signaled the need for export outlets, and the traditional East European markets were a primary target. Churchill stressed the need for Britain to "keep open our trade in every possible direction," particularly in view of the economic revival of German and Japanese competition. In the absence of an immediate strategic threat, West European governments saw no justification for allowing security concerns to outweigh economic considerations in the control process; they believed, in the words of a U.S. negotiator, that "the risk of general war is not great enough to warrant foregoing the gains from trade which would follow from a relaxation of controls."[71] West European officials anticipated political gains as well, since increased trade would reinforce any relaxation of East–West political tensions. Overall, the export control strategy that was judged necessary to protect national security in 1950 appeared in many ways to be counterproductive by 1954.

The adjustment of U.S. controls

I suggested earlier that restrictions on American exports to Western Europe might have provided leverage to extract East–West concessions from the allies. As was the case with military aid, however, American state officials were anxious to avoid such a linkage. Restrictions on intra-Western trade would compromise their commitment to organize and maintain a liberal world economy, the cornerstone of postwar American foreign economic policy. In fact, executive officials not only avoided using exports as a weapon, but were sufficiently concerned with maximizing the free flow of trans-Atlantic trade that they intentionally shaped America's national export controls to meet that objective.

The 1954 CoCom list reduction posed a problem for executive officials. The revision left a wide disparity between the CoCom list and the (much longer) U.S. list.[72] If U.S. officials did not adjust the latter, West European firms would have an advantage over American firms in Eastern markets. Given American business' disinterest in those markets, this was not (at least initially) a significant concern. The real problem was that, given a wide differential between the lists, Western European governments would take no part in preventing U.S.-controlled items, exported from the United States to Western Europe, from being transshipped to the East. This raised the danger of

71. See the National Intelligence Estimate, "Consequences of a Relaxation of Non-Communist Controls on Trade with the Soviet Bloc," 23 March 1954, reprinted in *FRUS*, vol. 1 (1952–54), pp. 1121–35, citation at 1131.

72. The 1954 revision left the CoCom List at 252 items; the U.S. control list, prior to its adjustment, contained 474 items (the pre-revision CoCom figure), plus 113 more controlled unilaterally by the United States. See "United States Security Export Controls," Report for the NSC by the NSC Planning Board, 11 June 1954, reprinted in *FRUS*, vol. 1 (1952–54), pp. 1191–97.

what U.S. officials referred to as a potentially "explosive" problem: the possibility of having to apply controls against Western Europe, and thereby interfere with intra-Western trade, to maintain the integrity of the national control list.[73] The problem would be minimized if U.S. officials simply adjusted their list downward to match the CoCom consensus. That, however, would provoke a conflict with congressional critics, who would accuse the executive of not only "allowing" the allies to trade strategic goods to the East, but permitting U.S. firms to do the same.

In the interest of minimizing interference with West–West trade, executive officials chose to adjust U.S. controls. New control criteria were enacted late in 1954, which would make the U.S. list conform to the CoCom list. Executive officials would make exceptions for items unique to U.S. producers, and for those considered "special political problems," that is, items not considered strategic by executive officials, but whose export would invoke an adverse political reaction at home.[74] As always, executive officials were wary of a negative reaction from Congress and the public, and sought to placate it; the overall thrust of their policy, however, was to maximize their broader alliance objectives and deal with Congress in the aftermath.

Executive officials did confront, and manage effectively, congressional opposition to their role in the adjustment of export controls. They took great pains to depict the CoCom revision as a strengthening of the control system (because of improved enforcement and "streamlined" lists),[75] rather than as a retreat from economic warfare. As a sop to hardliners, they persuaded the allies to maintain a "China differential"—a comprehensive embargo on trade with China, on the dubious assumption that China posed a special security threat to the West. (Since exports to the Soviet Union could be easily transshipped to China, the differential made little strategic sense, and eventually was formally abandoned in 1958.)[76] State officials also revised the Battle Act list downward, to match the CoCom list, and thus to bring the allies into compliance with the legislation. Finally, they sought to minimize adverse congressional reaction by depicting the adjustment as a boon to U.S. business, which could now export more easily to Western Europe.[77]

73. The concern of state officials over the possibility of having to apply controls against Western Europe is indicated in the Memorandum Prepared in the Economic Defense Advisory Committee for the NSC Planning Board, 9 March 1954, reprinted in *FRUS*, vol. 1 (1952–54), pp. 1103–07, citation at 1107.

74. The new U.S. criteria are laid out in NSC 152/3, Statement of Policy by the NSC on Economic Defense, 18 June 1954, reprinted in *FRUS*, vol. 1 (1952–54), pp. 1207–13, citation at 1211. The new U.S. list was "substantially comparable" to the CoCom list. *Battle Act Reports*, No. 5, 23 November 1954, p. 23.

75. U.S. officials successfully persuaded other CoCom members to improve their enforcement of export controls, as a tacit exchange for shorter lists. See *Battle Act Reports*, No. 5, 23 November 1954.

76. *Battle Act Reports*, No. 10, 24 January 1958, pp. 15–18.

77. Memorandum of Discussion at the 210th Meeting of the NSC, 12 August 1954, reprinted in *FRUS*, vol. 1 (1952–1954), pp. 1235–39, citation at 1237.

A minority in the Senate did protest the revisions forcefully.[78] However, the larger conflict between executive and Congress, which had peaked in 1950 and led to the Battle Act, had largely dissipated by 1954. Congressional critics were not powerful enough to mobilize a large-scale challenge to the executive, given the latter's careful management of the domestic politics of adjustment.

Conclusion

This article has reinterpreted the evolution of alliance export control policy in the first decade after World War II, and also the role of American executive officials in the determination of that policy. I have argued that the pattern of alliance outcomes is best explained not by the exercise of American power in the face of conflicting interests, but by whether or not congruent interests existed. In 1950 and 1954, executive officials possessed significant instruments of coercion; in both cases, they were constrained in their ability to use them, since their use would threaten to compromise more fundamental foreign policy objectives. Executive officials were fortunate in 1950, because West European preferences shifted, as the result of a perceived security crisis, to complement those of the United States. However, in 1954, when allied preferences had shifted again, U.S. officials were, in effect, powerless to prevent the revision of Western policy and in fact broader foreign economic policy considerations compelled them to adjust America's national export control list as well.

This argument may offer lessons for two important literatures in international political economy. First, international structural theories (for example, the theory of hegemonic stability, derived from structural realism) posit that international outcomes can be explained according to the distribution of power resources among nation-states.[79] Hegemonic powers, such as the United States in the early 1950s, are expected to translate their resources into influence and to shape decisively the outcome of diplomatic conflicts. Critics (sympathetic or otherwise) have found the "power fungibility" assumption of this approach problematic, and have noted that power-as-resources is not always easily translated into power-as-influence.[80]

Evidence from the early CoCom disputes supports the caveat of the critics

---

78. The best evidence of congressional discontent is found throughout the Senate Committee on Governmental Operations hearings, *East–West Trade* (note 59).

79. Useful discussions of hegemonic stability theory are found in Robert Keohane, *After Hegemony* (Princeton, N.J.: Princeton University Press, 1984), chaps. 3 and 9, and also Duncan Snidal, "The Limits of Hegemonic Stability Theory," *International Organization* 39 (Autumn 1985), pp. 579–614.

80. See David Baldwin, "Power Analysis and World Politics: New Trends versus Old Tendencies," *World Politics* 31 (January 1979), pp. 161–94, and Robert Keohane, "Theory of World Politics: Structural Realism and Beyond," in Keohane, ed., *Neorealism and its Critics* (New York: Columbia University Press, 1986), pp. 158–203, especially pp. 182–89.

and demonstrates the limits of American influence in the early postwar period. Moreover, the analysis suggests that the reason for the failure of the conversion process was the multiple objectives of state officials, which confounded each other when pursued simultaneously. State officials' willingness to translate their formidable resources into influence was not constrained by domestic interests, bureaucratic fragmentation, or the lack of policy instruments, but by the incompatibility of their own objectives. It is somewhat ironic that the more committed executive officials were to maintaining the strength of the alliance, the less influence they actually had over alliance policy. Indeed, America's commitment to the alliance proved to be an important source of leverage for the ostensibly weaker West European states, both in 1950 and 1954.[81] By implication, we may hypothesize that paradoxically, as the commitment of a hegemonic state to alliance management wanes, its influence over alliance affairs may actually increase.

The experience of the 1950s also has policy implications for the viability of economic warfare as alliance strategy. Since 1954, CoCom's control criteria have remained those of a strategic embargo. Recently, however, U.S. officials sparked an alliance conflict by seeking to revive economic warfare. In the Siberian pipeline episode, they attempted to coerce other Western governments into compliance, only to meet widespread defiance and ultimately to back down, in the interest of preventing the collapse of alliance cohesion. The Reagan administration appears to have learned by hard experience what earlier administrations intuited: that coercive tactics are likely to prove counterproductive in alliance disputes over the broad purpose and direction of export control strategy.[82] Furthermore, the early history of CoCom suggests that West European governments are likely to accept economic warfare only in the face of a direct and immediate threat to their security. U.S. officials attempted to depict events in Afghanistan and Poland as just such a threat, but they did not meet with success. The criteria of a strategic embargo governs CoCom policy, and is likely to continue unless and until the alliance faces a threat tantamount in perceived significance to the Korean invasion.

Second, the East–West trade case is instructive for the relationship between the state and its domestic environment. It was noted at the outset that the American state is considered relatively weak in foreign economic policy, in terms of its ability to articulate preferences and realize them in the face of domestic opposition. It is considered particularly weak in trade policy, since

---

81. An interesting examination of the idea that weaker alliance members may derive bargaining leverage over their dominant partners is Valerie Bunce, "The Empire Strikes Back: The Transformation of the Eastern Bloc from a Soviet Asset to a Soviet Liability," *International Organization* 39 (Winter 1985), pp. 1–46.

82. Reagan administration officials, of course, dispute this lesson and claim the pipeline dispute was actually constructive, because it sensitized Western Europe to the security risks of East–West trade. While there may be a kernel of truth in this, it is hard to deny that the administration was compelled to back down by the fear of maintaining a rupture in the alliance that threatened other areas of policy (e.g., the Euromissile deployment).

state officials are least insulated from societal pressures in that area.[83] The evidence presented in this article suggests we regard the scope of that generalization with caution, and also suggests that, in certain areas of trade policy, the American state may take on the attributes and capacities associated with stronger states. Export control policy is one such area; its direct relationship to national security and the East–West conflict, and its development in the crisis environment of the early cold war period, combined to provide executive officials with unusual (and enduring) sources of domestic strength. Executive officials were able to formulate and pursue a coherent strategy and to overcome congressional opposition to the way that strategy was coordinated internationally.

The possession of domestic strength, of course, did not enable U.S. officials to overcome the international constraint necessarily associated with export control policy—that is, the existence of alternative sources of supply. It is ironic that, in this particular instance, had the United States been weaker domestically, executive officials may have been more successful in realizing their issue-specific objectives internationally. Had Congress dominated the executive, or had the executive itself been more seriously divided, the linkage of American trade or aid to West European control efforts might have emerged as a more viable or credible option. As executive officials recognized, however, any success that resulted from such efforts would probably have come at the expense of transatlantic economic and security regimes, which were in their formative stages. In effect, the domestic strength of state officials afforded them the opportunity to concede in their issue-specific conflict, and thus avoid jeopardizing their broader economic and security interests.

As the crisis atmosphere associated with the early cold war receded in the 1960s and 1970s, state officials began to confront in East–West trade some of the domestic constraints that were characteristic of trade policy more generally. American exporters developed an interest in Eastern markets, Congress became more assertive and also more divided, and the executive itself faced an inter-agency conflict over the proper role of export controls in U.S. foreign policy.[84] Nevertheless, state officials have continued to enjoy the considerable export control authority granted to them in the extraordinary circumstances of the cold war, and have sought gradually to expand the scope of that power. Economic sanctions have become a routine instrument of foreign policy, employed for many reasons beyond the protection of national security, and against many targets other than the Soviet Union and Eastern Europe. What began as an extraordinary delegation of authority in a time of crisis has become institutionalized, and executive officials have used it to enhance their role more generally in foreign economic policy.

83. See Krasner, "External Strength and Internal Weakness."
84. For a discussion of the breakdown of the U.S. domestic consensus by the 1970s, see Jentleson, "From Consensus to Conflict" and *Pipeline Politics*.

Market solutions for state problems: the international and domestic politics of American oil decontrol G. John Ikenberry

The dramatic upheaval in oil prices in the 1970s posed difficult policy dilemmas for the United States. Like other industrial importing nations, the United States was forced to make decisions concerning how to adjust its economy and society to the new and troubling international energy reality. From the Nixon to the Carter administrations, government officials attempted to implement policies of energy adjustment. These efforts began with ill-fated international schemes to form a "consumer cartel" of industrial nations, and ended with the decision in 1979 to decontrol oil prices.

The problems of gaining agreement on a united industrial country response to Organization of Petroleum Exporting Countries' price increases were fundamentally rooted in structures of domestic politics. Despite all the ambitiousness of American energy diplomacy in the 1970s, the government could not back up its pledges with substantial changes in patterns of domestic production and consumption. By 1975, with only a modest emergency oil-sharing agreement in place, it was clear that the industrial countries would find separate paths to energy adjustment.

The decontrol of oil prices was the most important government action that emerged out of the energy policy turmoil of the last decade. For most industrial nations, the Organization of Petroleum Exporting Countries (OPEC) price shocks of 1973–74 passed directly through the economy and forced immediate adjustment.[1] The United States economy, however, at the mo-

The author would like to acknowledge the comments and suggestions of Beverly Crawford, Judith Goldstein, Joanne Gowa, Stephan Haggard, Peter Hall, David Lake, Charles Lipson, Mike Mastanduno, John Odell, Robert Putnam, Theda Skocpol, Peter Van Doren, and four *IO* referees.

1. See Edward N. Krapels, *Pricing Petroleum Products: Strategies of Eleven Industrial Nations* (New York: McGraw Hill, 1982).

International Organization 42, 1, Winter 1988

ment of the Arab oil embargo, was under the guidance of the Nixon administration's 1971 wage and price controls. These controls acted to regulate the
market and, as a result, domestic consumers were partially shielded from
rising world oil prices. When the wage and price controls lapsed in 1973, oil
price controls were extended in emergency legislation that Congress passed
to cope with the crisis. Although enacted as "temporary" measures, these
regulatory controls lasted for the better part of a decade and were periodically reformulated in successively more complicated programs.[2]

The price controls put the nation's petroleum markets in a position not
likely to respond to any of the government's energy goals: domestic production was discouraged while consumption was indirectly subsidized, and the
effective limit on imported oil did not allow for domestic shortages to be
made up with foreign supplies.[3] Oil pricing necessarily became politicized.
Consumers represented in Congress clutched tenaciously to the price controls while the large oil companies inveighed against them. At the same time,
beginning in 1975, the Ford administration, and later the Carter administration, sought in various ways to dismantle, circumvent, or abridge the
controls. Finally, in the spring of 1979, with new executive authority over
oil pricing, the Carter administration announced a program of phased oil
decontrol.

How do we explain the policy of decontrol? The dominant account of oil
pricing policy focuses on the play of interest groups.[4] The history of oil price
regulation and deregulation is imbued with the active involvement of interest groups and congressional politics. A "society-centered" explanation
would trace the persistence of regulatory controls and their eventual dismantlement to the efficacy of consumer and industry interests within the policy
process. Shifts in world oil markets and the domestic political environment
were followed by shifts in the bargaining position of these groups, and
change in public policy was the consequence.

Consumer and industry groups had substantial interests at stake in oil-
pricing policy. Yet an exclusive focus on interest groups cannot satisfacto-
rily explain the rise and decline of oil price controls. Societal interests were
strongly divided over the merits of decontrol and, without a consensus, had
reached a stalemate.

A second explanation, and one advanced here, gives attention to the inputs of executive officials and to the institutional structure of the American
state as it shaped the terrain for policy struggle and provided resources for

2. These regulatory policies are described in Joseph P. Kalt, *The Economics and Politics of
Oil Price Regulation* (Cambridge, Mass.: MIT Press, 1981).

3. Douglas R. Bohi and Milton Russell, *Limiting Oil Imports: An Economic Analysis* (Baltimore: Johns Hopkins University Press, 1978).

4. See, for example, David Glasner, *Politics, Prices and Petroleum: The Political Economy
of Energy* (Cambridge, Mass.: Ballinger, 1985).

executive officials to influence policy outcomes. An adequate explanation for the timing and content of oil decontrol must attend to the institutional structure of the state as it provided a basis for executive officials with their own agenda to respond to and influence the evolution of oil-pricing policy.[5]

While constrained within a fragmented and decentralized government structure, executive officials were able to marshal resources uniquely available to the state. Of particular importance was the special access state officials had to the international system. This privileged position was manifested in 1978 at the annual seven-power economic summit, when Carter administration officials maneuvered to tie an American pledge on oil decontrol to a German and Japanese agreement to reflate their economies. American regulation of domestic energy prices pressured prices upward on international markets, much to the displeasure of the other industrial importing nations. Price controls also indirectly encouraged imports and, by 1978, weakened an already sagging American dollar. Oil-pricing policy, therefore, came to impinge on other important foreign economic policy interests. Consequently, opportunities were provided for government officials to recast the issue of oil-pricing policy—of what was at stake and what could be accomplished. In turning decontrol into a foreign policy issue, government officials were able to call on special advantages they had relative to other actors who participated in the struggle to shape American oil policy.

In this context, we need to appreciate the structure of the state to understand the course of policy development. The state's institutional structure provided resource for and sites from which various factions, including government officials, pursued their interests. Executive officials were able to draw upon the state's unique role as the authoritative agent for foreign policy and recast the politics of oil pricing.

At the same time, this "state-centered" explanation for oil decontrol suggests the need to recast conceptions of the American state. The simple image of a "weak" American state—able to do little more than register interest group demands—is misleading. Yet the image of a "strong" state is equally misleading. We need a set of new terms that allow a more nuanced understanding of the inputs of government officials who are situated in institutions with various types of resources at their disposal.

This article presents an interpretation of the reconstruction of market pricing in petroleum. There are three parts to this analysis. First, I sketch and critique the society-centered explanation of oil pricing as it focuses exclusively on the activity of consumer and industry groups. Second, I present a state-centered interpretation that focuses on the role of govern-

---

5. As a policy area with many and diverse interest groups attempting to influence government decisions, the oil-pricing episode is a "least likely case" for the state-centered interpretation. To the extent that the explanation is persuasive in this case, the confidence in its significance across policy areas rises.

ment institutions and the activity of executive officials. Finally, I discuss these perspectives with reference to the sequence of oil-pricing policies that led to the 1979 decontrol decision.

Societal interests and oil-pricing policy

Throughout the 1970s, large and vocal groups arrayed themselves on all sides of the decontrol issue. Each policy alternative, ranging from the continuation of controls to the dismantlement of these controls, had identifiable social groups that would be advantaged by that policy. Yet an exercise that simply matches policy with social interests is not an adequate explanation. It is important, therefore, to take a close look at those interests and at their role in the course of policy development. Oil-pricing policy is not comprehensible as the straightforward translation of private interests into government action. The structure of the state, a structure that allowed executive officials to shape and influence the decontrol decision, mediated those interests.

Regulation and the entrenchment of interests

In the decades prior to the 1973 embargo, petroleum producers generally had their way in oil-pricing policy. The 1959 Oil Import Program, which remained in place until 1971, protected domestic producers from the less expensive imports generated by expanding Middle Eastern reserves. Throughout the 1960s, these import controls kept domestic oil prices at roughly 30 percent above the world market price. Petroleum policy was designed primarily to stabilize and protect the national petroleum industry from its own and foreign surpluses.[6] However, fundamental shifts in world petroleum production and pricing interacted with domestic regulations in the early 1970s to alter the politics of petroleum policy. Consumer interests, represented in Congress, became a substantial counterweight to industry interests.

Rising world oil prices and declining domestic production after 1969 put stress on import controls. While liberalization of petroleum markets seemed prudent, the broader problem of inflation in 1971 led to the first phase of wage and price controls; with this action, the regulation of petroleum was

6. For a discussion of the import program, see William J. Barber, "The Eisenhower Energy Policy: Reluctant Intervention," in Craufurd D. Goodwin, ed., *Energy Policy in Perspective: Today's Problems, Yesterday's Solutions* (Washington, D.C.: Brookings Institution, 1981), pp. 229–61. A more general discussion is Gerald D. Nash, *United States Oil Policy, 1890–1964 Business and Government in Twentieth Century America* (Pittsburgh: University of Pittsburgh Press, 1968).

reinvented in a new guise.[7] These wage and price controls, formulated and reformulated through four phases, were superimposed on international oil markets that were experiencing fundamental change. Most importantly, by the beginning of 1973, world oil prices were, for the first time in the postwar period, rising above domestic petroleum prices. In the months preceding 1973, the world supply of crude oil and refined products began to tighten, thus putting upward pressure on prices. Devaluation of the dollar also contributed to the higher oil import prices.[8]

These dislocations on a national scale mirrored similar dislocations with the domestic oil and refining industry and prompted demands for additional government regulation. During the earlier period of cheaper foreign sources of oil, the import quota had provided a regulatory basis for small independent refiners to buy the cheap oil and flourish domestically through marketing petroleum at cut-rate prices. But as domestic and international petroleum differentials reversed themselves and the quota system broke down, these refiners were forced to compete with the major companies. Thus, as the price controls began to have divergent impacts on refining and marketing firms, demands were created for government to intervene to allocate supplies for purposes of equity.[9] The changing differential prices of domestic and imported crude oil prices are summarized in Table 1.

Further pressure for allocation regulations came with Phase Four of price controls. Introduced in August 1973 in an attempt to encourage domestic production, Phase Four controls separated oil prices into two tiers. Crude oil produced from existing wells—"old" oil—would continue to be controlled. But "new" oil—defined as suppliers that exceeded 1972 production levels— was allowed to rise to world levels. Again, this created problems for many domestic refiners and marketers, because of differences among them in access to the cheaper controlled oil. Refiners and marketers dependent on imported oil (primarily in the Northeast) had higher costs, and this competitive disadvantage left the market with severe dislocations. Regional price

7. Authorization of this action was found in the Economic Stabilization Act of 1970. Pub. L. No. 91-379, 84 Stat. 796 (1970). On the wage and price control program see Craufurd D. Goodwin, ed., *Exhortation and Controls: The Search for a Wage Price Policy 1945-71* (Washington, D.C.: Brookings Institution, 1975); M. Kosters, *Controls and Inflation: The Economic Stabilization Program in Retrospect* (Washington, D.C.: American Enterprise Institute, 1975); J. Pohlman, *Economics of Wage and Price Controls* (Columbus: Grid, 1972); G. Haberler, *Incomes Policy and Inflation* (Washington, D.C.: American Enterprise Institute, 1971).

8. William A. Johnson, "The Impact of Price Controls on the Oil Industry: How to Worsen an Energy Crisis," in Gary Eppen, ed., *Energy: The Policy Issues* (Chicago: University of Chicago Press, 1974), p. 104.

9. Johnson, "Impact of Price Controls," p. 106; William C. Lane, Jr., "The Mandatory Petroleum Price and Allocation Regulations: A History and Analysis," report prepared for the American Petroleum Institute, 5 May 1981, pp. 23–24. See also, C. Owens, "History of Petroleum Price Controls," Department of Treasury, *Historical Working Papers on the Economic Stabilization Program* (Washington, D.C.: GPO, 1974), pp. 1253–54.

TABLE 1. *Domestic and imported crude oil prices, 1968–82 (in current dollars)*

	Domestic	Imported
1968	3.21	2.90
1969	3.37	2.80
1970	3.46	2.96
1971	3.68	3.17
1972	3.67	3.22
1973	4.17	4.08
1974	7.18	12.52
1975	8.39	13.93
1976	8.84	13.48
1977	9.55	14.53
1978	10.61	14.57
1979	14.27	21.67
1980	24.23	33.89
1981	34.33	37.05
1982	31.22	33.55

Note. Prices figured in terms of refiner acquisition costs.
Source. Energy Information Administration, *Annual Energy Review, 1984* (Washington, D.C.: Dept. of Energy, Energy Information Administration, April 1985), p. 123.

disparities and shortages prompted new efforts by industry and government officials to search for reform. Thus, the price control scheme was extended to include a mandatory allocation program.[10]

In the decades prior to 1973, when the threats to national oil producers involved declining world petroleum prices, the industry was able to enlist government in protecting prices. The price shocks of the 1970s, however, involved higher world prices, and government policy responded to a larger range of societal interests. The presence of price controls, moreover, had the unintended effect of strengthening the position of consumer groups and others who had a stake in the continuation of those controls. While the history of oil-pricing policy would lead one to expect policy to again respond primarily to the demands of oil producers, this did not happen. Congress extended and reworked price and allocation controls to insulate consumers from higher world prices. In the process, domestic producers were denied the full gains that OPEC pricing made possible. "[T]he interests of oil users," as one analyst notes, "had superseded those of oil producers in determining the direction and nature of government policies."[11]

10. Johnson, "Impact of Price Controls," pp. 109–10. See also Bohi and Russell, *Limiting Oil Imports,* pp. 225–26.
11. Arthur W. Wright, "The Case of the United States: Energy as a Political Good," *Journal of Comparative Economics* 2 (1978), p. 171.

Consumers voiced their interest in the maintenance of controls in Congress. While officials in the executive branch began to articulate the decontrol position in 1975, Congress repeatedly generated majority votes for the extension of controls. The costs to consumers would be onerous; when coupled with an excise tax, the burden of decontrol was estimated in 1975 to be approximately $24 billion.[12] In the view of many in Congress, moreover, decontrol would only benefit the large oil producers, and control of domestic pricing would be handed over to OPEC. This opposition to decontrol was manifested in the Energy Policy and Conservation Act (EPCA) of 1975. The price of domestic oil was rolled back and controls were extended for another forty months. At the end of that period, the president would need to take positive action to end controls, subject to congressional review.[13]

An explanation of the persistence of price controls does require a focus on societal interests, in particular those of consumers represented in Congress. The price controls unintentionally diminished the importance of the major oil firms in the policy process. In contrast to the pre-1973 period, oil producers were not at the center of oil-pricing policy. Regulatory controls enlarged the political struggle over pricing policy, and consumer interests demonstrated the ability to overwhelm the interests of oil producers and thwart, for a time, the designs of executive officials. While oil producers did gain from the subsequent decontrol decision, there is reason to be skeptical of their influence over pricing policy.

The oil industry and decontrol

An interest group explanation of the shift from controls to decontrol would examine the changing influence of consumer and industry groups in the policy process. In particular, one would expect to find the erosion of consumer interests in Congress on the one hand, and a more well-organized and active oil industry on the other. Indeed, the absence of strong oil producer influence over pricing policy throughout the period of controls suggests that the rise in industry influence would need to be quite remarkable. In fact, however, industry interests were not well-organized during the period of controls, and the controls fragmented the petroleum industry by creating winners and losers. Industry interest in decontrol was not unalloyed, and an explanation for policy change will need to look beyond those industry interests.

The regulatory controls redistributed very large amounts of income. As we have noted, the major losers in this program were the domestic crude oil

---

12. Testimony of Frank G. Zarb, in U.S. Congress, House, *Hearings on the Presidential Energy Program,* pp. 20–21. See also Richard H. K. Vietor, *Energy Policy in America Since 1945: A Study of Business-Government Relations* (London: Cambridge University Press, 1984), p. 249.

13. *Public Law* 94-163 (22 December 1975).

TABLE 2. *Estimated distributional effects of controls and entitlements, 1975–1980 (in billions of 1980 dollars)*

	Crude oil producers	Petroleum refiners	Petroleum product consumers
1975	− 23.9	+ 15.0	+ 6.9
1976	− 18.9	+ 10.2	+ 6.8
1977	− 18.7	+ 10.4	+ 6.4
1978	− 14.3	+ 8.5	+ 4.7
1979	− 32.6	+ 21.8	+ 8.3
1980	− 49.6	+ 31.7	+ 12.2

Note. 1980 figures are annual rate based on data for January–March.
Source. Joseph Kalt, *The Economics and Politics of Oil Price Regulation* (Cambridge, Mass.: MIT Press, 1981), p. 216.

producers; petroleum refiners and consumers were the winners. Joseph Kalt estimates that if these producers had been able to sell their production at unregulated prices, they would have enlarged their income in amounts ranging from $14 billion and $49 billion (1980 dollars) annually between 1975 and 1980.[14] The rents that would have gone to crude producers were instead captured by petroleum users—namely, domestic refiners and final users of petroleum products. A calculation of the redistributional effects of the price and allocation controls is provided in Table 2.

With domestic crude oil prices controlled, competition developed among crude oil users for access to the cheaper supplies. Initially, government regulations allowed access to this oil to be based on existing supply contracts. The result was the transfer of billions of dollars to some domestic refiners with preexisting access to price-controlled oil who could refine and sell their products at world prices. The Entitlements Program, enacted in November 1974, contained provisions to spread the subsidy to all domestic refiners. Price controls also created distortions in the downstream use of refined petroleum products, and this prompted demands for "priority access" to supplies. In effect, the growth of federal allocation regulations expanded the range of refiner and consumer groups that benefited from the regulation of prices.[15]

Thus, price and allocation regulations fragmented the interests of the American oil industry. Kalt notes: "Even among the largest integrated companies, the effect of federal policy was disparate. As the balance of opera-

14. Joseph Kalt, *Oil Price Regulation*, pp. 213–21.
15. Kalt, "The Creation, Growth, and Entrenchment of Special Interests in Oil Price Policy," in Roger G. Noll and Bruce M. Owen, *The Political Economy of Deregulation: Interest Groups in the Regulatory Process* (Washington, D.C.: American Enterprise Institute, 1983), p. 106.

tions shifted from domestic crude oil production (where regulatory burdens were imposed) to refining and international operations (where entitlements benefits were conferred), companies acquired vested interests in the overall regulatory program—as differences in companies' lobbying efforts on the issue of decontrol repeatedly testified."[16]

Regulatory controls provided gains to some and losses to others within the petroleum industry, and positions on control and decontrol varied accordingly. The positions of Standard Oil of Ohio and Marathon, both medium-sized oil companies, are illustrative. Sohio, with a large refining capacity and little oil production of its own, qualified as an independent refiner. Under the terms of the Allocation Act, it was able to buy subsidized crude oil from other domestic producers. The company, consequently, favored extension of the regulatory program. Marathon, on the other hand, was largely self-sufficient in petroleum production and was forced to sell some of that production. Unable to gain the full rents of its own petroleum production, Marathon vigorously opposed controls.[17]

The problem with a societal-centered explanation of decontrol is that group interests were highly mediated by the prevailing institutional structures of government. An analysis that takes the capabilities of societal actors as given is inadequate. The interests of consumers, which otherwise would have been diffused and difficult to organize, were crystallized in unanticipated ways by the preexisting price controls. This crystallization magnified their claims and created an effective counterweight to the interests of oil producers. At the same time, the regulatory program also fragmented the petroleum industry on the issue of decontrol. While most oil producers had a substantial stake in decontrol, the evolution of policy in that direction cannot be explained by changes in their capabilities. Indeed, as I shall argue, oil decontrol was accomplished in spite of, rather than because of, the interests of major oil producers. An understanding of the shift from controls to decontrol requires the appreciation of the role of executive officials as they drew upon resources uniquely available to them and, by so doing, redefined the issues at stake.

State structure and policy change

Federal petroleum regulations generated profits and losses to various societal groups, but they also had aggregate effects on the national economy and the nation's international position. Artificially low domestic prices created incentives for the overconsumption of imported crude oil and the underproduction of domestic reserves. Regulations put upward pressure on

16. Ibid., p. 109.
17. Vietor, *Energy Policy in America*, p. 247.

the world market price of oil, and the result strengthened the monopolistic pricing of OPEC and disadvantaged other industrial importing nations. Domestic controls prevented the production of domestic oil that, even at world prices, would have cost less than the imported oil that replaced it. Taken together, the amount of national wealth transferred to foreign suppliers by virtue of control has been estimated at between $1 and $5 billion (1982 dollars) per year over 1975–1980.[18] Executive officials, beginning in 1975, deliberately sought to address these national and international consequences of domestic regulations. The activity of these state officials shifted the balance of forces in favor of decontrol, a process that was accomplished by redefining what was at stake in oil-pricing policy.

American state structure

Analysts have studied the independent impacts of states on their societies and economies in a variety of ways. Most recent scholarship has given specificity to the state by focusing on the policy process and situating its organizational and instrumental characteristics within larger structures of state and society. Out of this literature has emerged general propositions about the capacities of the state, which locates the advanced industrial states along a continuum of "weak" and "strong."[19]

Scholars have identified a range of institutional structures that undergird autonomous administrative organization and that, in comparative perspective, differentiate states according to their capacities. Zysman, who is interested in the divergent abilities of advanced capitalist states to become involved as coherent and weighty actors in industrial adjustment, focuses on three structural elements: mechanisms of recruitment in the national civil service; the degree of centralization within government civil service; and the extent of independence from legislative oversight.[20] These characteristics of

18. Kalt, "Oil Price Policy," p. 101. On international market effects of domestic petroleum regulations, see Edward Fried and Charles Schultze, eds., *Higher Oil Prices and the World Economy: The Adjustment Problem* (Washington, D.C.: Brookings Institution, 1975), p. 67.

19. Peter J. Katzenstein, "International Relations and Domestic Structures: Foreign Economic Policies of Advanced Industrial States," *International Organization* 30 (Winter 1976); Peter Katzenstein, ed., *Between Power and Plenty: The Foreign Economic Policies of Advanced Industrial States* (Madison: University of Wisconsin Press, 1978); Stephen Krasner, *Defending the National Interest* (Princeton, N.J.: Princeton University Press, 1978); John Zysman, *Governments, Markets, and Growth: Financial Systems and the Politics of Industrial Change* (Ithaca, N.Y.: Cornell University Press, 1983).

20. Zysman, *Governments, Markets, and Growth*, p. 300. For discussions of the higher civil service, see Ezra Suleiman, *Politics, Power and Bureaucracy* (Princeton, N.J.: Princeton University Press, 1974); John A. Armstrong, *The European Administrative Elite* (Princeton, N.J.: Princeton University Press, 1977); Hugh Heclo, *A Government of Strangers* (Washington, D.C.: Brookings Institution, 1977); Ezra Suleiman, ed., *Bureaucrats and Policy Making* (New York: Holmes & Meier, 1984).

government structure, Zysman argues, can be combined into a single measure of a state's capacity for intervention.[21]

In this formulation, the most striking case is France, where permanent organizations of government officials have access to many policy tools and resources that may be legitimately deployed in the regulation of a wide range of social activities. Measured in terms of scope of state activities in the economy and society and the prominence of central bureaucratic institutions, there is every reason to place that state at the center of analysis. In his classic essay on the state as a conceptual variable, J. P. Nettl presented France as the paradigmatic case of "stateness" in modern industrial countries, a model adopted by political leaders who are intent on creating state-centered national identities in other parts of Europe.[22]

More recent comparative discussions of the state, referred to earlier, have repeatedly described France as a "strong" state, focusing on the autonomy and influence of central government institutions in forming societal and economic policy. Katzenstein focuses on the character of specific "policy networks" that are shaped by the larger structures of state and society. Thus, in a survey of trade, finance, and energy policy, he finds French policy networks are "state-centered" and American policy networks "society-centered."[23] Zysman, as we have seen, is much more concerned with the capacity of specific central bureaucratic institutions, such as ministries of finance and ministries of industry. Nonetheless, both have notions of broad differences in the capacities of states—differences rooted in historically derived forces of political and economic development. Fundamentally, this comparative literature suggests, state strength is reflected in the organization and resources of bureaucratic government as well as its insulation from competing actors.

In this literature, the United States serves as the counter-example, the "weak" state. The American state is fragmented and decentralized, possessing few of the instruments and resources necessary for strategic intervention in the economy and society. Despite repeated presidential attempts, there is no comprehensive, effective planning agency for even a single issue-area, much less for government as a whole. The frequent turnover of high-level executive officials and narrow divisions of bureaucratic authority create a

21. Zysman, *Governments, Markets, and Growth*, p. 300.
22. Nettl, "The State as a Conceptual Variable," *World Politics* 20 (July 1968), p. 567. This view is echoed elsewhere: "It is still possible even today to distinguish between political systems in which there is both a center and a state (France), a state but no center (Italy), center but no true state (Great Britain and the United States), and neither a center nor a true state (Switzerland). In the first two cases, the state dominates civil society and is responsible for its organization, albeit in different degrees. In the last two cases, civil society organizes itself." Bertrand Badie and Pierre Birnbaum, *The Sociology of the State* (Chicago: The University of Chicago Press, 1982), p. 103.
23. Katzenstein, "International Relations and Domestic Structures," p. 43.

"government of strangers" and severely hinder the emergence of effective bases of power.[24] The United States is not simply a late-bloomer; its political institutions are fundamentally malformed for the emergence of a strong state.

The image of a "weak" American state portrays a government able to do little more than register the demands of society. This image is confirmed when the goals of government officials are thwarted and when policy conforms to the interests of dominant social groups. Consequently, the notion of a "weak" state does not provide the basis for capturing the independent or intervening role of government officials in policymaking and the range of resources these officials can draw upon. In effect, this literature provides only a negative image of the American case; the state is defined by what it is not.

The image of the American state as a continually transformed, internally differentiated arena of conflict—rather than an integrated institution— necessitates a rethinking of the concept of state capacity. Rather than searching for analogues of the centralized, coordinated planning apparatus of the French state, attention is more usefully focused on the institutional configuration of government and the influence of evolving political institutions on the political position of, and resources available to, specific actors in the policy process, including executive officials. In this sense, the state is not directly understood to be a single integrated institutional actor, but rather a piece of strategically important terrain, which shapes the entire course of political battles and sometimes provides the resources and advantages necessary to win them. Among these resources, as I shall argue, is the special access of executive officials to the international system.

This approach, which focuses on institutional structures (or "state structure"), has been elaborated by Skocpol.[25] State structure, Skocpol argues, affects the possibilities for policy outcomes in two ways. First, state structures can provide the bulwark for government bureaucrats and policy experts to fashion proposals for action.[26] In effect, the institutions of government provide havens or sites for policy experts and executive officials to generate ideas and programs that address particular socioeconomic challenges. As we shall see, executive officials were provided an autonomous

24. Heclo, *A Government of Strangers.*
25. See articles by Theda Skocpol and her associates: Margaret Weir and Theda Skocpol, "State Structures and the Possibilities for 'Keynesian' Responses to the Great Depression in Sweden, Britain, and the United States," in Peter B. Evans, Dietrich Rueschemeyer, and Skocpol, eds., *Bringing the State Back In* (Cambridge: Cambridge University Press, 1985), pp. 107–63; Skocpol and Ikenberry, "The Political Formation of the American Welfare State in Historical and Comparative Perspective," *Comparative Social Research* 6 (Greenwich, Conn.: JAI Press, 1983), pp. 359–81. See also Peter A. Hall, *Governing the Economy: The Politics of State Intervention in Britain and France* (New York. Oxford University Press, 1986).
26. Weir and Skocpol, "State Structures," pp. 117–19.

position to push policy towards market pricing, and sought recourse to resources uniquely available to them.

State structure can have a second, and less direct, impact on policy outcomes by influencing societal groups' perceptions of what goals are possible and the ways to successfully pursue them. The institutional terrain upon which variously situated groups compete can shape the possibilities for successful group action. Weir and Skocpol argue that "the administrative, fiscal, coercive, and judicial arrangements of given states, as well as the policies that states are already pursuing, influence the conceptions that groups or their representatives are likely to develop about what is desirable, or possible at all, in the realm of governmental action."[27] As we have already seen, the wage and price controls that predated the October 1973 embargo politicized oil-pricing policy and enhanced the influence of consumers in the policy process. Analysis must focus not just on the interests of societal groups but also on the interaction of these group interests with institutional structures and preexisting policy.

An explanation for decontrol that focuses exclusively on the capabilities of social groups, as I have argued earlier, is inadequate. A state-centered focus, along the lines sketched here, considers the independent and intervening efforts of executive officials to recast the problem of oil pricing in ways that advance a set of goals larger than those embraced by any particular social group. While decontrol did provide benefits to national oil producers, it was the task of executive officials to redefine what goals market pricing of petroleum would serve. Redressing losses to national wealth and to the nation's international position required state officials to distance themselves from the interests of the oil producers. Their goals, as Bohi and Russell argue, were "clouded because of pervasive suspicion of the oil industry and because this national goal coincided so exactly with certain of its special interests."[28] The development of a foreign policy rationale for decontrol, most prominently achieved at the 1978 Bonn Summit, allowed that decision ultimately to be made. Let us now trace these developments.

The state and market strategy

During the Ford and early Carter administrations, executive officials articulated a "state interest" in market pricing, and related these goals to larger national economic and foreign policy. Both administrations labored under the regulatory programs championed in Congress. As we shall see, in 1978, new opportunities were provided for executive action on oil pricing—

27. Ibid., p. 118
28. Bohi and Russell, *Limiting Oil Imports.*

opportunities seized upon by the senior officials and linked to larger foreign economic policy objectives.

The Ford administration and market pricing

In 1975, while economic recession had restrained growth in oil consumption, import dependence continued to climb.[29] In this context, the new Ford administration began to articulate a national adjustment strategy—one that was organized around a return to market pricing of petroleum. This priority, which was to reemerge during the Carter administration, had an uneasy history. At each turn, the Ford administration was forced to compromise with Congress, diluting the thrust of the market strategy. Nonetheless, a small victory was won: congressional legislation contained the provisions for eventual presidential control over oil-pricing policy.

The Ford administration made a commitment to decontrol in January 1975 with the announcement of a proposed excise tax and import fee on foreign crude oil and a "presidential initiative to decontrol the price of domestic crude oil. . . ."[30] The rationale for decontrol was rather simple. The deputy administrator for the Federal Energy Administration argued before a congressional committee in August 1975: "The most efficient way to reduce demand and increase supplies (and thereby reduce imports) is, of course, through the price mechanism."[31] Beyond frustrating the goal of lower import dependence, the controls had further problems. The administrative official argued that the controls hindered competition in the petroleum industry and prevented rational corporate investment decision-making. Finally, the official argued that the controls prolonged distortions and inefficiencies in the adjustment process itself. "As domestic production continues to decline at differing rates in different parts of the country, necessary adjustments in crude oil distribution channels cannot be resolved through the operation of normal market mechanisms, and can only be accomplished [under present circumstances] by ad hoc action by the FEA, which is ill-equipped to deal with such matters."[32]

In addition to this immediate rationale for decontrol, several quarters in the administration voiced another set of arguments about foreign policy goals. The State Department's position was that leadership in the West hinged on gaining control of rising petroleum imports. International energy goals would necessarily involve domestic-pricing decisions to encourage

29. Oil imports from Arab OPEC members constituted the greatest increase. Department of Energy, *1982 Annual Energy Review* (Washington, D.C.: GPO, 1982), p. 57.

30. State of the Union Message, 13 January 1975. The price deregulation proposals made by the administration were contained in S. 594/H.R. 2650.

31. John A. Hill, Hearings before the Committee on Interior and Insular Affairs. U.S. Senate, "Oil Price Decontrol," 4 and 5 September 1975, p. 147.

32. Ibid., pp. 149–50.

conservation and the development of alternative energy technologies.[33] This indirect support for reformed pricing, based on broader foreign policy goals of allied energy cooperation, continued into the Carter administration and became an important force behind the final decontrol decision.

With this rationale for decontrol, the administration prepared itself for legislative maneuverings with a skeptical Congress. An import fee, proposed in the January speech by Ford, was designed as a bargaining chip with Congress. Ford intended to decontrol prices of domestic oil on 1 April 1975, if Congress did not veto decontrol as was allowed within the terms of the 1974 Emergency Petroleum Allocation Act. Consequently, Ford was eager to have Congress approve his excise tax proposals—he asked for passage within three months. To stimulate congressional passage, Ford warned that he would impose a $1 import fee on 1 February and a second $1 on 1 April.

This pressuring of Congress by the administration, however, was not effective. To begin with, Congress passed legislation that denied the president the authority to impose an import fee for ninety days. Ford quickly vetoed this legislation. Following this, negotiations took place between the two branches and Ford agreed to delay both the fee and the decontrol plan. The decontrol action was pushed back to 1 May; this was also the date by which Ford wanted Congress to act on his tax proposals. This deadline was again transgressed. On 30 April, Ford agreed to a phased program of decontrol.[34]

The president could have allowed prices to be decontrolled if he had let EPCA expire. This would have occurred on 31 August. Ford, however, wanted decontrol to be a shared decision with Congress. And because of this, he accepted the phased plan.[35] A second opportunity to veto energy legislation that extended EPCA controls came on 15 December 1975, when the EPCA was due to end. Again, the president chose not to decontrol by veto, waiting instead for the phased program to lapse in thirty-nine months. Thus, the president, although urging decontrol, was not willing to have it at any cost.

A victory of sorts was rescued from the congressional struggle. The EPCA legislation contained provisions for eventual presidential discretion over oil-pricing policy. While this authority was still several years off, the politics of oil pricing had shifted from a congressional–executive struggle to an intra-administrative struggle. In the early period of the Carter administration, officials were still bound by EPCA controls, and, as I shall note below, they

---

33. A report at the time noted: As formulated by Secretary of State Henry A. Kissinger, approved by principal officials of the Administration and accepted by President Ford, the high price concept lies at the heart of the government's foreign policy strategy in the energy field. *National Journal*, 8 March 1975, p. 357.

34. Congressional Quarterly, *Energy Policy*, 2d ed. (Washington, D.C.: Congressional Quarterly Press, 1981), pp. 34–35.

35. Ibid., pp. 35–36.

sought an ingenuous taxing scheme to artificially replicate market pricing. Nonetheless, as discretionary authority for pricing policy neared in 1978, the struggle moved into the executive branch, where foreign policy and energy officials sought to fashion a persuasive rationale for decontrol that would lift it above the troubling constraints of domestic politics.

Market pricing by artifice

The Carter administration came to office trailing campaign rhetoric that opposed petroleum decontrol. That this rhetoric came to embrace a taxing scheme that moved effective prices to world levels is, therefore, surprising. Once in office, however, energy planners moved quickly to propose a tax scheme that would bring domestic energy prices to the prevailing international level—the Crude Oil Equalization Tax (COET) proposal of 1977. This elaborate tax proposal languished in Congress and was ultimately defeated. As the energy prices moved upward again with the collapse of Iranian oil production, the Carter administration came to more fully embrace the strategy of market adjustment.

Carter's initial pricing proposals were included in the major policy package presented to Congress as the 1977 National Energy Plan. The oil price taxing aspects of this plan reflected the tactical problems of using the price mechanism to alter consumption patterns while also using it to meet obdurate political resistance in Congress (primarily among liberal Democrats in the House) to giving producers a free market in petroleum. The COET was designed as a tax on producers in an effort to limit their profits, while at the same time bringing the effective price of oil at the refining and marketing stages up to prevailing world prices. The taxes collected from oil producers were to be rebated back to lower- and middle-income families in order to offset the inflationary impact on these households. Other portions of the collected taxes would be channeled into mass transit projects and an energy investment fund.

The COET would only have addressed the consumption side of the problem by having costs to consumers reflect international prices. The tax would not create new production incentives. "One possible method for dealing with the consumer-to-producer transfer had been previously proposed; President Carter's crude-oil equalization tax would have prevented any of the revenue gain from decontrol from accruing to producers. While this would have maintained the demand-side benefits of decontrol, the supply-side benefits would have been lost; no additional domestic production would occur."[36]

---

36. Mark Steitz, "Oil Decontrol and the Windfall Profits Tax," in Raymond C. Scheppach and Evertt M. Ehrlich, eds., *Energy-Policy Analysis and Congressional Action* (Lexington, Mass.: Lexington, 1982), p. 82.

The emphasis on conservation rather than production allowed the National Energy Plan to use a tax to dampen consumption by moving prices to their replacement cost. The Carter policy innovation was its attempt to have it both ways: to continue controls in order to regulate the prices producers could charge, but also to introduce replacement cost pricing to energy. With this initiative, the administration affirmed the idea that price levels would have to be set in a larger context of demand and supply. Elaborate though this was, the new notion of pricing was a step away from the premises of the regulatory regime.

The distinctive Carter approach to gaining world prices in energy by continuing controls and adding taxes was slowly smothered in congressional committee. In the House, where Democratic leadership supported the package, the COET proposal survived committee and floor votes. However, the Senate was less supportive. The decisive obstacle to tax passage came from the Senate Finance Committee. Although Finance Chairman Russell Long from Louisiana initially endorsed COET, the committee refused to pass the tax proposal and it was left in Congress without any legislative life.

The transnational bargain

In early 1978, the Carter administration was caught between a looming $45 billion annual oil import bill and a failed COET proposal. At the same time, the leaders of other industrial nations began to voice criticism of excessive American consumption of oil. It was at this juncture that the administration's foreign economic policy officials began an effort to redefine the oil-pricing issue by linking oil decontrol to a larger set of international economic problems and to a diplomatic agreement that addressed those problems. In doing so, these officials drew on a resource uniquely available to them, namely, the special legitimacy of the state to manage foreign economic policy. In transforming the issue of decontrol, the position of these officials within the domestic policy process—and within the administration itself—was strengthened. Less than a year later, the administration began the process of decontrol.

While leaders from the major industrial countries had become highly critical of the rising American oil consumption, U.S. officials in 1978 were concerned with slow economic growth in Japan and Germany. With the annual summit conference as the forum, a transnational bargain linking these issues was attempted. Allied governments, Germany most prominently, were attempting to pressure the American government to bring the cost of domestic oil into accord with prevailing world market prices. Meanwhile, the Carter administration was attempting to convince Chancellor Helmut Schmidt to reflate the German economy in order to stimulate international growth. This set of counter-demands gave the decontrol decision large significance and also gave administration officials already in favor of market pricing a new rationale.[37]

In the winter and spring prior to the 1978 Bonn summit, several major international economic issues confronted the industrial nations. The German and Japanese economies were experiencing low inflation and low growth. The United States, on the other hand, was experiencing accelerating inflation, an increasing oil deficit, and a weakened currency. The Carter administration moved to reflate its economy and wished Germany and Japan to do the same. Also, the Multilateral Trade Negotiations were entering their final stage, and the British and French governments showed some reluctance to finish. Finally, there was the nagging issue of American energy consumption; oil imports had risen to an historic high by the end of 1977. The possibility for a package agreement presented itself.

Accounts suggest that British Prime Minister James Callaghan, in the early months of 1978, began to explore the possibilities for a package deal at the Bonn summit. An agreement linking these issues was discussed when Callaghan visited the White House in the winter. The key Carter officials for international economic policy—Richard Cooper at the State Department, Anthony Solomon at the Treasury, and Henry Owen, ambassador-at-large for economic summits—had also discussed the possibilities for a package at the first of the year.[38] Formal discussions that would link American energy policy and German growth policy began in March 1978 at meetings of the summit sherpas in Bonn.[39]

At the preparatory meeting in Bonn, the American representative, Henry Owen, met with Chancellor Schimdt to seek a commitment on German reflation. The German Chancellor countered and asked for American concessions. Schmidt contended that the continuation of controls on American domestic petroleum indirectly contributed to higher world oil prices. Not only did controls discourage the production of domestic American oil, he argued, but they also encouraged consumption, and therefore demand on supplies in the international market. In exchange for budgetary stimulus in Bonn, Schmidt asked for assurances from the United States on energy policy. The United States must move to cut down levels of imported oil, and go forward with its comprehensive energy policy. The result was a trade-off: German reflation for American world oil pricing.

Chancellor Schmidt suggested this "bargain" just prior to the summit:

---

37. The most complete description of this fascinating bargain is in Robert D. Putnam and C. Randall Henning, "The Bonn Summit of 1978: How Does International Economic Policy Coordination Actually Work?" Paper presented at a workshop on "Intergovernmental Consultations and Cooperation about Macroeconomic Policies," Brookings Institution, 6 April 1985. See also, George de Menil and Anthony M. Solomon, *Economic Summitry* (New York: Council on Foreign Relations, 1983); Robert D. Putnam and Nicholas Bayne, *Hanging Together: The Seven-Power Summits* (Cambridge, Mass.: Harvard University Press, 1984).

38. Interview, Henry Owen, 10 August 1985.

39. Putnam and Henning, "The Bonn Summit of 1978," p. 85.

"Governments of some participating countries believe that they have a recipe for me and for Germany. By way of compromise, if others would bring about some sacrifices or tackle some domestic hardships, I would be ready to do so in my country."[40] Carter also has indicated that a bargain had been struck. In his memoirs, Carter noted that he held a meeting with congressional leaders several weeks prior to the Bonn summit. "I got all of those who would speak out to advise me. . . to tell our partners at the Bonn Economic Summit Meeting that if Congress did not act to raise the domestic price up to the world level by 1980, then I would act administratively."[41]

The agreement at Bonn was not one that, strictly speaking, involved an exchange of concessions. Most participants suggest that the German pledge on growth and the American pledge on energy were desired by the respective heads of state themselves. Rather, the agreement was a form of cooperation that attempted to strengthen each leader's domestic position. Carter and Schmidt would be able to pursue their policy commitments, bolstered politically by the impression that a concession had been extracted from the other. Thus, it is useful to view the Bonn pledge as the outcome of a momentary "international coalition" of political leaders, each having domestic political problems, and each agreeing to create the convenient fiction that hard-fought concessions had been won.[42] Ironically, at an unusual moment when interests converged between the leaders of two powerful industrial nations, that agreement had to be presented to the world as a contest over concessions.

There was a great deal of ambiguity within the Carter administration concerning what the president had in fact pledged. The foreign policy officials understood that the Bonn statement was itself a policy decision on oil pricing. One participant suggests that the decision was made "in principle" at Bonn to move the effective price of domestic oil to world levels. However, this commitment might still be carried out through the COET, or other tax or administrative mechanisms.[43] Another participant argues even more

40. John Vinocur, "Schmidt Says U.S. Holds Key to Economic Accord," *New York Times,* 14 July 1978, p. 3.

41. Jimmy Carter, *Keeping Faith: Memoirs of a President* (New York: Bantam, 1982), p. 104.

42. An interpretation along these lines was suggested to me by Richard Cooper. Interview, 9 August 1985. The Japanese sherpa to the summit, Deputy Foreign Minister for Economic Affairs Hiromichi Miyazaki, argues that the issues of economic stimulation and energy were not explicitly linked, and that the Japanese, at least, had no intention of "bartering" over U.S. oil pricing policy. The Japanese did resist engaging in a "locomotive" expansion of American, German and Japanese economies. Nonetheless, a compromise emerged. "The Japanese," Miyazaki noted in an interview, "would do things that would look like reflation in U.S. eyes." In essence, Miyazaki's argument is that each side was able to use the other's public statements in the formulation of a domestic rationale for policy they already supported. In this sense, the summit pledges were used to strengthen the domestic position of the various leaders, and they were not, strictly speaking, a bargain built on mutual concessions. Interview with Ambassador Hiromichi Miyazaki, Bonn, Federal Republic of Germany, 22 July 1985.

43. Interview, Richard Cooper, 9 August 1985.

strongly that the decision on decontrol was made in Bonn. "Carter wanted oil decontrol," this official argues, "and welcomed Bonn as an opportunity to do it."[44] Carter himself argues that the inability to implement an energy policy was "becoming an international embarrassment." And he notes his commitment at Bonn to "let American oil prices rise to the world level. . . ."[45] Others, such as CEA Chairman Charles Schultze, thought that Carter had gone too far—exchanging a pledge on oil pricing for Schmidt's commitments on growth that the Germans would have pursued anyway. Schlesinger was hesitant to see the government make a foreign policy commitment when the issue hinged on domestic political circumstances.[46] The domestic policy staff, however, were the least aware or convinced that a decision had, in fact, been made at the summit. While attending several of the pre-summit meetings on the proposed pledge, Eizenstat and his staff were surprised and dismayed by the announcement at Bonn. Eizenstat faulted the foreign policy side of the administration for not being "sensitive to domestic considerations." No decision memorandum had been prepared prior to the summit, and the domestic implications of the pledge had not been discussed.[47]

A foreign policy rationale now added impetus to administration deliberations on oil-pricing policy. While the Bonn summit pledge was pushed by officials not directly involved in domestic policy discussions of oil pricing, it did encourage those discussions. The pledge, one domestic analyst noted, "gave people within the administration reason to keep working on this issue."[48] A study of the annual Western economic summit meetings concludes that "[i]nternational pressure played a significant part in convincing President Carter that the time had come to push for decontrol of the price of oil."[49] One Carter foreign economic policy official suggests that the Bonn pledge "tilted the balance" in the administration deliberations on oil pricing.[50] Another notes that it would have been "embarrassing for Carter to change his mind after Bonn."[51] A cabinet secretary argues that the Bonn

---

44. Interview, Henry Owen, 10 August 1985. In an essay, Owen described the outcome of the Bonn summit: ". . .the United States decontrolled oil prices (arguably the single most important step taken by the industrial countries to address the world energy problem), which Carter could only have done as part of an international economic bargain which also included stimulus and trade pledges from other countries." Owen, "Taking Stock of the Seven-Power Summits: Two Views," *International Affairs* 60 (Autumn 1984), p. 660. It would come as a surprise to other officials in the administration (particularly on the domestic side) that Carter decontrolled oil prices at the Bonn summit.

45. Jimmy Carter, *Keeping Faith,* pp. 103–4.

46. Interview, James Schlesinger, 22 August 1985.

47. Interview, Stuart Eizenstat, 19 June 1985.

48. Interview, Jim Voytka, 7 June 1985.

49. George de Menil, "From Rambouillet to Versailles," in Menil and Solomon, *Economic Summitry,* p. 24.

50. Interview, Richard Cooper, 9 August 1985.

51. Interview, Henry Owen, 10 August 1985.

pledge was a "significant but not preponderant" factor in the final decontrol decision.[52] Nonetheless, in internal discussions of oil pricing and the conflicting problem of inflation in early 1979, Carter clearly realized that to postpone decontrol would require persuading Schmidt and other leaders that inflation posed a greater international economic threat.[53] After Bonn, oil pricing was manifestly an international issue, even in meetings with domestic staff.

The true impact of the transnational bargain is difficult to measure. Robert D. Hormats, a State Department official who helped guide American summit planning efforts during the Ford and Carter administrations, has emphasized the summit's importance in countering domestic opposition to decontrol. He notes that the summit "helped Carter, who I think wanted to do it in the first place, but for a variety of reasons didn't."[54] In this interpretation, the summit was not the source of forcing the decontrol decision, but a source of support for the decision. Other officials have given a stronger significance to the summit politics. Putnam and Henning argue that the Bonn pledge served to break the deadlock on oil pricing within the administration by separating the question of whether to raise domestic oil prices from the means for doing so.[55] This overstates the role of the Bonn pledge. On at least two occasions in early 1979, Carter indicated privately to his staff that fighting inflation was perhaps of greater importance than living up to the Bonn pledge, and that he would be willing to suffer the consequences.[56] As I indicate below, the dilemma between meeting the Bonn commitments, energy conservation, and production goals, on the one hand, and fighting inflation through the continued use of controls, on the other, became the crux of the decision. In the end, the weak dollar problem apparently undercut the inflation-fighting argument. Treasury Secretary Michael Blumenthal and Anthony Solomon argued that the continuation of controls would further weaken the dollar, thus canceling the anti-inflation gains.[57]

The transnational bargain, struck at Bonn, had an agenda-setting effect. It moved the administration debate of oil pricing into a larger tangle of foreign policy and international economic issues. Energy officials were forced to place their domestic concerns alongside those addressing international political and economic problems. In the end, these officials became allies, articulating a rationale for decontrol that challenged those officials who addressed domestic political concerns and pursued the administration's inflation-fighting program.

52. Interview, James Schlesinger, 22 August 1985.
53. Carter meeting with Mondale, McIntyre, Bosworth, Schultz, Kahn and Eizenstat, 3 January 1979. Eizenstat diary.
54. Clyde H. Farnsworth, "Trade Notes, *New York Times,* 15 April 1984, p. F8.
55. Putnam and Henning, "The Bonn Summit of 1978," p. 91.
56. Eizenstat diary, 3 January and 15 March 1979.
57. Eizenstat diary, 18 January 1979.

Agenda setting and the decontrol decision

The Bonn agreement signaled a shift in the way the Carter administration characterized the oil-pricing issue. This, in turn, shifted the balance of forces in the struggle over decontrol, both within the administration and with Congress. Within the administration, senior officials who were concerned primarily with national and foreign economic policy, and who uniformly favored market pricing, gained the political upper hand. The administration's bargaining position with Congress also was strengthened. Price and allocation controls were due to expire in April 1979, and for the first time in almost four years, the president would have discretionary authority over the pricing issue. A decision would be necessary—a presidential choice to continue controls, abolish them, or phase them out. The struggle over pricing policy continued, but the strength of executive officials pursuing a larger foreign economic policy agenda had grown. It is this development that is necessary to explain policy change.

A number of circumstances external to the ongoing administrative rethinking of strategy pushed a decision on decontrol forward in late 1978 and early 1979. International oil markets were in turmoil. Triggered by the shutdown of Iranian production and skyrocketing prices on the spot market, OPEC made decisions in December 1978 and March 1979 that effectivley doubled world prices. At the same time, allied pressure continued on the Carter administration to stand by its 1978 Bonn pledge to bring domestic prices up to world levels. They had reason to complain. While Japanese and European countries had reduced import levels marginally, American oil import levels continued to remain high by historic standards. Finally, inflation continued to mount and compounded the seriousness of the oil-pricing decision.

All of Carter's senior domestic and foreign policy advisors were engaged in the debate over oil-pricing policy. No longer was decontrol framed simply as an energy issue; national economic and foreign policy considerations were explicitly incorporated into the decision process. This expansion of the policy debate is illustrated in the decision memorandum prepared for the president by his senior advisors. The list of issues summarized in that memorandum for President Carter is reprinted in Table 3.

The key issue before the president was summarized in the memorandum: "Should our energy policies and international commitments on energy be deferred or delayed in their implementation so as to minimize the near term inflation effects which an increase in United States prices to world levels would entail?"[58] Those advisors urging immediate decontrol included Energy Secretary Schlesinger, who saw its merits in terms of the achievement of production and conservation incentives and import reductions.[59] Treasury

58. Memorandum for the President, 3 January 1979.
59. Schlesinger thought that a "window of opportunity" had been created by the Iranian crisis in the early months of 1979 that would close by summer. Interview, 22 August 1985.

TABLE 3. *Oil pricing policy issues (reprint from presidential memorandum)*

Energy policy
— replacement cost pricing;
— provision of adequate incentives to stimulate maximum domestic production of oil;
— incentives for conservation and a reduction in oil imports;
— equity in the distribution of any windfalls associated with oil price increases;
— elimination of the current complex system of price controls, allocation, and entitlements.

Economic policy
— reducing inflation, and holding 1979 increases in the Consumer Price Index as low as possible;
— maintaining the strongest possible posture to urge major unions to remain within administration guidelines in upcoming contract negotiations;
— maintaining growth in the economy and in employment;
— improving the balance of trade and the strength of the dollar; and
— regulatory reform objectives.

Foreign policy
— the Bonn pledge to raise the price paid for oil in the U.S. to world prices by the end of 1980;
— the general international concern over inflation, including Bonn pledge to make reduction of inflation a top priority of U.S. economic policy;
— reducing U.S. dependence on oil imports, thereby reducing the trade deficit and strengthening the dollar;
— maintaining U.S. credibility among our key summit allies and assuring their continued efforts toward meeting their own Bonn pledges.

Source. From Jim Schlesinger, Mike Blumenthal, Richard Cooper, Charles Schultze, Alfred Kahn, Jim McIntyre, Henry Owen, Stu Eizenstat. Subject: Domestic Crude Oil Pricing—Information. 3 January 1979, pp. 2–3.

Secretary Blumenthal and his deputy, Anthony Solomon, urged decontrol as a means of improving the balance of trade and strengthening the dollar. Richard Cooper from the State Department and Henry Owen, along with Blumenthal, had been instrumental in the original Bonn pledge, and these officials continued to press for decontrol in accordance with foreign policy and international economic considerations.

Those giving special attention to inflation and domestic political considerations, and seeking a compromise position, included Charles Schultze of the CEA and Alfred Kahn, who headed the Council on Wage and Price Stability. Trade Representative Robert Strauss and Office of Management and Budget Director James McIntrye also sought a compromise solution. Finally, those most resistant to immediate decontrol, and with an eye on the Democratic party politics and constituencies, were Stuart Eizenstat and Vice-President Walter Mondale.

In the meantime, officials debated the relative impacts of the various options on production, conservation, inflation, and foreign policy. The critical meeting came at Camp David on 19 March. Gathered together with his cabinet secretaries, Carter listened to a vigorous debate on oil pricing.

Schlesinger presented what had become a narrow set of options: either immediate decontrol, or a gradual or phased raising of prices to world levels. Schlesinger argued that decontrol was necessary to meet the Bonn pledge, that it would be a symbol to the IEA and OPEC of the administration's seriousness in gaining control over imports, and that, in the absence of such a decision, Congress would get out in front of the issue.[60] Vice-President Mondale spoke in favor of continued control, with a phased program and a windfall tax as second best. Blumenthal argued that immediate decontrol would allow the president to be bold, as he had been with Anwar Sadat and Menachem Begin on the Middle East at Camp David. The decision would help the dollar, and the effect on inflation would only be marginal. Eizenstat argued that immediate decontrol would "kill us on inflation."[61] Carter ended the discussion suggesting that he was hesitant to decontrol without a tax—he could not just give $16 billion to the oil companies. He went on to suggest that total decontrol with a tax to allow for some "consumer compensation" would be his most desired option.[62]

Following the Camp David summit, discussions focused on what type of decontrol option would provide the most likely basis for congressional passage of a windfall profits tax. At a meeting on 23 March 1979, Carter again heard the foreign policy and economic arguments for decontrol. The Council of Economic Advisors, who had wavered on the issue, argued that a phased program would be complete by 1981. Warren Christopher from the State Department argued that decontrol would enhance Carter's world leadership image by keeping the Bonn pledge.

On 5 April 1979, Carter announced his decision to gradually lift price controls on domestic crude oil.[63] Existing law would have ended controls in September 1981; Carter moved to allow this to happen, but also to phase it in over several months. At one level, this was a dramatic turnaround by the Carter administration, as observers noted.[64] But in a more important way, it was not. Executive officials had consistently been looking for policy opportunities to discourage consumption and boost production. Earlier incarnations of proposed energy policy—such as the COET—had sought to insinuate price influences within prevailing political constraints. The new problems created by the second oil shock of 1978–79 also provided new opportunities for more extensive action. Indeed, the new policy was seen as a victory for the original planners of the first Carter energy plan.[65]

60. Eizenstat diary, 19 March 1979.
61. Ibid.
62. Ibid.
63. Martin Tolchin, "Carter to End Price Controls on U.S. Oil and Urge Congress to Tax any 'Windfall Profits,'" *New York Times,* 6 April 1979, p. 1
64. Steven Rattner, "Decontrol a Complete Turnaround in Strategy," *New York Times,* 6 April 1979, p. D3.
65. Richard Halloran, "A Schlesinger Victory Seen in Early Plan," *New York Times,* 7 April 1979, p. 38.

Strikingly, the other groups that struggled throughout the decade over oil pricing were on the outside of the process. Congressional opponents to decontrol were on the defensive. Several congressional representatives continued to attempt to discredit the administration's decision by linking it to the interests of the oil industry.[66] But Congress was no longer able to generate a majority vote for the continuation of controls. In the fall of 1979, Representative Toby Moffit of Connecticut proposed an amendment to a bill to continue price regulations. For the first time in history, the House voted against the extension of controls. The amendment never came up in the Senate.[67] Consumer interests in controls had not changed. Indeed, the 1979 oil shock made the controls more attractive. What had changed was the terms of the debate.

Finally, the oil industry was also outside the decontrol decision. The administration proposed a Windfall Profits Tax designed to capture half of the expected increase in oil revenues. In effect, a severance tax of 50 percent was applied to revenues gained from the release of controlled production. The large oil producers, while opposing the tax, were less disadvantaged by this tax than the earlier COET program. Independent producers, with revenues coming almost exclusively from domestic reserves, vigorously attacked the new tax. While Congress struggled over the tax plan, and old consumer and industry conflicts resurfaced, the final agreement preserved the general character of the Carter proposal. An estimated $227 billion in tax revenue would be transferred from the oil industry to the Federal Treasury by 1988.[68]

Neither consumer nor industry interests were satisfied with the final outcome. The final tax and decontrol plans bore their marks, but the movement towards market pricing was propelled by a distinct agenda that was embraced by executive officials. The position of these officials was strengthened as the issue of oil pricing became a foreign policy concern, which was most forcefully defined as such at the 1978 Bonn summit. In a contentious policy process, executive officials were able to resort to resources uniquely available to the state—the ability to gain special access to the international system and define issues in terms of the nation's foreign economic policy imperatives.

Conclusion

In an era of turbulent oil prices, the choice between regulatory and market policy engages powerful social and economic interests. For consumer and

---

66. Senator John Durkin, speaking for the New England delegation, argued that Secretary of Energy Schlesinger shared "the oil industry's self-serving illusion that all will be well if we only pay higher prices." Quoted in Vietor, *Energy Policy in America*, p. 265.

67. *Congressional Quarterly*, 13 October 1979, p. 2262.

68. Vietor, *Energy Policy in America*, p. 270.

producer groups, the struggle is over who will bear the burden of higher energy costs. In each policy direction there are winners and losers. For executive officials, with a broad political mandate, the problem is not simply one of mediating societal demands. Foreign policy and national economic goals are also at stake. Such were the circumstances in the protracted struggle over oil pricing in the 1970s.

In providing an explanation of oil pricing policy—of the persistence of price controls and their eventual abandonment—two approaches have been discussed. A "societal-centered" approach focuses exclusively on the play of interest groups in the policy process. This explanation accounts for policy change in terms of the changing power or influence of consumer and producer groups engaged in struggle over pricing policy. A second, "state-centered" approach incorporates the play of societal groups but argues that those interests are mediated in important ways by the structure of the state and by the activity of executive officials within it. At stake theoretically is how one is to conceptualize the forces at work in the conduct of American foreign economic policy. Is policy primarily an index of societal interests and influence? Or is there room for the state to make its own mark on policy?

The society-centered explanation is useful to understand the persistence of controls, but even here those interests were highly mediated by the prevailing structure of government. An analysis that takes the capabilities of consumer and industry groups as given is inadequate and cannot fully explain the movement towards decontrol. Price controls had the unintended effect of diminishing the importance of petroleum producers in the policy process. In contrast to the pre-1973 period, those industry groups were not at the center of pricing policy. Regulatory controls served to enlarge the struggle over policy, and consumer interests represented in Congress demonstrated the ability to perpetuate controls. While government officials pursuing their own agenda were also thwarted during this period, the societal divisions over pricing policy created opportunities for those officials to push forward their own positions.

The society-centered explanation of decontrol would account for the movement towards market pricing in terms of the rising influence of producer interests. These interests, however, were divided over oil policy. Indeed, the regulatory controls helped fragment the ranks of the petroleum industry by creating winners and losers. The decontrol decision did not respond directly or even indirectly to industry pressure. If executive officials were simply developing policy that echoed the most vocal and widely embraced societal interests, the continuation of controls would have been far more politically rewarding. A decontrol policy, as I have argued, was accomplished in spite of, rather than because of, industry interests in such a policy. The task of executive officials was in part to differentiate their position on market pricing from those of the petroleum industry. An understanding of the shift requires an appreciation of the role of executive officials as they drew upon resources uniquely available to them in the policy struggle.

A state-centered explanation allows a focus on the independent impacts of executive officials on policy development. In this case, executive officials, embracing national economic and foreign policy agendas, maneuvered to tie oil pricing to a larger set of international issues and, by so doing, recast what was at stake. When the moment arrived in 1979 when the executive had discretionary authority over oil pricing, the fact that this issue was now imbued with larger foreign policy and international economic significance tilted the balance in a political setting that otherwise favored the continuation of controls. The development of a foreign policy rationale for decontrol, codified at the 1978 Bonn summit, allowed the decision to go forward. While industry interests had a stake in that decision, the logic of decision lay elsewhere. Moreover, the simultaneous proposal by the Carter administration for a Wind Fall Profits Tax was in part designed to insure that the decontrol decision would not be an unmitigated financial boon to the industry.

While many groups struggled over oil-pricing policy, an explanation that fails to include the role of executive officials who were pursuing their own agenda and intervening to recast the issues at stake is incomplete and misleading. The struggle over oil-pricing policy unfolded within a distinctive set of government institutions. The American state helped shape the decontrol of oil, not in the guise of a single, integrated institutional actor, but as a piece of strategically important terrain that influenced the course of battle over pricing policy and that provided resources and advantages necessary to win. In the first instance, those institutional advantages went to consumers, who used price controls as an unexpected device to maintain shelter from adverse international economic change. Ultimately, the institutional advantages accrued to executive officials in their special access to the international system. Here the device took the form of a diplomatic commitment that changed the nature of what was at stake in the domestic debate.

The image of a "weak" American state is that of a government able to do little more than register the demands of societal groups. Policy in a "weak" state can best be traced to demands placed upon the state from the society and economy. The image is useful as a way of depicting the fragmentation and dispersal of power within government and the enduring constraints on government officials. However, the image is essentially negative, suggesting what the American state is not. It is not very effective in capturing the independent and intervening role of government officials in policymaking or the range of resources available to those officials. The image of a "strong" state is also inappropriate. As this case suggests, what is needed is a more nuanced understanding of the structure of the American state and the implications that structure has for influencing societal and government actors and for the course of policy development.

Ideas, institutions, and American trade policy
Judith Goldstein

Nowhere is America's hegemonic decline more evident than in changing trade patterns. The United States trade balance, a measure of the international demand for American goods, is suffering historic deficits. Lowered demand for American goods has led to the under-utilization of both labor and capital in a growing number of traditionally competitive American industries. Conversely, Americans' taste for foreign goods has never been so great. Japanese cars, European steel, Third World textiles, to name a few, are as well produced as their American counterparts and arrive on the U.S. market at a lower cost.

It is no surprise that as America's trade position suffers, the subject of commercial policy again looms large on the political agenda. The questioning of America's trade policy was common throughout the 19th and early 20th century. In the post-World War II period, however, a consensus arose that America should have an open, liberal trade posture. In the late 1960s, those who questioned that commitment found little support. By the 1980s, however, newspapers and journals were heralding the return of protectionism and sounding the death knell for America's liberal trade policies.

Changes in America's market position also have led academics to predict policy change. Such predictions are no surprise. They derive directly from current analyses of American politics. Among scholars, the explanation for protectionism is often presented as the flip side of a theory of trade liberalization. The lack of the causal structure that explains the choice to pursue openness predicts protection.

Earlier versions of this article were presented at the annual meeting of the American Political Science Association, New Orleans, 29 August–1 September 1985, and the Conference on the Political Economy of Trade Policy sponsored by the National Bureau of Economic Research, January 1986. I would like to thank Beverly Crawford, James Conrad, Jeff Frieden, Stephan Haggard, David Lake, William Lowry, Joanne Gowa, Cynthia Hody, G. John Ikenberry, Michael Mastanduno, and four anonymous reviewers for their excellent comments and assistance.

International Organization 42, 1, Winter 1988

Two genres of theory offer predictions for American trade policy. One looks to social pressures as an explanation for policy; the other looks to international structure. Of the two, the former dominates the study of American trade policy. Among American scholars, the seminal analysis of trade policy was conducted by E. E. Schattschneider.[1] His analysis of 1929–30 Smoot Hawley Act made tariff policy the prima facie proof of extensive interest group influence over the making of American laws. Although studies of later legislation led to revisions in the original analysis of the tariff-making process, an often implicit belief that interest group activity determines protectionism remains ingrained in analyses of American economic policy.[2]

The alternative approach used by international relations scholars considers trade as a foreign policy issue and looks to international structure as the determinant of state interest. These analysts argue that liberal trade and an absence of protectionism were prefaced by America's ascendancy to hegemony after World War II.[3] With a decline in American power has come a decline in interest and resources with which the U.S. can maintain a liberal trade regime. As in the interest group approach, the loss of American power and market share leads to the prediction of an increase in trade protectionism.

This article argues that neither of these approaches captures the dynamic of protectionism in the U.S. Both approaches envision government as a conduit translating either group pressure or international demands into state policy. Neither approach looks at the institutional arrangements through which domestic demands and international constraints are filtered. In this article, state structure is used to explain policy. The argument made is that state structures are historically determined and reflect the biases of decision-makers present at their creation. Critical in decisions of protection is the evaluation by the state of the legitimacy of claims brought forth by social actors. What the law designates as a legitimate claim for aid has varied systematically over time. This article explains the origins and scope of three types of legitimate claims for state aid.

---

1. E. E. Schattschneider, *Politics, Pressures and the Tariff* (New York: Prentice-Hall, 1935).

2. See, for example: Robert Baldwin, "The Political Economy of Postwar U.S. Trade Policy," *Bulletin,* 1976–4. (New York: N.Y.U. Graduate School of Business, 1976); *The Political Economy of U.S. Import Policy* (Cambridge: MIT Press, 1985); "The Inefficacy of Trade Policy," *Essays in International Finance* 150 (December 1982), pp. 1–26. See also Raymond Bauer, Ithiel DeSola Pool, and Lewis Anthony Dexter, *American Business and Public Policy: The Politics of Foreign Trade* (Chicago: Aldine, 1983); and J. Pincus, "Pressure Groups and the Pattern of Tariffs," *Journal of Political Economy* 83 (August 1975), pp. 757–78.

3. Robert O. Keohane and Joseph Nye, *Power and Interdependence* (Boston: Little, Brown, 1977); Keohane, "The Theory of Hegemonic Stability and Changes in International Economic Regimes, 1967–1977," in Oli Holsti, Randolph M. Siverson, and Alexander L. George, *Change in the International System* (Boulder: Westview, 1980); and Stephen Krasner, "State Power and the Structure of International Trade," *World Politics* 28 (April 1976), pp. 317–47.

Understanding protectionism

The explanation for American protectionism or the systematic exclusion of industries from general American trade policy has three components. First, policy-making is dominated by a belief in the efficacy of free trade. That belief has been encased in post-World War II laws and institutional structures that service continued trade liberalization and ensure minimal legitimacy for social claims for protectionism. Second, U.S. policy has a "fair" trade component. Previous to America's move towards openness in the mid-1930s, policy was protectionist. From the end of the Civil War to 1934, policy reflected the belief that the U.S. could maintain an isolationist policy with respect to imports and still expand trade in foreign markets. The impact of this period is evident in laws and institutions that legitimate social claims for state intervention to favor domestic producers over foreign competitors. Third, there is a welfare component to U.S. policy. Policies exist that are redistributive. The state both compensates uncompetitive sectors and helps industries adjust to foreign competition that results from liberalization. Viewing America's policy on protectionism, an analyst finds state policies based on often contradictory ideas about the correct relationship between state and society. Laissez-faire, intervention against foreign producers, and intervention to redistribute social goods all coexist as legitimate state policies.

How can the coexistence of three apparently contradictory policies be explained? Most simply, these different policies exist because institutions, once created, live substantially beyond the mandate they originally served. Government organizations do change but more slowly than does their environment. In the U.S., a society embalmed in the "rule of law," legal constraints encourage the layering, rather than the replacing, of government institutions.[4]

As in geological surveys, the institutions of American government can be organized by the historical period of their birth. Institutions are created to serve a particular legal mandate. Mandates evolve from a political consensus that was generated to support a particular response to a government or social need. Institutions, then, reflect a set of dominant ideas translated through legal mechanisms into formal government organizations. If ideas become encased in institutions through legal procedures, they will continue to have policy impact over time. Generally, this institutional influence derives from the existence of formal organizations whose rules, norms, expectations, and traditions establish constraints on individuals within these

---

4. For an interesting argument on the force of legal constraints in trade policy, see Alan Wolff, "The Role of America's Trade Policy in the International Competitiveness of American Industry," Harvard Business School, 1984.

organizations, on elected leaders outside these organizations, and on society in general.[5]

Institutional structures alone are an insufficient explanation for postwar American trade policies. As critical is the belief system of those individuals who enforce laws.[6] In the U.S., liberal beliefs about trade policy have dominated the debate and thinking of those involved with policymaking. In the post-Depression period, liberalism gave decision-makers both a design for economic reconstruction and organizing principles that directed what was then seen as a problematic relationship between government and society. The Great Depression was the necessary prerequisite for the acceptance of liberalism. The Depression not only led to international decline and war but also led to a domestic crisis emanating from the fear that congressional pork-barrel politics had caused or at least contributed in a major way to great economic and political dislocation. Crisis was a requisite, a necessary but not sufficient cause, for liberalism to take on an ideological character. In its early years, liberalism can be explained in that it served the interest of the U.S. and its central decision-makers. However, the existence of unprecedented postwar affluence and power for the U.S., which came to be associ-

---

5. See James March and Johan Olsen, "The New Institutionalism: Organizational Factors in Political Life," *American Political Science Review* 78 (September 1984), pp. 734–50, for an overview of the institutional perspective.

6. There is a vast and growing literature on the role of ideas, cognitions, values, norms, and ideologies in the political process. In this essay, ideas refer to shared intellectual outlooks. In particular, the shared outlook is the efficacy of government pursuing one economic policy rather than another. In this essay, I do not address questions of why one set of ideas dominates the process by which society transmits particular outlooks or the cognitive process associated with having a particular outlook. Following closely on the way that John Odell uses ideas as a variable in *U.S. International Monetary Policy: Markets, Power, and Ideas as Sources of Change* (Princeton, N.J.: Princeton University Press, 1982), the emphasis of the essay is on the political influence of the content of an idea, not the cognitive processes. It is assumed that ideas reflect more than the translation of international needs into domestic policy. Rather, we assume that there are competing interpretations of optimal economic policy for a given environment and the ascendance of one policy idea, rather than another, has important policy ramifications.

This way of viewing ideas and, on a macro level, ideology is similar to that used in a variety of subfields within political science. For instance, Philip Converse defines belief systems as "a configuration of ideas and attitudes in which the elements are bound together by some form of constraint or functional interdependence." Converse, "The Nature of Belief Systems in Mass Publics" in David Apter, *Ideology and Discontent* (New York: Free Press, 1964), p. 207. Looking at organizations, Franz Schurmann suggests that organizations can be characterized by "a manner of thinking" and concludes that there are ideologies of organization in addition to those of classes and individuals. An organizational ideology is defined as "a systematic set of ideas with action consequences serving the purpose of creating and using organization." *Ideology and Organization in Communist China* (Berkeley: University of California Press, 1966), p. 18. As defined by Douglass North, "Ideologies are intellectual efforts to rationalize the behavioral patterns of individuals and groups." *Structure and Change in Economic History* (New York: W. W. Norton, 1981), p. 48. These scholars agree on a definition of ideas or ideology; variations exist on the explanatory value and independence of ideas. A number of other social scientists, in addition to those mentioned above, look to "ideas" as explanation for policy. See, for instance, Anthony King, "Ideas, Institutions and the Policies of Governments: A Comparative Analysis," *British Journal of Political Science* 2 (July 1973); and Louis Hartz, *The Liberal Tradition in America* (New York: Harcourt, 1955).

ated with a particular international economic policy, elevated liberalism into a realm untouchable by interest group politics. Crisis followed by affluence became the necessary and sufficient criteria for the entrenchment of liberal doctrine.[7]

In sum, this article reexamines protectionism in the U.S. In particular, it attempts an explanation for patterns of aid. We begin with the observation that over time, societal actors have become increasingly threatened by foreign producers. In the postwar period, the U.S. has continually lowered barriers to trade at home. The result has been that American producers have encountered increasingly stiff competition at home as well as abroad. Average ad valorem tariffs have declined dramatically since the 1930s (see Table 1). Import penetration has increased more quickly than either exports or GNP. In the 30 years following World War II, Americans have almost tripled their consumption of foreign goods. Whereas only 5 percent of personal consumption expenditures were for imports in 1945, that proportion increased to 14 percent by 1984. Both industry and labor have responded to loss in market share by attempting to gain state aid. Petitions for aid increased dramatically in the 1970s in all the categories examined below. Although Congress showed little interest in protectionist legislation in the 1960s, it entertained hundreds of bills pertaining to some aspect of America's trade program in the 1970s and 1980s.

This article focuses on five particular mechanisms available to these complainants. They are differentiated by the historical period in which Congress first created each form of aid. The article maintains that variation in aid is greater across the various forms of protectionism than within each form. Types of aid should be differentiated by the legal criteria used by the government to adjudicate cases. These differences in laws reflect historic shifts in ideas about what constitutes a legitimate claim for state aid. Laws alone, however, cannot explain the pattern of aid in the U.S. Equally important are the beliefs of those who adjudicate the laws. Thus, "ideas" appear twice in the explanation of protectionism. First, they are critical independent variables that explain why different laws arise in different historical periods. Second, the ideas or beliefs of those who administer the laws affect outcomes. However, contemporary beliefs of decision-makers affect the ability of groups to obtain aid only to the extent that there is room for discretion in the administration of these laws.

This article does not seek to give a general theory of American trade policy. Rather, its purpose is to show the value of studying the institutional

7. Within government, a number of mechanisms reinforced the policy dominance of free trade ideas. For example, in the mid-1970s, members of the House Ways and Means Committee had to pass a "free trade" test to be recruited onto the committee. Throughout the postwar period, economists have been united in support for free trade, influencing economic options presented to central decision-makers. In a third example, shared perceptions by a cohort of government officials about the causes of the Depression continue to influence policy.

TABLE 1. *Change in U.S. GNP, imports, and tariffs, 1948–84 (%)*

Years	GNP	Imports	Tariff
1948–58	74	80	− 20
1958–68	93	160	+ 2
1968–78	146	423	− 47
1978–84	155	223	− 42

Source. Calculated from U.S. Government, *Historical Statistics of the United States: Colonial Times to the Present* (Washington, D.C.: GPO), part 1, 1970, 1975, p. 224; Part 2, pp. 884–900; *Statistical Abstract of the U.S.* (Washington, D.C.: GPO), 1973, pp. 778–90; 1980, pp. 439, 872–74; 1982–83, pp. 833–44; 1984, pp. 448–49, 831–41.

and cognitive bases for American policy. We argue that neither the disintegration of American power nor the rise of interest group activity fully explains the pattern of protectionism. A more complete explanation resides in the study of state institutions themselves.

The role of the state

Models traditionally used to explain commercial policy underplay the autonomy of the state. Government is an important variable in both societal and international structural theories, but one portrayed as essentially regulated by variables external to government institutions. The state is either an arena in which social groups fight over the allocation of scarce resources or a necessary vehicle for translating international constraints and opportunities into public policy. Studies abound on the functioning of American government institutions. Few, however, attempt to explain policy as the result of the interests and beliefs of the state. Rather, independent state action is not expected. When found, such policy is explained away as the anomalous result of unintended actions. In essence, the state is often portrayed in modern American scholarship as epiphenomenal.

In the 1970s, scholars reacted to the lack of a shared ontological conception of the state. From both the field of comparative politics and the field of international relations, questions of national development, of economic policy, and of national interest led analysts to seek a common definition of the state.[8] Following Krasner, four definitions have emerged from this discussion.[9]

1. The state both as a legal order and a public bureaucracy (or administrative apparatus) modeled as a coherent totality.

8. E. Nordlinger, *On the Autonomy of the Democratic State* (Cambridge: Harvard University Press, 1981). Theda Skocpol, *States and Social Revolutions* (Cambridge: Cambridge University Press, 1979). Charles Tilly, ed., *The Formation of National States in Western Europe* (Princeton, N.J.: Princeton University Press, 1975).

9. Stephen Krasner, "Approaches to the State: Alternative Conceptions and Historical Dynamics," *Comparative Politics* 16 (January 1984).

2. The state as the collective set of personnel who occupy positions of decisional authority in the polity.

3. The state as ruling class.

4. The state as normative order.

Given these choices, what is the view of the state taken here? There are two. The state, when seen as an exogenous source of explanation for phenomena, as in much of this article, is implicitly being defined as in the first definition. The state itself, its institutional design, its legal precepts, and its normative views explain particular policy options. Use of such a shorthand explanation for public policy is, however, time-bound. It is bound by crucial periods in which social forces, not state institutions, determine policy. At these times, the state is better conceptualized as in the second definition— that is, merely as a collective set of personnel more or less representing social groupings. The plasticity of the state suggested in the second definition is, however, temporary. Winning coalitions cement their victory by creating institutions which, by design, protect their interests. Change then occurs slowly and only under duress. The state moves forward according to its inner logic even as those social groupings, so influential in the past, find that changes in their needs do not lead to changes in state policy.

The First definition is closest to the view of the state used in most studies of international relations. When the national interest for a single state is deduced from the distribution of power of all states, government is portrayed as a totality.[10] Few international relations scholars, however, are willing to ignore domestic variables in favor of "black boxing" government processes. Still, many favor international structure as a primary determinant of a nation's interests and policies. The compromise is to define the state explicitly as in the first definition. Although bringing back the politics of the nation-state unit, policies do not reduce the push and pull of the societal actors. Rather, the state is the institution which interprets, more or less correctly, national needs. Thus, international structure can remain the basic determinant of the national interest. States do, however, vary in their ability to act on these interests. Administrative units vary in their ability to extract from society resources necessary to pursue optimal national policies.[11]

There exists a major difference between this international structural approach and the one used here. The difference relates not to the definition of the state nor to qualifications about the capabilities of state, but rather to the importance of international structure of our understanding of behavior. The international distribution of power is not accorded a central

10. Kenneth Waltz, *Theory of International Politics* (Reading, Mass: Addison-Wesley, 1979).

11. Peter J. Katzenstein, "Introduction: Domestic and International Forces and Strategies of Foreign Economic Policy," *International Organization* 31 (Autumn 1977), pp. 587–607.

role in the explanation of American policy in this article. Since we seek to explain the lack of change in American trade policy in the face of changing international power relations, international structure cannot be the explanation. Instead, the explanation is rooted in American politics and American history.

In sum, two sets of domestic variables are essential to the explanation of state-society relations. These variables are only tangentially related to foreign policy goals; they do not constitute ad hoc additions to the core of a structural theory.[12] To the point, instead of arguing that ideas and institutions become operative at times when structural constraints are not present, it is argued here that ideas and institutions are always operative and are isomorphic with state needs, as detailed by an international structure approach only in periods of international crisis. The status of ideas and institutions in normal times moves from that of intervening variable, as in other statist analyses, into an independent role.

An analysis of trade policy would be incomplete without consideration of state institutions. Public organizations establish, maintain, and monitor the rules under which social actors seek protection. Variables rooted in social action alone are not sufficient to explain variation in the amount of aid groups receive from government. Government preferences, too, affect outcomes. Although in the long term groups may be able to organize and change the general character of American institutions, in the short term laws and norms have significant impact on their ability to translate social action into public goods.

This article maintains that social actors do not face a uniform set of constraints in obtaining protection. Analogously, state and social actors are interacting in a number of different ''games'' of protection. These games vary in their rules; they vary in their payoff matrices. This variation makes it easier for groups to receive one type of aid than another and encourages actors to pursue particular strategies.

The next sections examine three types of protectionist policy. Two themes are repeated. First, each section argues for the uniqueness of that type of policy. Each policy is identified with a set of legitimating ideas, with an organizational design that translates these ideas into law, and with a unique set of political processes. Once established that there exist three different types of legal institutions, data on the extent of change in protectionist institutions are examined. Highlighted is the finding that the U.S. is not simply becoming more protectionist over time. Although state responsiveness has risen, the more interesting variations are between types of aid, not over time.

12. Imre Lakatos, ''Falsification and the Methodology of Scientific Research Programs,'' in Lakatos and Alan Musgrave, eds., *Criticism and the Growth of Knowledge* (Cambridge: Cambridge University Press, 1970); Robert Keohane, ''Theory of World Politics: Structural Realism and Beyond,'' in Ada W. Finifter, ed., *Political Science: The State of the Discipline* (Washington, D.C.: APSA, 1983).

The liberal idea

In the postwar period, America's commercial policy has centered on the creation and perpetuation of a liberal trade regime. As envisioned after World War II, that regime called for the opening of national borders to the free flow of goods, services, and capital. Although many aspects of the liberal regime were never accepted by America's trading partners, the U.S. has continually attempted to inculcate the neoclassical economic view of trade into international practice.

Although components of the liberal regime, most particularly the General Agreement in Tariffs and Trade (GATT), have come under criticism, support for liberalism has only minimally eroded among American central decision-makers. Liberalism still holds a social position not unlike a "sacred cow" in the policymaking community. In content, America's liberal ideas stem from two intellectual roots: 19th-century British thought and 18th-century American political philosophy.

The institutionalization of the liberal idea of free trade can be dated to 1934. Although entertained as a policy earlier in the 19th century (for example, see debate on Walker tariff, 1846), it was only after 1934 that American central decision-makers looked to free trade ideas as a basis of policy. The primary event that prefaces this move to liberalism is the Great Depression. The failure of the Smoot–Hawley tariff of 1929–30 to deal with economic decline set up a policymaking crisis. The delegitimization of protectionism forced the political community to search for an alternative theoretical approach to explain past errors and provide guidelines for future behavior.

Economic decline breeds numerous interpretations. The Great Depression was no exception. Two sets of events allowed for the particular shift towards free trade. First, institutional responsibility for tariff-making shifted to the executive. A Democratic Congress relinquished its constitutionally granted mandate under the guidance of a strong Democratic president. Party discipline alone, however, does not explain this change. The president needed to have a cognitive explanation of the interconnections between electoral misfortune, the Great Depression, and the protectionist policies of earlier administrations to gain congressional agreement. These connections were made repeatedly to the President and Congress by "free traders" such as Secretary of State Cordell Hull.

Liberalism began as one policy alternative among many. It became a policy bias only after the U.S. began to prosper under the free trade regime. Although in 1934 Congress undertook a policy of liberalization, there was no immediate opening of America's borders. The lesson of the Depression was far more modest. It was clear that Congress could no longer protect noncompetitive sectors of the American economy. Market forces could not be ignored in the rush to aid constituents. Politically, this meant that powerful private interests wishing protection would have to be ignored. In the 1930s, however, central decision-makers did not agree that free trade was the only policy option for the U.S. Liberalism became ingrained as a policy bias as intellectuals and elected officials attributed the return to abundance and postwar growth to the successive, although incremental, policy of reducing barriers to trade. Success was taken to mean that those who argued that liberalism was the optimal policy for the U.S. were correct. By the early 1970s, liberalism had become more than a policy option, it was a policy bias and a policy constraint.[13]

Liberalization after 1934 was characterized by two processes. First, state mechanisms were developed that supported liberal trade. Not only did Congress allocate tariff-making authority to the executive, but it repeatedly endorsed the right of the U.S. to engage in negotiations to lower tariffs while nurturing bureaucracies whose mandate was to foster liberal trade relations.[14] And second, liberalism was accepted only with safeguards. Understanding that interest groups would continue to demand particularistic import preferences, Congress created a set of safeguards to protect its policies from group interference. The method used was to create alternative mechanisms through which groups could articulate their needs. Instead of going to Congress, interest groups could go to bureaucratic agencies whose legal task was to placate potential congressional clients. As an example of this process, we turn to the escape clause.

Escape clause

In the postwar years, Congress has instituted a number of measures that protect constituents unable to compete with foreign producers within the U.S. The measure with the longest history of both legislation and adjudication is the "escape clause." As compared with protectionist legislation written before America's move towards liberalism, the escape clause is more difficult to obtain, may be overruled at a number of decision points, and once received, needs repeated renewals to keep protection in force. In short, although potentially a device that could create great barriers to trade, the escape clause was created in a manner making attainment a difficult and arduous process. As such, this legislation has deterred a rise in protectionism and helped maintain liberalism. Cases are decided by the International Trade Commission (ITC), an independent bureaucracy, that selects recipients based on a set of objective criteria established by Congress. As opposed

13. See Stephen Blank, "Britain: The Politics of Foreign Economic Policy, the Domestic Economy and the Problem of Pluralist Stagnation," *International Organization* 31 (Autumn 1977), pp. 673–721 for a similar explanation of British monetary policy.

14. A number of good accounts of the liberalization process have been written. See, for example: Robert Pastor, *Congress and the Politics of U.S. Foreign Economic Policy: 1929–1976* (Berkeley: University of California Press, 1980); and Ernest Preeg, *Trades and Diplomats: An Analyses of the Kennedy Round Negotiations under the General Agreement on Tariff and Trade* (Washington, D.C.: Brookings Institution, 1973).

to the pre-1934 period, the ITC, not Congress, deals with formal petitions for aid. By distancing congressional representatives, the ITC acts as a buffer, mediating potentially disruptive political pressures.

Since the escape clause was instituted by Executive Order in 1947 and incorporated into statute in 1951, the U.S. has always included safeguard provisions in trade treaties and legislation. The escape clause provision allows an industry that has been seriously injured by imports to be exempted from an American trade agreement that would lower its tariff. The initial intent of the escape clause was to accomplish what the old peril point had failed to do—that is, to keep imports at a level that precluded injury to domestic producers.

The concept of the escape clause was first used as a provision in a 1942 trade agreement with Mexico. The idea reappeared in debate over the 1945 trade act as a compromise by the executive following congressional transference of increased tariff-making authority. In return for legislation, Truman issued Executive Order 9381 (1/25/48), establishing that all future trade agreements were to include escape clause provisions.[15]

To ensure congressional assent, the U.S. backed inclusion of an escape clause provision, similar to domestic law, in the GATT. The provision, Article XIX, was condemned by then President Truman as "an embarrassment to be avoided in the interest of maintaining an image of American leadership and dependability in world and foreign affairs."[16] Once the escape provision was in place, however, the U.S. was the first to invoke it four years later, in a case involving hatter's fur. Under American tutelage, GATT held that the U.S. was "entitled to the benefit of the doubt" in its estimation of criteria of injury. This somewhat loose interpretation of Article XIX led to the prediction that the liberal tenets of GATT would be defeated in an onslaught of cases using a nation's own definition of injury as grounds for protection. However, the use of Article XIX to escape liberalization by the U.S. or any of its trading partners has been limited. In effect, the magnitude of changes in trade patterns over the postwar period has *not* been reflected in use of Article XIX.

Although the earlier intent of the escape clause procedure was frozen into GATT rules, its American counterpart has evolved over time. In fact, escape clause procedures have been reexamined each time Congress has mandated further liberalization; in substance, however, much of the original program remains. By statute, a request from the president, Congress, Senate Committee on Finance, or House Ways and Means Committee, an ITC motion, or an application from an interested party (industry, union, or association) will induce an escape clause investigation. The investigation, according to the 1951 law, determines whether any industry "product on which a trade

---

15. William Ris, "Escape Clause Relief Under the Trade Act of 1974: New Standards, Same Results," *Columbia Journal of Transnational Law* 16 (1977), p. 299.
16. Ibid., p. 300.

agreement concession has been granted is *as a result,* in whole or in part, of the customs treatment reflecting such concession being imported in such increased quantities either *actual or relative,* as to *cause or threaten to cause injury* to the domestic industry producing like or directly competitive products" (emphasis mine). If the ITC rules that imports did threaten an industry, it can recommend an increased import barrier. The finding, however, is by statute only a recommendation to the president. The president could choose to ignore the finding, to accept the finding but choose a different remedy, or to accept the advice of the ITC.

Since 1951, Congress has reviewed this legislation three times. An examination of the textual changes in the law reveals the 1962 criteria to be the most difficult to fulfill. This becomes obvious by looking at the evolution of the phrases emphasized above.

First, the 1951 Act required imports to have "contributed substantially" to injury or threat of injury. In 1962, this criterion was considered too permissive; instead, imports had to be "the main factor" in causing injury in order to justify aid. Under the Trade Act of 1974, the criteria again eased. Increased imports had to be only "a substantial cause" rather than "the major cause" of injury.[17]

Second, the early law required proof that injury resulted from a customs concession. Again, Congress in 1962 voted to stipulate more strictly that causal connection. The 1962 Trade Expansion Act stipulates that injury must have resulted "in major part" from the concession not just "in whole or in part." When reexamined in 1974, the newer requirement was dropped.

Third, the specification of whether imports have to increase in absolute or in relative terms to constitute grounds for protection has varied. In 1951, either constituted just cause; in 1962, however, the tightening of aid criteria led to legislation which specified that only an absolute increase in imports warranted aid. This interpretation was again overturned in 1974 for the earlier, more flexible interpretation.

The one criterion that has been consistently eased is the specification of what constitutes serious injury. In 1951, the ITC was mandated to consider, among other things, "a downward trend of product, employment, prices, profits, or wages in the domestic industry concerned, or a decline in sales, an increase in imports, either actual or relative to domestic production, a higher or growing inventory, or a decline in the proportion of the domestic market supplied by domestic producers."[18] In 1962 this mandate to the ITC was expanded to include "all economic factors which it considered relevant, including idling of productive facilities, inability to operate at a level of reasonable profit, and unemployment or underemployment."[19] The factors

17. Substantial cause was defined as one "which is important and not less than any other cause."

18. Stanley Metzger, "The Trade Expansion Act of 1962," *Columbia Law Review* 61 (Spring 1961), p. 444.

19. Ibid., p. 445.

to be considered were further expanded in 1974. Congress declared that the ITC must consider, among other things, the "idling of productive facilities, the ability to reap a profit, unemployment and underemployment and downward trends in production, profits, wages, or employment in the affected industries."[20]

Although these procedural issues have been addressed and changed by Congress, a basic relationship between the executive and the legislature has not been violated. In particular, Congress has never taken from the executive his jurisdiction as final judge on escape clause cases. Although sentiment has been expressed for a renewal of a congressional role in aiding industries injured by imports, the reaction of Congress has been to give more power to the bureaucracy through easing aid requirements, not to take authority from the president. As early as the 1962 hearings, the position expressed on aid was that "relief ought not to be denied for reasons that have nothing whatever to do with the merits of the case. . . . In particular . . . no U.S. industry which has suffered serious injury should be cut off from relief for foreign policy reasons."[21]

Yet the 1962 Act was the most antiprotectionist to come out of committee. During these hearings, Congress expanded executive discretion with the inclusion of adjustment assistance as an additional alternative to using the escape clause without establishing enforceable rules to dictate presidential choice. It was not that curtailment of executive privilege was not discussed. Congress dictated guidelines for the president but did not choose to make them mandatory.

For instance, Congress has expressed preferences for one type of aid to be given over others in positive escape clause cases. In 1974 hearings, a popular opinion espoused in Congress was that in the choice between consumer interests and the interests of those unemployed, "the President should adopt the latter course and protect the industry and the jobs associated with the industry."[22] In terms of referred remedies, Congress stated that an import duty was to be considered and used first while an Orderly Marketing Agreement (OMA) was to be considered last. This advice has been repeatedly ignored.

In sum, although Congress has argued about the form, amount, and duration of escape clause aid to industries affected by imports, the power to make those decisions has remained with the president. In legislation aimed at affecting the decision-making criteria used by the bureaucracy, Congress has maintained guidelines established in the 1950s, a time when there was little interest and minimal pressure for protectionism. Although a presidential veto of an ITC decision could be overturned by Congress with increased ease over time, the power has never been exercised. Rather,

20. Ris, "Escape Clause Relief," p. 306.
21. Ibid., p. 307.
22. Ibid., p. 309.

Congress is content with what appears to be symbolic measures to aid industry.

That Congress plays only a symbolic role in aiding industry is counterintuitive, given the structural relationship between Congress and powerful private groups. Congress has been a focal point for societal pressures aimed at gaining relief from imports. Even though negotiating authority was given to the president in 1934, the ability to legislate protective duties remains with Congress. Yet Congress has not responded to industry malaise with legislation—on the occasions when a quota was passed by one of the houses, executive intervention has forestalled implementation. Although the 1980s have been filled with accounts of impending congressional intervention, the large increase in bills entered in the *Congressional Record* has led to relatively few changes in law. The fear of a "slippery slope" to protectionism continues to affect the legislative process.

The role Congress does play is to establish criteria by which the technocrats in the ITC or the other trade-related bureaucracies adjudicate cases. As more pressure is placed on Congress, it responds by expanding the powers of the bureaucracy, not by intervention. Congress retains the right to hold hearings and has done so for key sectors such as the steel and automobile industries. However, once a hearing is completed, it is executive, not congressional, action that dictates whether that industry will receive effective aid. Congressional consent is necessary to appoint commissioners to the ITC. And congressional hearings and pressures from interested private groups affect the constitution of the ITC itself. But, since even a pro-protectionist ruling by the ITC in an escape clause case will be meaningless if the executive does not accept the ITC's advice, the role of Congress is severely constrained.[23]

In sum, two facts emerge from this review of the legal history of the escape clause. First, legislation has changed, but in only marginal ways, over the postwar period. In the periods before 1962 and after 1974, the criteria for escape clause aid were easier to meet than under the 1962 Act. We expect that ITC decisions will reflect these changes in law. Second, although Congress has changed the legal criteria over time, the basic design of the legislation has remained substantially the same. Congress sets standards, the ITC adjudicates cases, but the president makes all final decisions on relief and amount. In short, the law gives much latitude to the president. The power of the executive office to maintain trade policy is the institutional design that has fostered liberalism in the postwar period.

Escape clause data

To illustrate the points discussed above, two types of data are presented. Both evaluate the state's behavior in granting aid to import-sensitive indus-

---

23. For an analysis of executive–congressional relations, see Pastor, *Congress and Politics*.

TABLE 2. *Escape clause cases (in effect 1958–81)*

Year[a]	Average no. petitions/year (total)	ITC acceptance rate[b]	Presidential acceptance rate	
			Approved[c]	Approved with ITC relief
1958–62	11 (56)	.27	.14	.07
1963–74	3 (31)	.30	.13	.03
1975–78	10 (40)	.60	.23(.20)[d]	.03
1979–83	4 (18)	.56	.39(.23)[d]	.11

a. Organized by legislative periods.
b. Includes split votes and cases to extend relief due to expire.
c. An award of adjustment assistance alone is not considered aid.
d. Number in parentheses indicates acceptance rate for an industry not already covered by escape clause action.
Source. U.S. International Trade Commission, *Annual Report* (Washington, D.C.: GPO, 1975–82); U.S. President, *Annual Report of the President of the U.S. on the Trade Agreements Program* (Washington, D.C.: GPO, 1958–82); U.S. Tariff Commission, *Annual Report* (Washington, D.C.: GPO, 1958–74).

tries. Table 2 gives the petition activity, ITC response, and final presidential decisions on all escape clause cases in effect between 1958 and 1983. Table 3 looks at cases adjudicated for a sample twenty-year period and models the attributes of those who get aid.

Table 2 presents data according to the major legislative periods discussed above. Two points are noteworthy. First, petition activity is not a good predictor of either ITC or presidential acceptance rates. The years of lowest acceptance rate by the ITC are during the period of highest interest. Conversely, the highest acceptance rate is in the most recent period, when there have been relatively fewer petitions for aid. Thus, the ITC does not simply respond to increasing numbers of petitions by increasing aid. Presidential acceptance, too, seems unresponsive to petition activity. The president was most responsive to petitions after 1979, a period of relatively few escape clause petitions. Furthermore, in the periods before 1962 and after 1979, the president was most likely to accept both the form and amount of aid recommended by the ITC. Yet petition activity varied greatly in these periods.

Second, better explanations for acceptance rates are legislated changes in the law. The ITC has increased its rate of acceptance from 27 to 62 percent in the time period examined. As expected, the ITC acceptance rate increased sharply after passage of the 1974 law. This relationship between congressional legislation and ITC votes is less apparent in the 1958–62 period. Although the legislation was similar to that found after 1974, the acceptance rate was low. This probably reflects fewer industries meeting the criteria of injury as a result of a yet unlowered tariff.

Although ITC behavior seems predicated on congressional action, presidential behavior is less explicable from these tables. Two aspects of presidential behavior are revealed. First, presidents have routinely vetoed ITC decisions. More than half the time the ITC decides an industry has met the legal criteria for aid, the president overrules that decision on grounds of the national economic interest. On the whole, presidential action has served to minimize the potentially protectionist decisions of the ITC. The presidential acceptance rate, however, is on the rise. The rate was stable in the period through 1974, but the president accepted more cases in the following years. Second, presidents who accept ITC decisions do not necessarily accept the ITC remedies. This presidential authority is one of the more obscure but important forms of influence he has on trade policy. We can assume that ITC decisions on amount of aid reflect the advice of technical experts. Still, the president has repeatedly accepted the finding of injury while awarding a remedy below that needed for industrial recovery. This pattern suggests that the president uses his authority to minimize closure of the American market.

The effect of aid that was "too little, too late" is reflected in measures of market penetration. Looking at market shares in 1981, in only 1.6 percent of the escape clause cases decided by 1978 did aid receipt lead to either domestic market growth or maintenance.[24] In short, very few industries receive effective aid. The U.S. may be giving aid, but it is not necessarily aid that explicitly stops imports. And, although there has been an increase in the president's acceptance rate since 1979, the number declines if only new cases are considered; the data show that it is easier to garner a continuance in aid than to qualify initially for protection.

In sum, the escape clause reflects the biases of its creators. As compared with the legislation considered in the next section, the escape clause allows much discretion on the part of both the ITC and the president. Although elements of the law have been scrutinized in the postwar period, the criteria for aid are more open-ended than in other types of protectionist legislation. The ability of the president to veto an ITC decision or accept the decision and change the remedy is further evidence that Congress sees executive discretion to be legitimate in trade policy. The effect of executive discretion has been to maintain openness whenever possible, thus counteracting the more protectionist pressures felt by Congress. This is not to say that the executive has never granted protection. Under sufficient pressure, any elected leader will respond to the demands of his constituency. Rather, we argue that the institutional arrangement of the escape clause has allowed liberal presidents to be more isolated from constituent pressure than would otherwise be the case. We see less protectionism than is predicted from shifting constituent and international interests.

24. Judith Goldstein, "The Political Economy of Trade: The Institutions of Protection," *American Political Science Review* 80 (March 1986), pp. 161–84.

TABLE 3. *Predicting escape clause aid, 1958–78*

Variable	B (Standard error)
Change in number of employees	−1.51[a]
	(.32)
Government petitions	.28[b]
	(.17)
New capital expenditures	10.78[a]
	(2.09)
Association petitions	−1.18[a]
	(.26)
Average import penetration	−6.29[a]
	(1.30)
Industry petitions	.93[a]
	(.17)
Weight	1.16
	(.179)

a. Significant at .01 level.
b. Significant at .05 level.
Source. See Table 2; U.S. Department of Commerce, *Census of Manufactures* (Washington, D.C.: GPO, 1964, 1967, 1972, 1977, 1982); U.S. Department of Commerce, *U.S. Imports, SIC Based Products, FT 210 Annual* (Washington, D.C.: GPO, 1964, 1972, 1978, 1979, 1980, 1981); U.S. Department of Commerce, *U.S. Exports, SIC Based Products, FT 610 Annual* (Washington, D.C.: GPO, 1965, 1972, 1978, 1979, 1980, 1981).

A second way of assessing legitimacy is to model the traits of social groups who are successful in gaining state aid. This is done for a twenty-year period in Table 3. By comparing the variables that actually predict a successful petition with the legal rules, we can assess the relative weight of legislation and decision-making discretion. This exercise is particularly interesting when we compare these models across aid programs.

If the aggregate data portray the escape clause as legitimating freer trade, so too does our regression model. The data on petitions filed between 1958 and 1978 show that a number of variables significantly affect the decision of who gets escape clause aid. As grouped, four of seven sets of factors that were entered into this and subsequent aid equations appeared as important.[25]

25. The data that appear in Table 2, 4, and 6 were modeled from the same data set. That data set included all industries that applied for any of these three aid types between 1958 and 1983. Petitions were disaggregated by 8-digit product categories and then reorganized into 4-digit Standard Industrial Classification (SIC) codes. This method allows petitions covering large product groups to be appropriately weighted. The estimations to the model were produced using a weighted least square method. For computation of weights, see Judith Goldstein, "A Re-examination of American Trade Policy: An Inquiry into the Causes of Protectionism," Ph.D. diss., UCLA, 1983; and A. Zeller and T. H. Lee, "Joint Estimation of Relationships Involving Discrete Random Variables," *Econometrica* 33 (April 1965). In total, 313 industries (4-digit) petitioned for at least one of these aid types.

In modeling an explanation for government response, industry variables were organized into the following analytic groups: (1) indicators of international competitiveness; (2) measures of

First, who petitions is explanatory. Data were collected on five types of petitioners—single industries, trade associations, government, unions, and unions and industries filing jointly. Three of these petitioners appear in the regression. Government petitions and industry petitions had a better chance of gaining aid; conversely, petitions from associations were inversely related to success-rate. That government petitions would be more favorably received was expected—these petitions to the ITC, either from Congress, the president, or the ITC itself, designate cases of special attention. Often they are cases that have been refused before. Although repeated petitioning generally does not seem to increase an industry's propensity to receive aid, a repeat of a petition from a government agency probably does. Why industry petitions are more likely to get aid than association petitions are is less clear. The explanation may lie in the types of cases filed by single industries and those filed by associations. If association petitions represent smaller industries or ones that have had less previous contact with the government petition process, they may have a more difficult time receiving government assistance. When examined, this proves to be the case. Petitions from industries were from larger manufacturers with relatively high petition activity. Although size and total number of petitions filed do not directly enter the model, who petitions may be considered an indirect surrogate for these factors.[26]

Three other factors weigh into the explanation of who gets escape clause aid: change in number of employees is negatively related to success; new capital expenditures are positively related to success; and average import penetration is negatively related. All three of these findings contradict what is commonly envisioned as the typical aided industry. Of those industries who have asked for aid, those who receive escape clause aid are *not* the industries that are relatively less sophisticated nor the ones suffering from the greatest import penetration. They are, however, the industries having relatively large declines in employment, which perhaps makes an executive veto politically unfeasible.

These regression findings are suggestive. First, those who have received aid do not necessarily fit the criteria for aid established by Congress. Most striking, aid receipt is not related in the expected direction to import penetration. All the industries in the sample were import-competing. However, those who did receive aid were not necessarily those with the most penetrated markets. Second, who petitions seems to matter as much as the merits of the case. This finding suggests a political, rather than economic, explana-

import penetration or export strength; (3) indicators of relative industrial size; (4) measures of relative industrial strength; (5) a measure of previous petition success; (6) measures of change in industry characteristics (whether or not due to imports); (7) for a subgroup, the country that would be affected if a positive ruling were made.

26. The Pearson correlation between average employment (1963–77) and petition activity is .69 ($P = .00$). The correlation between employment and petitioning as an industry (not through an association) is .45 ($P = .00$).

tion for protectionism. Third, industries that received aid were relatively "healthier" than the bulk of industries in the sample. These industries still invested in capital improvements, which in these equations serves as a proxy for a range of other industry attributes. In short, it appears that the more competitive members of the sample received aid. Last, we find a strong relationship between the size of the industry and aid receipt. Large industries suffering declines in employment are apt to get a favorable state response.

These results are compatible with our explanation of the politics of escape clause protectionism. The findings that who petitions affects outcome, that employment declines elicit a state response, and that aid goes to the most competitive of the industries that petition speak to the discretion built into this trade legislation. These results also indicate that an interest group model of politics alone does not explain the pattern of aid. Industries that are the worst off may be repeatedly articulating their need for aid, but it is the upper strata of manufacturers that receive government protection. The more interesting finding from this exercise, however, is in comparisons across types of aid. This comparison of models of aid suggests that three different political processes drive American policy.

The defense of fair trade

The escape clause is only one mechanism open to industries needing import protection. The other forms of aid, to which we now turn, are based on differing notions of what constitutes a legitimate claim for protection. These laws, conceived before the Great Depression, reflect a period when the ideas of List and Hamilton dominated those of Smith and Ricardo. It is this period, from the end of the Civil War to Smoot–Hawley, in which ideas of "autarky" led policymakers to see gains from trade only in terms of export expansion. (By 1913, liberal ideas had gained increased acceptance among a subset of policymakers. Only after 1934, however, did legal and institutional changes allow these ideas to be translated into policy.) This period gave rise to what is labeled here as a "fair" trade law.

Indicative of differing views on trade, the legislative debates on tariffs in this earlier period are distinguishable. The question addressed by those debating the tariff in the earlier period was whether a tariff's primary purpose should be to raise revenue or to protect national industry; in the later period the debate turned on the tariff as a foreign policy instrument. In the earlier period, the tariff was subject to congressional logrolling; after 1934, tariff-making authority was given to the executive. Finally, the first set of tariffs was more reflective of the nexus of competing interests of the time. Since no one position on what was an optimal tariff had emerged, the type of tariff passed was a function of the capabilities of particular groups within and

outside Congress. After 1934, agreement on one position on tariff policy—
that is, liberalism—substantially transformed the interest group process.[27]

What is somewhat unusual in the U.S. move to free trade is that liberalization occurred without the dismantling of pre-liberal norms, values, and institutions. Laws written in America's pre-liberal period reveal a far different
set of state interests than would be the case after the Depression. In design
these "mercantile" statutes reflect earlier American concerns with economic nationalism, not with later interest in the international gains free trade
would afford. These laws changed little, even as the U.S. revamped her
basic approach to trade policy. Thus, even in America's most liberal period,
a legal mandate existed to exclude imports under these sets of laws.

Three laws are examined in this section. All have their legal roots in the
pre-1934 period of American tariff history. All establish a set of criteria for
"fair" trade based on a narrow interpretation of legitimate market behavior.
Created in a period in which the U.S. wanted to discourage imports, these
laws establish criteria for fair trading and state involvement in the production process that could exclude the majority of America's current trading
partners. A philosophical difference exists between how cases of "fair"
competitive trade that adversely affects an American producer and cases of
"unfair" trade that may cause the same result are viewed. Belief in the long-
term beneficial aspects of the market has translated into a condemnation by
American decision-makers of foreign governments and foreign industries
that attempt to interfere with "natural" market mechanisms, especially if
the goal of that manipulation is predatory. The relationship between the
American state and private industry is the model used to evaluate actions
taken by other nations. The law stipulates that no country assist home
industries or interfere with consumer market preferences to a greater extent
than is done in the U.S.

A number of problems exist in the administration of these "fair" trade
laws. First, there is a problem in the discovery and definition of a violation.
Rulings in all three types discussed below are subject to difficulties with data
collection; administrators must rely on domestic and foreign producers to
supply information, which is often incomplete and difficult to assess. In laws
in which the intent of the foreign producer to undercut an American producer is critical to the state's ruling, it is even more difficult for American
complainants to prove their case. Foreign producers do engage in what
Americans view as unfair practices but often without predatory intent. There
is a dilemma in how to judge, for example, national pricing policies or
subsidized research and development programs. In such cases foreign prac-

---

27. For analysis of pre-1934 tariffs, see G. W. Taussig, *The Tariff History of the United
States* (New York: Knickerbocker, 1914); and *International Trade* (New York: Augustus Kel-
ley, 1966); Tom E. Terril, *The Tariff, Politics and American Foreign Policy, 1874–1901* (Westport, Conn.: Greenwood, 1973); David Lake, *Structure and Strategy: The International
Sources of American Trade Policy, 1887–1939*, Ph.D. diss., Cornell University, 1984.

tices were often not created to gain a market advantage but merely reflect national goals.

Second, administrators must adjudicate cases based on overly ethnocentric standards. States vary greatly in their philosophical and historical relationship to producers. The relationship found in the U.S. is not characteristic of that found in other polities. To use the U.S. case as a benchmark establishes criteria on the extreme end of a continuum. The enforcement of American values of the state-industry relationship not only interferes with a set of foreign policy goals that seek prosperity in non-communist states but also translates into interference into other states' domestic politics. Such interference alienates allies and in principle deviates from the regime norm of sovereignty.

These issues were not of great importance in the early years of the liberalization program. As competition increased in the American market, however, these laws were rediscovered. Industries filed better claims and increasingly qualified under the narrow interpretation of "fair" trade as embodied in early law. This presented a dilemma for liberal central decision-makers who thought it in the nation's economic interest to keep the American market open. Administrators responded, whenever possible, by obfuscating the law through delays, noncollection of extra duties, and loose interpretations of findings. Such practices are no longer broadly accepted. Unfair trade issues are viewed by Congress, by the population, and by many administrators as more legitimate than their escape clause counterpart. "Cheating" remains antithetical to liberal norms. The problem facing central decision-makers who accept the principle of fair trade, however, is how to maintain openness while adhering to the narrow interpretation of fairness established in American statutes.

Antidumping legislation

Antidumping legislation appeared in its modern form in 1921, although earlier, in the Revenue Act of 1916, a similar condemnation of unfair trade practices was legislated. The intent of an antidumping law is to counter international price discrimination.[28] Legislation protects home producers from competition arising from imports being sold at values below those at which they are sold in their home market or below their cost of production. If such a practice is found to exist, an additional duty equal to that price differential is assessed on the product.

Until the Trade Act of 1979, the request of a domestic producer to the

---

28. See Frederick Davis, "The Regulation and Control of Foreign Trade," *Columbia Law Review* 66 (December 1966), pp. 1428–59; and Lowell E. Baier, "Substantive Interpretations under the Antidumping Act and the Foreign Trade Policy of the United States," *Stanford Law Review* 17 (March 1965), pp. 428–46. Since antidumping laws are aimed at international price discrimination, they have a domestic analogue in the Robinson–Patman Act.

Customs Bureau of the Treasury Department would trigger a preliminary appraisal of whether just cause existed for an antidumping investigation. If the appraisal was negative, the case was rejected. This preliminary judgment process, which determined the fate of many cases, was often inconsistent and highly discretionary.

Upon a positive preliminary determination, the Treasury Department would launch an investigation. The major component of the investigation determined whether sales were at Less Than Fair Value (LTFV). Compared with the other forms of aid examined in this essay, the criteria for such a determination were quite detailed. Dumping is defined by 300 lines of text in the Antidumping Act with an additional 1,000 lines on administrative regulation in the *Federal Register*. In contrast, the only criterion the Trade Act of 1974 imposed on the president's escape clause decisions was "the national economic interest of the United States," and the criteria by which the 1974 Trade Act charged the ITC with judging injury take up only thirty-five lines.[29]

If a LTFV ruling is made by the Treasury Department, the case goes to the ITC for a determination of whether there has been domestic "injury" as a result of the dumping activity.[30] Until 1979 the ITC had a wide amount of discretion in its determination. No hearing was necessary, even if requested by the petitioners. If the ITC found in the affirmative, a report was issued to the secretary of the treasury, who issued a "finding of dumping." As opposed to escape clause cases, a tie vote in the ITC became an affirmative finding. Until 1979, some redundancy existed between the Treasury Department and the ITC mandate. In particular, the information the ITC studied in making its final determination did not necessarily have to apply only to the injury determination. The ITC could find no injury based on a redetermination that the foreign producer was not, in its judgment, dumping, and overturn the Treasury Department ruling.[31]

The discretionary nature of the injury determination was of central concern to foreign producers in the Tokyo Round of GATT negotiations. The antidumping code agreed to in Geneva incorporated the notion of "material injury," not just any injury, by reason of LTFV imports. In previous hearings on the Kennedy Round of negotiated agreements, Congress had held that the international codes signed in 1967 did not change the 1954 revisions of the antidumping law. In question was whether any degree of injury other than *de minimus* constituted injury. The U.S. agreed that it did, although this conflicted with the view of other signatories of the agreement. To conform

29. J. M. Finger, H. Keith Hall, and Douglass R. Nelson, "The Political Economy of Administered Protection," *American Economic Review* 72 (June 1982), pp. 452–66.

30. This additional criterion was instituted in 1954.

31. This ITC practice is cited by Davis, "Regulation and Control of Foreign Trade," p. 1442; and Baier, "Substantive Interpretations," p. 418. The most frequently noted example is the case of 1964 Vital Wheat Glut in Canada.

with international standards, the Senate instructed the ITC to define "material" as "harm which is not inconsequential, immaterial or unimportant." This move was more symbolic than substantive. The ITC had never determined injury using the "more than *de minimus*" criterion, and had used its discretion to undercut, not increase, dumping rulings.

The changes made in 1979 trade legislation point directly to the weaknesses in the administration of antidumping law. New time limits were set for the assessment of dumping duties. In the past, duties could be delayed for long periods; for example, $400 million worth of duties were delayed seven years in the case of television receivers from Japan.[32] That the Treasury Department did not move quickly to collect these duties reflects the original intent of dumping legislation. In the past, if dumping margins were found to exist, yet were corrected before new merchandise entered the American market, no penalty was levied. It was assumed that foreign producers would change their prices when charged with a dumping finding. The Customs Department never developed the administrative structure necessary to collect back taxes from intransigent producers. Legislation was aimed at stopping future infringements, not punishing past infractions. The incentive thus existed to dump, at least until caught, onto the American market. Since 1979, however, a one-year statutory time limit has been set for collection.

In the period through 1979, when an investigation was in process, an importer was required to make a deposit through a customs bond for the merchandise under question. There were limited direct costs attributed to this bond and thus no incentive to stop a dumping practice until a final judgment or to provide necessary information to the Treasury Department or the ITC. After 1979, deposits of estimated dumping duties on merchandise imposed a far more substantial financial burden on importers. This new practice is consistent with the administrative practices of the European community, with GATT codes, and with the intent of American law; it is not a form of "new protectionism."

Finally, and perhaps most basically, after 1979 LTFV determinations were made by the Department of Commerce, which, as proponents of the bureaucratic transfer suggested, may be more responsive than the Treasury Department to domestic producers. Although the administrative organization has changed, the legal mandate has not. The Treasury Department did use the latitude it was granted under the law to maintain a liberal American market. Commerce may choose not to use its discretionary authority in that way. If adjudicated to the letter of the law, antidumping actions will lead to increased closure of the American market.

---

32. Matthew Marks, "Recent Changes in American Law on Regulatory Trade Measures," *The World Economy* 2 (February 1980), p. 434.

Countervailing duty legislation

If a nation is directly or indirectly giving a bounty or a grant—that is, a subsidy—to a domestic producer, U.S. law stipulates that an additional duty equal to the net amount of the subsidy should be levied on that product upon its importation into the country. In the U.S., the imposition of a countervailing duty follows a distinct set of procedures; conversely, in most other countries, subsidized exports are not distinguished from sales below cost.[33] The current form of legislation appeared in the Tariff Act of 1930, but similar mandates against such foreign practices appeared in both 1909 and 1913 legislation. In 1909, countervailing duties appeared as part of the maximum and minimum arrangements. This arrangement stipulated two tariff schedules, with the higher schedule being applied to nations using undue discrimination against the U.S. in the way of "tariff rates or provisions, trade or other regulations, charges, exactions in any other manner" or on export bounty or duty.[34] Again in 1913, the Secretary of the Treasury was authorized "to impose additional duties equal to the amount of any grant or bounty on exportation given by any foreign country."[35]

The procedures in countervailing duty cases are straightforward. Upon complaint, the Customs Bureau (Department of Commerce after 1979) initiates an investigation. Until 1979 there was no delineation of how the investigation should be conducted or of the appropriate criteria. Rather, upon completion of the investigation the secretary of the treasury would decide whether to impose the duty, and the appropriate "equalizing" amount. The 1974 and 1979 Trade Acts added an injury requirement in order to make U.S. law consistent with the GATT codes.[36] The 1979 law also specifies, for the first time, procedure and guidelines for the new overseeing agency, the Department of Commerce.[37]

The period between 1930 and 1979 was characterized by great latitude in countervailing duty cases. The size of the duty imposed was not subject to judicial review, and in general the Treasury Department had much freedom to interpret the law. The 1979 reforms came about because of the belief that such freedoms had been at the cost of the petitioner.[38] The laws themselves were repeatedly defended by the Congress. It was the administrative agencies that were seen as undermining the intent of congressional legislation. As with antidumping legislation, the discretionary nature of the legislation had allowed liberal administrators to undercut protectionism. With the move to

33. David, "Regulation and Control," p. 1445.
34. Taussig, *International Trade*, p. 403.
35. Ibid., p. 443.
36. The United States opposed the inclusion of an injury criteria for both countervailing duty and antidumping cases under the "grandfather clause," which exempted legislation in effect prior to the General Agreements signing in October 1947.
37. Marks, "Recent Changes," pp. 430–34.
38. See prepared statement of Charles Carlisle to the *U.S. Senate Committee on Finance Hearings on 1979 Act*, 10 July 1979, pp. 489–96.

the Department of Commerce and the mandate from Congress to enforce its legislation, countervailing duty laws could increasingly become an impediment to trade.

Section 337

Section 337 of the Tariff Act of 1930 empowers the ITC to investigate complaints of unfair competition in the importation or sales of items from foreign producers.[39] Section 337 has the potential of applying to a wide variety of predatory import practices. In general, most cases have dealt with patent violations. Under this law, if the ITC found that such practices destroyed or substantially injured an industry "efficiently and economically operated in the U.S.," the product could be excluded from entry into the U.S. Following an ITC exclusion order (a cease-and-desist order after 1974) the president had sixty days (under 1974 law) in which to intervene and override the ITC's decision "where he determines it necessary because of overriding policy reasons." Unlike countervailing duties or cases of dumping, the administration of unfair trade did not change under the 1979 law.

This review leads to three general conclusions about the politics behind unfair trade laws. First, there appears to be significant flexibility in the prosecution of these laws. Such flexibility has undercut the protectionist potential of these statutes. Even with the delineation of the LTFV criteria, the Treasury Department was never fully constrained by Congress to enact a particular type of policy in dumping and countervailing duty cases. In effect, Congress gave to the Treasury Department the right to regulate in this area as it saw fit. And, as the data show, it often decided not to grant protection. In the case of Section 337 violations, Congress gave to the ITC guidelines, but allowed the ITC's decisions to be sidestepped through both legal and extralegal means. Both the courts and the office of the president encouraged settlements.

Second, and related, there appears no clear criterion in the legislative histories by which to assess whether these laws are becoming more or less protectionist. Rather, continuity has existed in the form, basic organization, and use of these laws, even though administrative agencies have changed. This is true even with the 1979 legislation. In the countervailing duty and antidumping cases, the injury determination makes it somewhat more difficult to obtain aid; the change of administrative responsibility to the Department of Commerce may make it easier.

Third, what separates unfair trade laws from escape clause legislation is the autonomy vested in the bureaucracy. In the escape clause cases, the president has the authority to ignore an ITC finding if it is in the national interest. This has been an effective mechanism used by executives to keep the Amer-

39. For basis of statutory language, see George Bronze, "The Tariff Commission as a Regulatory Agency," *Columbia Law Review* 61 (Spring 1961), p. 483.

ican market open. Most post-Depression legislation has so aggrandized the rights of the president. Of the unfair trade laws studied, only one includes a role for the executive. Neither antidumping nor countervailing duty legislation allows the executive to counteract a protectionist ruling by the bureaucracy. Beginning in the 1970s, this presented a foreign policy problem to central decision-makers. Since the end of World War II, American security interests dictated that the U.S. maintain a strong economic alliance with both Europe and Japan. Analysts who studied postwar trade policy argue that America was willing to allow the EEC and Japan to protect their markets because American security interests took precedence over the establishment of a worldwide liberal trade regime. The onset of negative sanctions in the early 1960s, however, cannot be explained as a sharp reversal in security policy. Rather, the U.S. was able to allow the Japanese and Europeans latitude in the first twenty years after the war because their products posed no threat to American producers. As soon as foreign products began to threaten home producers, the government responded, even though sanctions conflicted with other elements of foreign policy. Although escape clause cases were sidestepped, unfair trade petitions forced central decision-makers to sanction Japan and Europe. These statutes withheld from the executive prerogative he had gained in other foreign policy areas since the 1940s.[40]

In short, unfair trade laws posed little threat to the trade regime in the 1960s. Although infringements of these statutes were prosecuted when found, American producers had little need to resort to them. In the 1970s, however, as competition intensified, producers found that state-society relations in most nations qualified them for state aid under unfair trade statutes. The rise in petitions with potentially positive rulings led liberal administrators to obscure the intent of these laws. The executive, too, in this period attempted circumvention of these statutes. Two examples are noteworthy. First, the 1974 law included a provision allowing a cabinet member, the secretary of the treasury, to waive a countervailing duty if necessary for the nation's interest. Second, negotiation and administration of the extralegal form of aid, trigger prices, gave the executive authority in dumping cases denied him by law. In essence, trigger prices created a powerful alternative to the Treasury Department route for steel petitioners.

With more public attention given to the issues of fair trade, the laws began to be administered more closely to their legislative mandates. Such attention undercut the flexibility members of government had had in interpreting the laws in line with general foreign policy or regime interests. Taken in conjunction with increasing import pressures and growing awareness on the part

40. For the growth of executive power and foreign policy, see Theodore Lowi, *The Personal President: Power Invested, Power Unfilled* (Ithaca, N.Y.: Cornell University Press, 1985); and Franz Schuman, *The Logic of World Power* (New York: Pantheon, 1974).

of producers of their legal rights in these cases, these laws have increasingly posed a problem for government officials who want to maintain openness. Some prosecution of unfair trade laws is helpful to liberalization; the U.S. never understood liberalism to mean that she take the "sucker's payoff." The problem facing central decision-makers, however, is that America's unfair trade laws hold an overly narrow interpretation of the legitimate relationship between producers and the state.

Unfair trade data

Table 4 displays petition activity and acceptance rates for the three unfair trade laws discussed above. None of the forms of aid showed the radical increase in acceptance rates found in escape clause cases. Although petition activity increased rather dramatically in the 1970s, government response has not mirrored increasing societal interest. In the case of countervailing duties, the acceptance rate has declined; for antidumping petitions, the rate rose after 1962, but has not significantly changed since then. The acceptance rate of Section 337s rose under the 1974 law and stayed the same for the next ten years.

In countervailing duty cases, the high rate of acceptance in the early period reinforces the notion that subsidies were never considered legitimate. As the number of cases accelerated, however, the high acceptance rate undercut America's commitment to the further liberalization of world commerce. The waiver provision, used for over 90 percent of the products that had technically qualified for aid, was an executive-centered mechanism for circumventing duty increases. After the completion of the Tokyo Round, the acceptance rate almost mirrored what it would have been without executive privilege.

Perhaps most striking about the antidumping law is its long history of use. The antidumping law has been used consistently since the early 1960s as a mechanism to keep the American market "fair." Low approval rates in the late 1950s may be attributed to American economic preponderance—few foreign manufactures had yet acquired the capacity to endanger American producers at home. With postwar recovery, antidumping legislation again became a central element of American trade policy. From an acceptance rate of under 5 percent in the early 1960s, dumping duties increased to an average 23 percent after 1963. After the 1979 shift of administration to the Department of Commerce, acceptance rates for dumping cases did increase from the previous period. Low rates under the 1974 Act, however, were partially due to the use of the trigger price mechanism to "pull back" steel cases. In conjunction with the slight increase in acceptance rates in countervailing duty cases, these changes suggest that if acceptance rates continue to rise, even with countervailing duty cases being subject to an additional material injury test, this shift in administrative responsibility will have a great impact on American trade policy.

TABLE 4. *Antidumping (AD), Countervailing Duty (CD), and Section 337 cases, 1958–83*

Year[a]	Average petitions per year			Acceptance rate		
	AD	CD	337	AD	CD	337
1958–62	28	1	1	.04	1.00	0
1963–74	24	1	4	.22	.93	.13
1975–78	42	37	12	.15	.30	.28
					(.08)[b]	
1979–83	32	24	22	.33	.34	.28

a. Organized by legislative periods.
b. Number in parentheses is acceptance rate if waived cases are counted as negative.
Source. See Table 2; U.S. Government, *Federal Register* (Washington, D.C.: GPO, 1958–83).

The procedure for obtaining a market exclusion as a result of a claim under Section 337 is the most technical of the types of protectionism examined. Section 337 cases typically involve complex issues relating to patent law or antitrust violation, or both. Adjudication is conducted by one or two ITC administrative law judges who conduct hearings and make recommendations to the ITC as a whole. The procedure encourages settlement between parties. Overall, in the period studied, the number of settlements was greater than the number of positive findings. The average rate of acceptance in the 1958–83 period for Section 337s has been 16 percent. That rate, however, has varied from 0 percent in the late 1950s and early 1960s to 28 percent in the late 1970s. It is noteworthy that, although the president is so empowered, he intervened in almost none of these cases. There are two explanations. First, in most cases a positive finding clearly represents an international predatory practice on the part of a particular foreign producer towards American technology. Violated are both international and domestic norms. Patent violations or other forms of industrial espionage are not viewed anywhere as legitimate. Second, a positive ruling arises from a complex process. The ITC clout resides in the sophistication of the procedures used to adjudicate the cases. Thus, both the content of the ruling and the method of its determination serve to dampen the incidence of a presidential veto. The nature of the cases too may explain why presidential action is unlikely. High settlement rates, especially after 1974, undercut the government's need to exclude many of these products as private parties arrived at some form of agreement.

The comparison of these laws with each other and with escape clause cases reveals a number of things about the institutional history of each of these laws. First, since the 1960s, societal interest in stopping unfair trade has increased dramatically. Although there was increasing interest in the escape clause after 1974, it was neither as great nor as sustained as the interest in these three unfair trade statutes. Although antidumping legislation had always been used by American producers, it is only after 1974 that manufacturers discovered the clout of countervailing duty petitions and Section 337s as a potential remedy to rising competition on the home market. And given the close relationship between governments and producers among America's chief trading rivals, the claim that subsidies were the cause for trade problems was easier to prove and received a far better reception from government officials than did the assertion that manufacturers could not compete due to lowered tariffs.

Second, although the majority of affirmative findings occurred after 1968, they did not occur at significantly higher rates than in the earlier period. It is correct to note an increase in the aggregate number of positive rulings. The success rate, however, is more constant. As the number of petitions rose and more industries qualified by legal standards, the number of political vetoes and extralegal settlements increased. Compared with escape clause data, which show a dramatic increase in positive determinations after 1974, the data on unfair trade laws show constancy rather than change.

Third, to predict protectionism, analysts need to consider both the administrative agency and the legal statute. Agency alone is an insufficient explanation. The ITC decides both Section 337 and escape clause cases, yet they tend to rule favorably twice as often in the latter cases. Conversely, the law alone may not explain all the variation in aceptance rates. Changes in law do not explain variation within unfair trade statutes or between these laws and escape clause rulings. The views of individuals and agencies assigned to monitor laws may be as important as the laws themselves. The Treasury Department acted as did the president in escape clause cases; given the mandate, it waived the vast majority of countervailing duty cases. Criticism of this role led Congress to give the Department of Commerce jurisdiction in these cases. It is still too early to determine whether Commerce will look more favorably on petitions for aid. But as will be discussed below, Commerce gave almost all petitioners adjustment assistance, suggesting that the slight rise in acceptance rates we see in the first four years of its tenure will continue in the future.

The second manner in which unfair trade laws may be compared with the escape clause is to repeat the modeling exercise presented in Table 3. The unfair trade model is presented in Table 5.

When all of these agencies' decisions are grouped, they reveal a pattern of aid receipt that varies greatly from that found for escape clause cases. As well as the variables studied in Table 3 (see note 25), the nation affected by the unfair trade suit was added to the list of possible explanations for aid receipt. Four variables appear as predictors. First, a country bias is apparent. Although Japan is the nation most often named in petitions for relief, it is the European petitions that appear to have a higher propensity for receiving aid. This high rate of success cannot be explained by a higher incidence

TABLE 5. *Unfair trade aid model, 1958–78*

Variable	B (Standard error)
Petitions from Europe	1.23[a]
	(.35)
Total number of unfair trade petitions	−0.42[a]
	(.12)
Average value of export shipments	2.04[a]
	(.73)
Average new capital expenditures	−6.24[b]
	(2.82)
Weight	.85
	(.13)

a. Significant at the .01 level.
b. Significant at .05 level.
Source. See Tables 3 and 4.

of "cheating." Rather, it is probably related to these cases being easier to document.

Three other attributes of the petitioning party explain variation in petition success rate. Industries that are relatively more export-oriented gain aid. Industries that have spent relatively less on new capital expenditures gain aid. And, finally, those that have petitioned less often seem to gain a positive government response.

The finding of a negative relationship between aid and capital expenditures is the most intuitive of the three. The industries that receive aid are the relatively least competitive of the applicant pool—they have chosen not to reinvest in their industries, perhaps because business practices of other nations have led to a more competitive foreign product. Most analysts agree that it is these noncompetitive industries that are expected to apply and receive protectionism. This finding itself is not exceptional; it is the absence of this variable in the escape clause model that is more noteworthy.

The other two findings need more explanation. The negative relationship between number of attempts at aid receipt is counterintuitive. Most theories of American politics look to pressure upon government officials as the primary explanation for protectionism. Here the relationship runs in the opposite direction. One explanation may be that if it is the weight of the case based on legal interpretation that explains aid, the need to repetition may indicate relatively weak cases. The more one needs to apply, the less likely it is that one initially had a strong case.[41]

---

41. Alternatively, the data may be picking up the effects of the trigger price mechanism. The president controlled steel dumping duties in the late 1970s by convincing petitioners to voluntarily pull back their petitions. Since it is coded as a petition that did not receive aid, the model could be picking up this dynamic.

The relationship between exports and aid can be explained in a similar way. The firms that are most involved with world trade are most affected by the trading practices of their competitors. They are also most aware of the trading practices of different countries and firms. Both contribute to the legitimacy of their legal claim. In effect, these laws were tailored for the company that is able to compete well on foreign markets but faces unfair competition at home.

In sum, the politics of getting unfair trade aid is nothing like that for the escape clause. Although the same industries apply for relief under both sets of laws, different laws dictate a different purpose for each type of aid. There is not one formula for gaining state aid from import pressures. This point is even more obvious when the last type of aid program, what we label here as redistributive aid, is examined.

The idea of trade adjustment

As with the other two tenets of American commercial policy, the origins of American adjustment policies trace to a cognitive model of the proper relationship between state and society. At issue here is the extent of state involvement in mitigating the social effects of economic fluctuations. After the 1930s, such active state participation gained increased legitimacy. Exigencies due to the business cycle, technological advances, or capital migration, to name but a few, were accepted by state leaders as costs of maintaining the capitalist economy. The role accepted by the government, however, was only that of adjustment; by the 1950s, the position of direct state intervention into the economy, a position that had gained some acceptance in the 1930s, was rejected.

At heart, trade adjustment policies reflect post-New Deal political norms. Adjustment policies are essentially compensatory. The state compensates industries and labor groups adversely affected by trade policy, from an ever-expanding economic "pie."[42] If trade policy had adversely affected constituents, they were entitled to state aid.

Trade Adjustment Assistance (TAA) was first proposed during the Eisenhower administration in a minority opinion to the Randall Commission report.[43] Adjustment was envisioned as a substitute, in the form of federal financial aid, for escape clause aid. With limited support, a weak version of TAA appeared in the 1962 Trade Act, was used in the Automotive Products Trade Act of 1965, and was ultimately expanded in the 1974 bill. Those who

42. For a similar argument, see Charles Maier, "The Politics of Productivity: Foundations of American International Economic Policy after World War II," *International Organization* 31 (Autumn 1977).
43. Daniel Mitchell, *Labor Issues of American International Trade and Investment* (Baltimore: Johns Hopkins University Press, 1976), p. 33.

understand TAA only as a method to sell trade liberalization fail to appreciate the welfare function the program has played. Though clearly not so conceived in the early 1960s, adjustment assistance evolved as an important component of trade policy as the state was forced to react to the rise in industry petitions for protection.

Under the 1962 Trade Act, workers and firms were eligible for aid. Petitions were filed with the Tariff Commission, which conducted investigations (limited to sixty days) to determine whether the petitioners fulfilled the legislative criteria. The criteria of eligibility were fulfilled (1) if injury was due in major part to a trade concession, (2) if injury resulted in increased quantities of a like or directly competitive product, and (3) if imports were a major factor in causing or threatening to cause serious injury to the applicant firm, domestic industry, or group of workers. Once passed by the Tariff Commission, the president certified the petitions; if the Commission vote was tied, the president was empowered to decide the case. In just about all cases, the president approved aid. Since the criteria used in TAA cases were similar to those dictating escape clause relief, a dilemma existed. In a sense, the Tariff Commission "could not be liberal in approving adjustment assistance petitions without being liberal in approving escape clause petitions. Thus, adjustment assistance—which was supposed to foster freer trade— was included in the Trade Expansion Act in such a way as to make its actual use inconsistent with that objective."[44]

As a response, TAA was revamped under the 1974 law. First, coverage was extended to communities as well as firms and workers. Second, the investigatory responsibilities and determination of injury were given to the Labor Department for worker cases, and to the Department of Commerce for cases involving firms and communities. And third, eligibility criteria changed from the earlier stricter requirements to the following: (1) that a significant number of workers be affected, (2) that there be an absolute decrease in sales and production, and (3) that imports of a like or directly competitive article contributed importantly to a decline in sales or production. "Contributed importantly" was interpreted as a cause that is important but not necessarily more important than any other cause.[45] This last criterion, that imports be of a similar nature to a product made in the U.S., served to disqualify a number of otherwise qualified applicants, especially in cases involving auto production. In the late 1970s, manufacturers of auto parts such as bumpers were being laid off as a result of the sale of foreign cars. Yet, because no foreign bumper was being imported, their case did not meet the necessary criteria.

Once certified, firms and communities received low-cost loans and other development assistance. Workers were paid a weekly adjustment allowance

44. Ibid., p. 43.
45. This adjustment assistance language was modeled on that used for the escape clause, which required imports after 1974 to be a "substantial cause" of injury. The main difference was that, in adjustment assistance cases, imports could be a less important "cause."

of 65 percent (in the 1962 Act) or 70 percent (in the 1974 Act) of their average weekly wage for up to fifty-two weeks, with a twenty-six-week extension for workers in training or workers over sixty years of age. In no case was aid to exceed 65 percent (70 percent in the 1974 Act) of the average weekly manufacturing wage. Employment services and relocation allowances were offered to facilitate re-employment, but these constituted a small part of the program.

The original 1974 program was extended in 1981 for two years. However, early in the Reagan administration it was announced that the program would be eliminated, and in October 1981, in the Budget Reconciliation Act (Title 25), the benefit program was changed. After 1981, and for the life of the program, aid would be given as an extension to unemployment insurance for the long-term unemployed. The previous concept of an additional payment to those unemployed due to imports (which brought income to 70 percent of previous levels) ceased. Furthermore, after 9 February 1982, cases had to show "substantial cause"—that is, imports had to be the primary cause of industry malaise, the criterion used under the 1962 Trade Act.

In essence, TAA was a program of transfer payments. Liberalism incurs differential costs and benefits. Adjustment assistance was an institutional response to these costs, and has acted both as a welfare policy and as a way to diffuse potential opposition. It was the latter function that propelled its creation, but the former that was its engine for growth. Adjustment assistance or its functional equivalent is a necessary ingredient in a liberal American trade policy. The program ensures support for free trade through redistribution. Liberal trade policy was accepted because it brought wealth; if an unregulated market leads to visible economic upheaval, the cognitive basis of liberalism will be questioned. The following section seeks to show that adjustment assistance served the critical role of "buying off" potential opposition to state policy. Without some agency playing this role, increasing dissonance over free trade is inevitable.

Adjustment assistance data

As in the previous two sections, two types of data were examined for trade adjustment assistance. Table 6 presents the aggregate list of petitions and acceptance rates over time. Table 7 models the determinants of this form of aid. The aggregate data show large increases in aid requests over time. Requests increased from under twenty a year while the program was administered by the ITC to over 1,000 a year under the 1974 Act and over 2,000 a year after 1979. The 1974 changes, which eased aid requirements and changed administrative responsibility, were followed by a significant increase in interest in the program. TAA numbers dwarf the number of requests for the escape clause, although these two laws served the same constituency. The number of petitions receiving aid is also much greater

TABLE 6. *Adjustment-assistance cases, 1963–81*

| | Average petitions per year | | Acceptance rate | |
Year[a]	Commerce[b]	Labor	Industry	Worker
1963–75[b]	5	19	.37	.30
1975–78	8	882	.91	.45
1979–81	623[c]	2071	.81	.28

a. By legislative periods.
b. Prescreening at regional offices reduces number of cases and increases possibility of aid.
c. Data do not include 1981.
Source. Department of Labor data; Department of Commerce data: ITC, *Annual Reports* (Washington, D.C.: GPO), various years.

than with the escape clause. As opposed to other aid types, a majority of those who applied for aid did receive aid. Table 6, however, does not reflect changes to the program during the Reagan administration. In 1981 alone, worker aid receipts declined to 9 percent, as compared with 41 percent during the previous two years.

This decline was not unexpected. The Reagan administration was committed to the state playing a reduced role. Thus, the initial premises of an adjustment program were considered illegitimate. The administration did not agree that governments bear a burden for either economic redistribution or compensation. Sympathetic with the arguments of neoclassical economists, Reagan's advisors argued for the benefits of trade unfettered by state involvement.

The welfare function of TAA is clear in our regression model. Contrary to the model produced for escape clause aid, adjustment assistance seems predicated on variables more commonly argued to predict import aid. The industries most often thought to need and receive aid are industries losing their competitive position; import penetration is indicative of general industrial decline.

Table 7 lists ten predictors of adjustment aid. These variables show that the industries that received aid faced heavy import competition, were relatively small in size, had declining exports, were closing factories, and showed increasing labor costs.

The other attributes of those that received aid were less expected. In looking at these industries, we tried to measure how they had fared for the twenty-year period covered by this model. Although all these industries began to decline after 1968, their membership included the large "boom" industries of the postwar period. These "boom" industries, which included steel and autos, received significant amounts of adjustment assistance in this period. These cases are reflected in the regression results. Relative to all industries that applied for adjustment assistance, those that were successful were more capital intensive and had gone through relatively greater changes

TABLE 7. *Adjustment assistance model, 1963–78*

Variable	B Standard error
Average value of imports	5.76[a]
	(.74)
Value of shipments	.34
	(.05)
Growth in exports	− .24[a]
	(.03)
Change in number of production plants	− .14[a]
	(.03)
Change in labor costs	.28[a]
	(.07)
Average capital intensity	.03[a]
	(.01)
Change in capital intensity	1.15[a]
	(.19)
Change in number of employees	.02[a]
	(.004)
Change in export shipments	.21[a]
	(.04)
Change in level of technological sophistication	.34[b]
	(.16)
Weight	− 5.53
	(.63)

a. Significant at .01 level.
b. Significant at .05 level.
Source. See Tables 3, 4, and 6.

in industry technology in the years of this study—they were industries which had had large export sectors in the postwar period that are now in a decline and had experienced fluctuations in the numbers employed in the industry.

Escape clause and adjustment assistance legislation have one important element in common. Both were created in America's liberal period to serve industries adversely affected by trade policy. In reading the general legislation, this joint purpose is apparent. Philosophical differences between the two, however, have led to substantial variation between who qualifies for one form of aid rather than the other. The discretionary nature of escape clause legislation translates into a state policy that uses criteria other than need. Comparatively, as a transfer payment or an illusory form of protectionism, adjustment assistance is given to industries that *are* suffering from the openness of the American market. Although the same industries demand both forms of aid, the state differentiates its rewards. This pattern of aid led us to distinguish categorically between the two. Variations, however, are not due to legislative mandate alone. They result because individuals who are entrusted to carry out laws are biased in their interpretation of the law.

Conclusion

Two types of conclusions are offered here. The first are more theoretical. The points addressed center on the ability to defend the role of institutions and ideas as important determinants of American politics. The second are substantial. The remarks address the trade data and their implications for the future of general trade policy in the U.S.

This article offers an alternative method for understanding protectionism in the U.S. Neither of the two dominant genres of analysis looks towards the state as the critical variable in explaining policy outcomes. Societally based explanations look to social forces; international explanations look to power structures. Our explanation does not deny the validity of either of these approaches. Rather, we argue they are insufficient in their explanation of American protectionism. This article looks to a dominant role for ideas, as embedded in institutional design and laws, and the beliefs of central decision-makers as an additional explanation for policy.

Protectionism should be viewed in its historical context. Viewed over time, it can be organized by the time period in which protectionist legislation was first written. In particular, laws have varied on what constitutes a legitimate claim against the state for aid, on the institutional structures used to adjudicate forms of aid, and on the discretion granted to administrators. The first type of aid examined we labeled liberal, created after the U.S. moved towards opening up its borders to trade. Philosophically, the period is characterized by limited state intervention; governments serve their societies most efficiently when they do not interfere with market mechanisms. The institutional structure is executive centered, and administrators have considerable discretion in adjudicating cases. The second set of ideas were labeled as "fair" trade. Here the legitimate role of government in trade is to ensure that American producers compete in a fair market. Written in the years preceding World War II, these laws are more Congress centered, are more detailed in the criteria administrators use to adjudicate the case, and on the whole allow less discretion than do other trade laws. The overt use of discretion to counter the intent of these laws by the Treasury Department was the central issue that led Congress to move administrative control to the Department of Commerce.

The third set of beliefs we labeled redistributive. Here, the government is portrayed as having some responsibility for abrogating the ill effects of the market. As with the escape clause, these laws are executive centered. And, as above, the president has the right to overturn decisions. The administration of these laws, however, was given to sympathetic departments with strong ties to affected communities. From the start, this form of aid was envisioned as a method of alleviating the painful aspects of liberalism.

This article shows that each of these three types of protectionism operated according to a different logic and aided a different type of constituent. By examining laws that direct the relationship between the state and society on trade matters, we saw that legislation reflected differing notions about the legitimate role of the state. Viewing laws over time, we saw that each functioned with a different internal logic and a different calculus of politics. Even though the escape clause was potentially a protectionist instrument, the structure of the statute encouraged liberal central decision-makers to undercut the ability of groups to use the law effectively. Conversely, the laws we designated as "fair" trade legislation have consistently forced central decision-makers to protect the American market. Liberal central decision-makers have done *whatever* is possible to undercut these laws. This too is reflected in the data. However, these laws were structured in a period of congressional ascendance. The executive is not granted the rights he gained in post-Depression legislation. To illustrate the third component of policy, we turned to Trade Adjustment Assistance. Adjustment assistance was argued to be a transfer payment to industries hurt by imports.

It is both interesting and important that in the period through the early 1970s these laws did not interfere with America's international commitment to the liberal trading regime. By pushing for fair trade, unfair trade laws served to reinforce the norm that market mechanisms, not government policy, should determine comparative advantage. Later, however, unfair trade laws, with their narrow interpretation of legitimate government policies, posed a problem to the continuation of free trade. Similarly, the TAA program served liberalism during the 1970s. By creating an alternative to a trade barrier, TAA diffused potential industrial pressures on government for a more substantial response. However, TAA became overwhelmed by petitioners in the late 1970s who took financial aid but continued to file more potent suits against the state. Neither of these programs created much interest among central decision-makers in the 1960s; both were seen as problematic to some aspect of American trade policy two decades later.

A general review of the data presented reveals a number of counterintuitive empirical findings. First, it is clear that as the U.S. became increasingly more open, domestic groups put up resistance. Increased resistance, however, is not the explanation for aid receipt. Rather, it is the fit between the strategy employed by groups and state structures that explains state response.

Second, a free trade bias seems to exist among central decision-makers and is part of an explanation for policy. In particular, the Office of the President has been active in protecting America's liberal position. Although the congressional position on trade has varied, the position of the executive has been unambiguous. When confronted by a choice between giving aid or not, the executive gave no aid. When protectionism was mandated by the bureaucracy, the president often chose to give a transfer payment, to give less than recommended, or in the case of countervailing duties, to sanction a tariff waiver. In dumping cases, legislation precludes direct executive action. In response, the president has attempted to control petition activity, using a variety of incentives to convince petitioners to halt the dumping investigation voluntarily.

It is in the category of circumvention of protectionism that we find VERs and OMAs. All were used as mechanisms to give industries less than they would have received either from an ITC, Treasury Department, or Department of Commerce ruling. In terms of fiscal impact, these marketing arrangements constitute a transfer of funds from the American treasury (funds which would have been collected from an equivalent tariff) to foreign governments. They are only rational as a presidential attempt to reconcile systemic interests in maintaining liberalism with a domestic need to respond to industries that fulfill the legal requisites for aid. They are not explicable as a response to group demands for such agreements, as the most efficient mechanism to aid industries, or as a new form of the old protectionism.

Third, of the ideas that have contributed to current trade policy, the notion of redistribution has had the weakest hold on the policymaking community. With budget deficits and a decline in wealth, this policy directive was abandoned. The explanation for the need for adjustment was never as developed as the explanation for free trade or as institutionalized as fair trade practices. Given our review of the functioning of trade policy within the U.S., this lack of an adjustment assistance strategy may ultimately undermine liberalism. The structure of politics in the U.S. places great pressure on government leaders. Some mechanism is necessary to act as a pressure valve. Without this support for groups adversely affected by imports, the pressures on government will lead to a questioning of their cognitive beliefs and make alternative approaches to trade more attractive.

Finally, what is the future of free trade in the U.S.? The U.S.-sponsored trade regime has had a unique character. The U.S. never confronted the political trade-offs associated with free trade doctrine, despite being the major force behind the liberalization of world trade. From free trade's inception, the U.S. never had the institutional capability to maintain all aspects of liberalization. Although accepting the norms of free trade, there was no consensus in Congress to repeal the traditional protections afforded to domestic industry. Thus, the norms and institutions of fair trade coexisted with their liberal counterparts. It is these laws that have the potential of undercutting the regime itself. It is no surprise that of the solutions suggested to America's declining trade balance, it is the call for fair trade and expanded access to export markets, not for the protection of noncompetitive sectors, that has received the greatest attention.

The prosecution of unfair trade laws, however, should not be interpreted as the first step down a "slippery slope" towards high barriers to trade. Liberalism still retains overwhelming support in the U.S. Ideas such as liberalism, however, do have life cycles. The inevitable conflict between free and fair trade in a period of chronic trade imbalance has led to a questioning of the tenets of American trade policy. Currently, however, there is no legitimate theoretical alternative to liberalism. The protectionism of the inter-war period has no support. Welfare-redistributive policies are fiscally not viable. Thus, although there is discontent, a radical change in American policy is unlikely.

Conclusion: an institutional approach to American foreign economic policy
G. John Ikenberry

It may well be that Poincaré's observation is correct, that natural scientists discuss their results and social scientists their methods. If so, it is because our guides to social reality are so frail. Approaches to political investigation are difficult to separate from the substantive puzzles that drive inquiry and the results that follow. In collective enterprises, such as this volume, the problem of approach or method becomes all the more central. We are left with no choice but to reflect on the tools that we use as well as on the social reality that they promise to reveal.

This volume began by identifying three major approaches to the study of American foreign economic policy. System-centered approaches trace policy to demands or opportunities generated within the international political economy. Prevailing distributions of power, the norms and principles embedded in international regimes, or the imperatives of international economic structures have all been invoked as systemic explanations of American foreign economic policy. Society-centered approaches trace policy to the demands placed on government by private groups, sectors, or classes within the national political system. State-centered approaches trace policy to either the active role of government officials pursuing autonomous goals or to the shaping and contraining role of the state's organizational structure.

In the historical cases that followed, the authors drew upon these perspectives in various ways to develop explanations for policy outcomes. Individually, the contributors differ in the emphasis and weight they give to these

I gratefully acknowledge the comments and suggestions of David Lake and Michael Mastanduno as well as the other authors in this volume. I have also received helpful comments from David Bachman, Peter Hall, Stephen Krasner, Charles Kupchan, Ken Oye, Theda Skocpol, and participants in the conference on "The American State in the International Political Economy," sponsored by the Program on Interdependent Political Economy, University of Chicago, 29 April 1987.

International Organization 42, 1, Winter 1988

three categories or varieties of explanation. Taken together, however, the articles suggest two general conclusions. First, societal and international approaches can be significantly enhanced by incorporating a conception of the state as an independent or intervening variable in the explanation. Second, in the historical account of American foreign economic policy, the conventional view of a "weak" state is inadequate. In a variety of historical cases, the authors found that government officials play a more active and innovative role and that state structures play a more crucial shaping and constraining role than the conventional wisdom predicts.

Both societal and international-centered explanations of foreign economic policy suffer from a "black box" understanding of policymaking. Each approach posits a set of forces that encourage or inhibit particular types of policy. How these social or international forces shape policy is unclear. International forces may manifest in a variety of ways. States might respond in a unitary and rational manner to changing international constraints and imperatives. Alternatively, policy might conform to international incentives through a process of selection or emulation. Similarly, social forces may manifest through direct actions of groups or classes, or more indirectly, through anticipatory and entrepreneurial actions of government representatives. An understanding of how these social and international forces are transmitted and mediated within the black box of government is particularly important when analysts are investigating small numbers of policy choices in a single country. If the analyst were only interested in predicting general tendencies over long stretches of time, the simplicity of these approaches might be compelling. The types of investigations presented in this volume, however, are more focused and historically bounded. In these cases, the authors, taken as a group, are more interested in explaining variations in American foreign economic policy. Such an agenda requires a more differentiated analysis, and because of this, intervening factors such as the state's organizational structure and the independent actions of executive officials increase in importance.

This is the theoretical warrant for incorporating a theory of the state in the explanation of American foreign economic policy, and this leads to our second conclusion. The state as a conceptual variable is important in two respects. First, as several of the authors have argued, politicians and executive officials, embracing a distinctive set of policy objectives, may be of decisive importance in shaping outcomes. State officials may be instrumental in interpreting the nature of international pressures or imperatives. Moreover, these officials at various moments may be able to activate and reshape the play of societal groups, influence the character of their preferences, or ignore them altogether. Second, the organizational structure of the state exerts an influence over policy choice. The state is not simply a collection of officials, but it is also a piece of strategically important terrain, which shapes the entire course of political battles and sometimes provides the resources and advantages necessary to win them. In the long run, the political institutions that undergird policymaking may well reflect more basic social and international forces. However, in the short run or in the absence of a major socioeconomic crisis to induce change, state structures are important in setting the framework that facilitates or inhibits access to political resources and the policymaking apparatus, including the role and influence of government officials themselves.

When American foreign economic policy is explored from a state-centered perspective, the conventional "weak" state interpretation appears misleading. The strong state/weak state idea was developed primarily to situate and compare the United States with other advanced industrial countries.[1] While the labels of "weak" and "strong" may have some utility for comparative investigations, they are wholly inadequate for historical analysis of the American case. Many of the authors in this volume have found that the image of a "weak" state, with government officials highly constrained by private groups, is not sustained in important episodes of foreign economic policy. Taken as a whole, the authors suggest that more differentiated and nuanced conceptions of the American state are needed that allow for variations in the role and efficacy of state and society.

In this conclusion, I build upon these arguments to address the larger theoretical research agenda on American foreign economic policy. In particular, I argue that many strains in the authors' arguments contribute to and advance an "institutional" approach to foreign economic policy.[2] The task ahead is to examine this institutional approach and the research program it proposes.

Constructing theory of foreign economic policy

The arguments presented above suggest the importance of systematic and historically grounded studies of the American state in the conduct of foreign economic policy. Even in the United States, with a political system marked by its fragmentation of political authority and diffusion of power, the shaping and constraining role of state officials and the institutions they inhabit remain considerable. The implication of this conclusion, however, is not that, in a contest of approaches, the state-centered models of foreign economic policy won. The conclusion is not that scholars embracing society and system-centered perspectives should pack their theoretical tents and steal

---

1. Peter J. Katzenstein, "International Relations and Domestic Structures: Foreign Economic Policies of Advanced Industrial States," *International Organization* 30 (Winter 1976), pp. 1–45; Katzenstein, "Introduction" and "Conclusion: Domestic Structures and Strategies of Foreign Economic Policy," in Katzenstein, ed., *Between Power and Plenty* (Madison: University of Wisconsin Press, 1978).

2. This point is my own judgment. My characterization of the volume should not suggest that the contributors have reached an explicit consensus.

away into the night. In fact, the research presented in this volume suggests a very different message. The most useful analysis explores the interplay and the historically contingent role of international-, societal-, and state-centered variables. In effect, we need a more encompassing set of reference points that provide guidance in selecting and incorporating the array of explanatory variables.

Moreover, the contributions to this volume also point to the importance of *institutional setting* for understanding particular policy outcomes. It is not enough simply to explore the immediate struggle over policy by societal, governmental, and transnational actors. While the process of policymaking is important, that process itself rests upon larger structures that influence, guide, redirect, magnify, and inhibit policy battles. Consequently, we need a better appreciation of the shaping and constraining role of the policy or institutional setting, as well as the historical dynamics that shape this institutional setting.

There are several ways to arrive at a theoretical appreciation of the interplay of system, society, and state-centered variables. One approach focuses on the properties of issue-areas. In that approach, the influences of societal groups and state officials are understood to follow from the characteristics of the political goods to be provided. Joanne Gowa develops this approach early in this volume, and in a later section, I return to this theme. I argue that this issue-area approach leads the analyst to questions of agenda-setting and institutional structure. A focus of the characteristics of policy does provide some leverage for explaining variations in the role and involvement of societal and governmental actors, but the approach begs the question of how and why policy becomes defined in ways that encourage or inhibit political action.

A second approach focuses on the shaping and constraining role of institutional structures of state and society, and on the historical dynamics of continuity and change that underlie these structures. The central claim of this perspective is that institutional structures mediate the interests and capacities of the groups and individuals within them. Large-scale and historically evolving organizational structures of state and society shape and constrain the interests that actors come to embrace and the resources they wield. In what follows, I argue that an "institutional" approach that focuses on the dynamics of institutional structures and on the manner in which those structures shape and constrain societal and governmental actors provides a promising, if as yet poorly elaborated, research program for the study of American foreign economic policy.

Institutional structures and historical dynamics

The struggle over foreign economic policy—the demands of societal groups and the imperatives of the international political economy—are mediated by the institutional setting in which it takes place. That institutional setting is the outcome of a confluence of historical forces that shape and reshape the state's organizational structure. From this "institutional" perspective, the challenge for scholars is to uncover the historical dynamics—both domestic and international—that shape the organizational structures of state and society, and the way that these structures shape, constrain, inhibit, and enable societal and governmental actors. The assumption behind this approach is that the relative importance of specific variables is time-bound, and theories of foreign economic policy must therefore be placed within a larger historical and institutional framework.

Institutionalist claims

The institutional approach, often called "path dependent" analysis, carries with it a variety of theoretical claims. First, there is a structuralist claim. Institutional structures shape and constrain the capacities of groups and individuals within them. Institutional structures refer both to the organizational characteristics of groups and to the rules and norms that guide the relationships between actors. These structures, as James March and Johan Olsen note, can be understood as "a collection of institutions, rules of behavior, norms, roles, physical arrangements, buildings, and archives that are relatively resilient to the idiosyncratic preferences and expectations of individuals."[3] Institutions have structural characteristics because they are not simply or straightforward reflections of social forces.[4] "Organization does more than transmit the preferences of particular groups," Peter Hall argues, "it combines and ultimately alters them." Because of this, economic policy "may not faithfully reflect a struggle among competing economic interests precisely because organization refracts that struggle."[5] It is not enough to delineate the preferences of social groups and government officials themselves. Those preferences will be constrained, and perhaps even shaped, by the larger institutional setting within which they are situated.[6]

A second claim is that institutional change is episodic and "sticky," rather than continuous and incremental.[7] Institutional structures, once established,

3. James G. March and Johan P. Olsen, "The New Institutionalism: Organizational Factors in Political Life," *American Political Science Review* 78 (September 1984), p. 735.

4. Huntington makes a similar distinction between social forces and political institutions or organizations. "A social force is an ethnic, religious, territorial, economic or status group . . . A political organization or procedure, on the other hand, is an arrangement for maintaining order, resolving disputes, selecting authoritative leaders, and thus promoting community among two or more social forces." *Political Order in Changing Societies* (New Haven, Conn.: Yale University Press, 1968), pp. 8–9.

5. Peter Hall, *Governing the Economy: The Politics of State Intervention in Britain and France* (New York: Oxford University Press, 1986), p. 233.

6. Stephen Lukes provides a helpful discussion of "structural" constraints. See "Power and Structure," in Lukes, *Essays in Social Theory* (New York: Columbia University Press, 1977), pp. 12–13.

7. Stephen Krasner, "Approaches to the State: Alternative Conceptions and Historical Dynamics," *Comparative Politics* 16 (January 1984), p. 234.

are difficult to change even when underlying social forces continue to evolve. This is true for several reasons. Particular institutional arrangements create privileged positions for individuals and groups who work to perpetuate those arrangements. At the microscopic level, individuals within organizations seek to perserve and protect their missions and responsibilities even when the specific circumstances that brought the organization into existence have changed.[8] At the macroscopic level, institutional reform is carried out within an existing array of organizations and structures that shape and constrain any efforts at change.[9]

Moreover, even when new institutional structures might provide benefits to a majority of groups and individuals, the costs of change and uncertainty concerning those benefits that will, in fact, accrue generate countervailing incentives for the maintainance of existing institutions. "Thus," as Stephen Krasner argues, "even if there is widespread societal dissatisfaction with a particular set of institutions, it may be irrational to change them. The variable costs of maintaining the existing institutions may be less than the total costs of creating and maintaining new ones."[10] Institutions, therefore, are likely to persist even when the social forces and circumstances that forged those institutions have gradually changed.

Arthur Stinchcombe has explained the dynamics of discontinuous institutional change in terms of the "liability of newness." When circumstances prompt the need for institutional change, Stinchcombe argues, the newer organization has to be "much more beneficial than the old before the flow of benefits compensates for the relative weakness of the newer social structure." For this reason, successful organizational change tends to take place "only when the alternatives are stark (generally in wartime)."[11] Without a crisis, the liability of newness makes organizational change difficult.

Consequently, change is likely to be episodic and occur at moments of crisis (war or depression), when existing institutions break down or are discredited and when struggles over basic rules of the game emerge. Political or economic crisis acts as a solvent, throwing into relief discontinuities between underlying social forces and existing institutions.[12] Moreover, polit-

---

8. A large literature in organizational theory explores this point. See discussion in Huntington, *Political Order in Changing Societies,* pp. 15–17. See also James Q. Wilson, *Political Organizations* (New York: Basic Books, 1973); Herbert Kaufman, *The Limits of Organizational Change* (University, Ala.: University of Alabama Press, 1971).

9. See Steven Skowronek, *Building a New American State: The Expansion of National Administrative Capacities* (New York: Cambridge University Press, 1982).

10. Krasner, "Approaches to the State," p. 235.

11. Arthur L. Stinchcombe, "Social Structure and Organizations," in James G. March, ed., *Handbook of Organizations* (Chicago: Rand McNally, 1965), p. 148.

12. For a general discussion of the logic of developmental explanation, see Gabriel A. Almond, "Approaches to Developmental Causation," in Almond, Scott G. Flanagan, and Robert J. Mundt, eds., *Crisis, Choice, and Change: Historical Studies of Political Development* (Boston: Little, Brown, 1973), pp. 1–42. The role of domestic political crisis and discontinuous policy change is emphasized in a new study of postwar Japanese politics. See Kent E. Calder,

ical elites may define and manipulate the role of crisis. If crisis is, as Harold Lasswell suggests, a "situation in which there is a great stress towards action, towards the resolution of conflict," then such conditions might well be encouraged or harnessed by officials seeking change.[13]

The logic of discontinuous institutional change parallels similar arguments that have been made at the international level for hegemonic systems and regime change. Robert Gilpin argues that change in the international system is likely to occur as the disjuncture grows between "the existing system of governance of the system" and the underlying "power in the system."[14] Likewise, the autonomy of international regimes, as Krasner argues, also may manifest when those regimes persist, even as the underlying distribution of power and interests that created them have changed.[15] While theories of institutional change (as well as their international-level counterparts) do not provide clear guidance on the thresholds necessary to induce change, change is likely to be highly episodic and follow from substantial disjunctures between evolving social and international forces and prevailing institutional structures.

A third claim of the institutional approach is causal complexity. In effect, there are interactive lines of causation between the social and economic environment and institutional structures. Large-scale social crises at one moment are likely to have profound effects on the institutions of the state. At a later moment, executive officials and politicians within the state itself may be in a position to influence or mediate the institutional position and efficacy of social forces. From this perspective, historical sequence and phasing become crucial to explanation. A dependent variable at T1 may become an independent or intervening variable at T2. Choices made at one juncture limit choices made at subsequent junctures. A historical branching process takes shape with earlier political choices creating the circumstances and limiting the options in the intervening period.

This claim of causal complexity complicates the theoretical enterprise, and leads to a final methodological claim on the primacy of contingent historical analysis. The institutional structures of countries emerge from distinctive national experiences. Consequently, theory must remain historically grounded and sufficiently contingent to allow for the variations in institu-

---

Crisis and Compensation: Policy and Stability in Changing Postwar Japan (Princeton, N.J.: Princeton University Press, 1988).

13. H. D. Lasswell, "Attention Structure and Social Structure," in Lyman Bryson, ed., *The Communication of Ideas* (New York: Harper, 1948), p. 262. The importance of the instrumental use of crisis was aptly expressed by Carl Schmitt: "Sovereign is he who decides the emergency situation." Cited by Franz Neumann in "Approaches to the Study of Political Power," *Political Science Quarterly* 65 (June 1950), p. 178. Albert Hirschman brought these references to my attention.

14. Robert Gilpin, *War and Change in World Politics* (New York: Cambridge University Press, 1981), p. 186.

15. Krasner, "Regimes and the Limits of Realism: Regimes as Autonomous Variables," in Krasner, ed., *International Regimes* (Ithaca: Cornell University Press, 1983), p. 359–61.

tional structures.[16] The fundamental premise of this approach is that political outcomes do not simply result from instrumental behavior by groups nor are they explicable in terms of functional or efficient social processes.[17] The institutional perspective leads the analyst to focus on the preexisting structures of social relations and their often unintended outcomes. Past historical circumstance, or what I have elsewhere termed the "shadow of the past," weighs heavily on what is possible and what is perceived to be desirable at specific moments.[18]

Varieties of institutional structure

What are these institutional structures? The earlier description by March and Olsen, which includes "rules of behavior, norms, roles," and even "physical arrangements," would suggest that they could be just about anything that serves as an external constraint on the behavior of individuals and groups. It is useful, therefore, to distinguish between different levels or varieties of institutional structure. These levels range from specific characteristics of government institutions, to the more overarching structures of state, to the nation's normative social order. Uniting these conceptions of institutional structure is the view that collections of norms and rules—large or small—manifest a certain political autonomy. Institutions provide the rules and the arenas within which social forces contend. Yet they also, to varying degrees, set the terms and provide the resources for that struggle. These various levels of institutional structure are summarized in Table 1.

At its narrowest definition, institutional structure refers to the administrative, legislative, and regulatory rules that guide the adjudication of conflict. Rules and procedures at this level are extensive, and they undergird the making of foreign economic policy. For example, guidelines set down in the 1974 Trade Agreements Act structured the U.S. Senate's review of the 1979 Tokyo Round Agreements. These guidelines channeled and constrained the role of private interests throughout the negotiation and ratification process.[19]

16. The theoretical enterprise within an institutional approach remains untidy. Yet this does not mean that large-scale theoretical generalizations are not possible. See John A. Hall, *Powers and Liberties: The Causes and Consequences of the Rise of the West* (New York: Penguin, 1986), p. 22. In many respects, the institutional perspective discussed here is congenial with the broader field of historical sociology. See Theda Skocpol, "Emerging Agendas and Recurrent Strategies in Historical Sociology," in Skocpol, ed., *Vision and Method in Historical Sociology* (New York: Cambridge University Press, 1984), pp. 356–91.

17. March and Olsen, "The New Institutionalism."

18. Ikenberry, *Reasons of State: The Oil Shocks of the 1970s and the Capacities of American Government* (Ithaca: Cornell University Press, 1988).

19. On the ratification procedures, see I.M. Destler, *Making Foreign Economic Policy* (Washington, D.C.: Brookings Institution, 1980), pp. 170–78. On their implementation, see I.M. Destler and Thomas Graham, "United States and the Tokyo Round: Lessons of a Success Story," *The World Economy* 3 (June 1980), pp. 53–70; Destler, "Trade Consensus–SALT Stalemate: Congress and Foreign Policy in the Seventies," in Thomas Mann and Norman J. Ornstein, eds., *The New Congress* (Washington, D.C.: American Enterprise Institute, 1981),

TABLE 1. *Levels of institutional structure*

Institutional structure	Characteristics	Nature of constraint
1. Administrative, congressional, and regulatory rules and procedures	Decision-making rules; standards; mechanisms to process claims	Channels of access to policy; availability and levels of benefits
2. Centralization and dispersion of power within the state	Balance of power between representative and executive bodies; centralization and coherence of bureaucracy; types of policy instruments	Capacities and resources of executive and congressional actors
3. Normative order defining relations between state and society	Prevailing national ideological proscriptions and prescriptions for state involvement in economy	Legitimacy and illegitimacy of alternative types of policy

In another case, the 1971 Wage and Price Controls played an important, if unanticipated, role in shaping the array of private interests that would struggle over oil pricing policy after 1973. In the many areas of American trade policy, as Goldstein illustrates, the accumulation of administrative and legal procedures shapes and constrains the provision of protection. Similarly, Robert Baldwin argues that "institutional arrangements . . . significantly reduced the ability of pressure groups to influence protection levels in particular industries."[20] These myriad rules and procedures provide the institutional bulwark within which social groups and government officials must contend. Institutional structures of this sort render some potential actions unavailable or unacceptable and make others possible.

A broader conception of institutional structure refers to the centralization and diffusion of power within the state. The capacities and resources of the various organizations that comprise the state are of concern here: the balance of power between Congress and the executive, the centralization and coherence of the bureaucracy, and the policy instruments available to incumbents within these organizations. In relating these institutional structures to foreign economic policy, scholars have given special attention to the role and efficacy of executive officials within the state. Developing a comparative framework, for example, Katzenstein focuses on variations among advanced industrial states in the centrality and autonomy of bureaucratic organizations capable of programmatic policy planning.[21] John Zysman, who

pp. 319–59; and Robert Cassidy, "Negotiating about Negotiations," in Thomas M. Franck, ed., *The Tethered Presidency* (New York: New York University Press, 1981), pp. 264–82.

20. Robert E. Baldwin, *The Political Economy of U.S. Import Policy* (Cambridge, Mass.: MIT Press, 1985), pp. 177–78.

21. Katzenstein, "Conclusion."

is interested in the divergent abilities of advanced capitalist states to shape industrial adjustment, focuses on three structural elements: mechanisms of recruitment in the national civic service; the degree of centralization within government civil service; and the extent of independence from legislative oversight.[22] Variations along these dimensions of institutional structure, Zysman argues, lead to differences in the ability of capitalist states to shape the course of industrial adjustment. In the American case, scholars have emphasized the fragmentation of power within the state and, as a result, the prominent role Congress plays in policy formation.[23] It is at this level of institutional structure that many of the contributions to this volume situate their analyses.

Finally, a still broader conception of institutional structure refers to the norms that govern the relations between state and society. Rather than identifying concrete rules and procedures or characteristics of the state's organizational structure, this level focuses on the often implicit normative boundaries that define the relations between state and society. Nations differ in terms of the reigning political beliefs that render legitimate particular types of state involvements in the economy and society The *étatist* tradition in France and the market ideology of the United States each exerts an influence on the conduct of foreign economic policy. "Among the Americans," as Andrew Shonfield has observed, "there is a general commitment to the view, shared by both political parties, of the natural predominance of private enterprise in the economic sphere and of the subordinate role of public initiative in any other than a manifest national emergency."[24]

The sway of this normative order may be found in particular historical episodes when economic distress generates proposals that appear to transgress prevailing normative conceptions of public and private. During World War II, for example, declining domestic petroleum production and British dominance in Middle Eastern oil fields prompted officials within the Roosevelt administration to develop plans for direct government involvement in foreign petroleum production. Despite elaborate plans and a national security rationale, major oil producers wielding normative claims of private market control blocked these efforts.[25] Broadly speaking, the prevailing set

22. John Zysman, *Government, Markets, and Growth: Financial Systems and the Politics of Industrial Change* (Ithaca, N.Y.: Cornell University Press, 1983), p. 300.

23. Robert Pastor, *Congress and the Politics of U.S. Foreign Economic Policy, 1929–1976* (Berkeley: University of California Press, 1980); Destler, *Making Foreign Economic Policy*.

24. Andrew Shonfield, *Modern Capitalism: The Changing Balance of Public and Private Power* (New York: Oxford University Press, 1965), p. 298.

25. An extensive literature discusses this episode. The most complete analysis is Irvine H. Anderson, *ARAMCO, the United States and Saudi Arabia: A Study of the Dynamics of Foreign Oil Policy, 1933–1950* (Princeton, N.J.: Princeton University Press, 1981), pp. 42–56. See also Michael B. Stoff, *Oil, War, and American Security: The Search for a National Policy on Foreign Oil, 1941–1947* (New Haven, Conn.: Yale University Press, 1980), pp. 84–86; and David Aaron Miller, *Search for Security: Saudi Arabian Oil and American Foreign Policy* (Chapel Hill: University of North Carolina Press, 1980), pp. 81–82.

of normative expectations about the proper role of state intervention in the society and economy strengthens the position of some actors and weakens that of others—political efficacy coming from the degree to which an actor's position resonates with the larger ideological structure.

These conceptions of institutional structure prompt a variety of questions that focus research on American foreign economic policy. Across the levels of institutional structure, they direct attention to the ways that rules and norms constrain the ability of groups to achieve their goals as well as influence the nature of those goals. Consequently, the analysis of the impact of institutions on policy cannot be separated from an analysis of the underlying configurations of power and interests. The claims made by Judith Goldstein and Robert Baldwin, for example, carry a set of expectations about what protectionist forces would want and could accomplish in the absence of institutional restraints. In this way, the institutional perspective is particularly useful when explored in the context of changing societal and economic forces. It is precisely when discontinuities can be found between underlying social forces and policy outcomes that institutional structures gain explanatory importance. For this reason, it is best to pay attention to historical turning points or junctures when social and international forces are changing rapidly.

A second set of questions concern the forces that shape institutional structure. This analysis focuses on the historical logic that accounts for particular structural outcomes, such as the distribution of power within the state. At this level, scholars turn to the general processes of political and economic development. The "general laws" of historical development, as they relate to the institutional setting of policymaking, also need further theoretical attention. Nonetheless, large-scale processes of political and economic change can relate to the circumstances of policy formation. I shall now sketch these institutional lines of analysis, with special attention to phases of historical development and the impact of crisis on institutional change.

Phases of historical development

The institutional claim is that the organizational structures of state and society shape and constrain foreign economic policy, and that, at periodic moments of crisis, those structures themselves may be reworked or transformed in the process of policymaking. Understanding the structures of state and society and the dynamics of change requires attention to phases of political and economic development. In these large-scale processes of historical development, the basic characteristics of organizational structure emerge. The balance of power between legislature and executive, the centralization and coherence of bureaucratic organizations, and the resources and policy instruments available to executive officials are all aspects of the prevailing organizational structures of state and society.

Scholars have identified a variety of historical forces that shape the origins and trajectories of modern states and give them distinctive organizational characteristics. Variations in the sequencing and timing of political and economic development and the state-building responses to economic depression and war powerfully affect the centralization and capacities of the representative and bureaucratic institutions of the state. Many European nations, for example, constructed powerful administrative organizations in advance of the spread of democratic institutions, which served to strengthen the role that executive officials could play in subsequent periods of economic and political development.[26] War and geopolitical conflict from the early modern period onward also had centralizing effects on European state bureaucracies; they also created incentives for developing extensive capacities for economic intervention and extraction.[27]

In the United States, the constitution preserved and codified a loose federal system that dispersed sovereignty across national, state, and local levels and between judicial, congressional, and executive branches. In the nineteenth century, when European state bureaucracies were expanding, the United States remained a government of "courts and parties," with highly competitive political parties and patronage-oriented domestic politics strengthening the role of congressional-centered government. Unlike their European counterparts, the spread of a mass-based democratic political system in the United States preceded the establishment of centralizing administrative institutions, and this sequencing of political development constrained bureaucratic centralization throughout the nineteenth century.[28]

The relatively insular economic and geopolitical position of the United

26. Charles Tilly, ed., *The Formation of National States in Western Europe* (Princeton, N.J.: Princeton University Press, 1975); Gianfranco Poggi, *The Development of the Modern State* (Stanford: Stanford University Press, 1978); Reinhard Bendix, *Kings and People: Power and the Mandate to Rule* (Berkeley: University of California Press, 1978); Micahel Mann, "The Autonomous Power of the State: Its Origins, Mechanisms and Results," *Archives Européenes de Sociologie* 25 (1984), pp. 185–213.

27. The relationship between war and state-building is an issue of ongoing research. See Charles Tilly, "Reflections on the History of European State-Making," in Tilly, ed., *The Formation of National States in Western Europe*; and Tilly, "War Making and State Making as Organized Crime," in Peter B. Evans, Dietrich Rueschemeyer, and Theda Skocpol, eds., *Bringing the State Back In* (New York: Cambridge University Press, 1985). Michael Mann, in the reconstruction of English state finance, demonstrates that the major expenditure of the British state was on warfare, and that war or the investment in war-related capacities prompted major expansions in levels of expenditure. Michael Mann, "State and Society, 1130–1815: An Analysis of English State Finances," in Maurice Zeitlin, ed., *Political Power and Social Theory*, vol. 1 (Greenwich, Conn.: JAI Press, 1980). Similar conclusions, explored comparatively, are reached by Karen A. Rasler and William R. Thompson, "War Making and State Making: Governmental Expenditures, Tax Revenues, and Global Wars," *American Political Science Review* 79 (June 1985), pp. 491–507. See also Art Stein, *The Nation at War* (Baltimore: Johns Hopkins University Press, 1980).

28. Skowronek, *Building a New American State* (New York: Cambridge University Press, 1982); J. Roger Hollingsworth, "The United States," in Raymond Grew, ed., *Crises of Political Development in Europe and the United States* (Princeton, N.J.: Princeton University Press, 1978).

States in the decades prior to World War I also reinforced a congressionally dominated political system.[29] The large internal market allowed the emergence of hierarchical and integrated business enterprises in the late nineteenth century to grow in the absence of a large and capable state apparatus. Where continental European nations, as Alexander Gerschenkron argues, developed extensive institutional relations between business and the state in this formative, industrial period, American public officials were left to play a subsidiary role in economic development.[30]

These basic organizational features of the American state were built upon, but not radically changed, during the world wars and Great Depression of the 20th century. United States involvement in the world wars did not have the same effect on state-building in continental Europe.[31] Mobilization for war occurred through a variety of temporary administrative programs that brought private businesspeople directly into the offices of the state. These state-sponsored, but privately run, emergency programs were easily disas-

29. Weber noted the importance of basic historical differences between the United States and Germany, including international position, for political development. "Destiny," Weber argues, has encumbered Germany "with a dense population and an intensive culture, which has forced us to maintain the splendor of our old culture, so to speak, in an armed camp within a world bristling with arms . . . The United States does not yet know such problems. This nation will probably never encounter some of them. It has no old aristocracy; hence the tensions caused by the contrast between authoritarian tradition and the purely commercial character of modern economic conditions do not exist. Rightly it celebrates the purchase of this immense territory . . . without this acquisition, with powerful and warlike neighbors at its side, it would be forced to wear the coat of mail like ourselves, who constantly keep in the drawer of our desks the march order in case of war." Weber, "Capitalism and Rural Society in Germany," in H. H. Gerth and C. Wright Mills, eds., *From Max Weber: Essays in Sociology* (New York: Oxford University Press, 1946), pp. 384–85. The importance of the state's geopolitical position in political development is stressed by Otto Hintze. See Felix Gilbert, ed., *The Historical Essays of Otto Hintze* (New York: Oxford University Press, 1975); and Hintze "The State in Historical Perspective," in Reinhard Bendix, ed., *State and Society: A Reader in Comparative Historical Sociology* (Berkeley: University of California Press, 1973), pp. 154–69.

30. Alexander Gerschenkron, "Economic Backwardness in Historical Perspective," in Gerschenkron, *Economic Backwardness in Historical Perspective: A Book of Essays* (Cambridge, Mass.: Harvard University Press, 1962), pp. 5–30. The argument has been developed further by James R. Kurth, "The Political Consequences of the Product Cycle: Industrial History and Political Outcomes," *International Organization* 33 (Winter 1979), pp. 1–34; and Kurth, "Industrial Change and Political Change: A European Perspective," in David Collier, ed., *The New Authoritarianism of Latin America* (Princeton, N.J.: Princeton University Press, 1979). A discussion of this theme in terms of the U.S. case is presented by Alfred D. Chandler, Jr., "Government versus Business: An American Phenomenon," in John T. Dunlop, ed., *Business and Public Policy* (Cambridge, Mass.: Harvard University Press, 1980); Chandler, *The Visible Hand: The Managerial Revolution in American Business* (Cambridge, Mass.: Harvard University Press, 1978); and Chandler, "The Coming of Big Business," in C. Vann Woodward, ed., *The Comparative Approach to American History* (New York: Basic Books, 1968), pp. 220–35. David Vogel, "Why Businessmen Distrust Their State: The Political Consciousness of American Corporate Executives," *British Journal of Political Science* 8 (January 1978), pp. 45–78. See also Andrew Shonfield, *Modern Capitalism*, pp. 298–329.

31. World War I did have some institutional repercussions. In the area of labor relations, see Julie Strickland, "War, the State, and Labor: The Case of the United States, 1917–1935," paper prepared for delivery at the annual meeting of the American Political Science Association, 28–31 August 1986, Washington, D.C.

sembled in the postwar years, and the decentralized organizational features of the state were largely preserved.[32]

While large-scale continuity can be found in the basic organizational features of state and society, long-term shifts in the nation's international political and economic position, and the more narrow evolution in state institutions, induced changes in the struggle over foreign economic policy. Through much of the post-Civil War period, for example, the American economy remained substantially insulated from the larger international economy. Consequently, the structure of the international system did not significantly influence tariff levels and government-business relations. At the same time, the American government apparatus was not developed in ways that allowed policymakers to pursue systematic and autonomous "state interests." If only because these other forces were absent, therefore, societal groups played a dominant role in shaping or influencing foreign economic policy. Tariff policy was both a source of revenue for government and a tool of pork barrel politics.[33] For these reasons, the interest group perspective is a good explanation of foreign economic policy during this period.

The politics of foreign economic policy began to shift, however, in the last decades of the nineteenth century. First, the United States became increasingly integrated into the international economy in ways that transformed the character of trade policy. Lake develops this argument in his essay.[34] As the United States moved into a position to influence patterns of behavior in the world economy, tariff policy became less an object of pork barrel politics and more an instrument of trade negotiation. The long-term shift in the American international economic position, coupled with a general decline in British dominance, signaled a shift in the politics of trade policymaking. Thus, the international economic position of the United States became increasingly important in the decades spanning the turn of the century.

Second, and somewhat later, the state became more central to trade policy. Passage of the 1934 Reciprocal Trade Agreements Act signaled a long-term move towards centralizing trade policymaking. As Haggard, Goldstein, and others discussed, in the five decades following 1934, trade policy responsibility gradually was transferred from Congress to the executive. The result was a decline in the influence of societal groups over policy. "Shifting decision-making towards the executive resulted in a relative decline in the influence of protectionist forces," Haggard argues.[35] Accordingly, the his-

32. For a discussion of wartime mobilization, see Robert A. Dahl and Charles E. Lindblom, *Politics, Economics, and Welfare* (New York: Harper & Bros., 1953), pp. 402–12.

33. See David M. Pletcher, "1861–1898: Economic Growth and Diplomatic Adjustment," in William H. Becker and Samuel F. Wells, Jr., eds., *Economics and World Power: An Assessment of American Diplomacy Since 1789* (New York: Columbia University Press, 1985).

34. David Lake, "The State and American Trade Strategy in the Pre-Hegemonic Era."

35. Haggard, "The Institutional Foundations of Hegemony: Explaining the Reciprocal Trade Agreements Act of 1934," p. 93; Goldstein, "Ideas, Institutions, and American Trade Policy"; Pastor, *Congress and the Politics of U.S. Foreign Economic Policy, 1929–1976*; I. M. Destler, *American Trade Politics: System Under Stress* (Washington, D.C.: Institute for International Economics, 1986).

torical evolution in the institutional locus of policymaking requires shifts in the explanatory weight of societal and state-centered variables.

It is clear from this discussion that the historical evolution of the nation's international economic position and the trajectory of state-building are interactive. On the one hand, the increasing exposure of the national economy to the international system was a decisive impetus for the centralization of trade policymaking. Haggard, for example, argues that the international trade environment in the 1930s, when bilateral trade agreements and the establishment of preference schemes became prominent, created incentives for flexible and autonomous government capacity to negotiate abroad.[36] The increasing salience of international economic threats and opportunities triggered efforts to enhance the capacities of the state.[37] On the other hand, independent developments in the structure of the state create new opportunities to react to and participate in the international economy. The changing nature of the American tax system, for example, diminished the importance of the tariff as a source of government revenue, shifting the government's stake in that issue.[38]

The general point that emerges from this perspective is that the appropriateness of system-, society-, and state-centered theory is grounded in the larger set of historical dynamics that undergird institutional structures and policymaking. Moreover, by placing particular explanations in historical and developmental perspective, interactive aspects of these variables become more evident. The logic of the institutional perspective can be further specified by looking at critical junctures that drive its progress.

Crises and critical junctures

The institutional approach, as noted above, gives special attention to specific historical junctures when economic or political crises reshape social relations and the institutions of policymaking. "Critical junctures" or episodic events refer to unanticipated and exogenous events that drive institution-building and, in turn, foreign economic policy. Depression and war are critical catalysts of change from this perspective.

---

36. Haggard, "The Institutional Foundations of Hegemony," p. 118. See also David A. Lake, *Power, Protection, and Free Trade: International Sources of U.S. Commercial Strategy, 1887–1939* (Ithaca, N.Y.: Cornell University Press, 1988), chap. 6.

37. There is a growing literature on this relationship. Overviews of it can be found in Peter Gourevitch, "The Second Image Reversed," *International Organization* 32 (Autumn 1978), pp. 881–912; and Gabriel A. Almond, "Roundtable on Internal vs. External Factors in Political Development," paper presented at the annual meeting of the American Political Science Association, New Orleans, 31 August 1985.

38. This issue is disputed. The new economic history strongly argues that the income tax was adopted because of the economic needs to reduce tariffs. See Ben Baack and Edward John Ray, "The Political Economy of the Origins and Development of the Federal Income Tax," *Research in Economic History*, supplement 4 (Greenwich, Conn.: JAI Press, 1985), pp. 121–38. On the post-Civil War role of tarrifs in raising revenue, see J. B. Condliffe, *The Commerce of Nations* (New York: Norton, 1950), pp. 229–30.

The importance of crisis stems from the intransigence of political institutions and relations. Politicians and administrators are continuously engaged in coping with socioeconomic challenges; responses are channeled through existing institutions. At particular moments, however, these challenges call into question existing rules of the game and the repertoires of state action. Extraordinary events prompt not just policy change, but also changes in institutional structure.[39] The impact of socioeconomic crisis on the institutional foundations of American foreign economic policy is evident, although scholars do not sufficiently understand its theoretical dimensions. The reason is that crisis plays a *catalytic* role in institutional development, and a multitude of intervening variables mediate the manner in which crisis will be manifest.

The onset of economic depression in the late 1920s, for example, was a catastrophic event that triggered the interest group politics of Smoot–Hawley. The precipitating events began in 1927 with the depression in American agriculture. At this juncture, farmers began to leave their historic position within the free trade coalition.[40] As that coalition broke down, the countervailing pressure on trade policy eroded and tariff policy became, as Schattschneider called it, the "strategy of reciprocal noninterferences."[41] A radically changed economic environment activated more societal groups and intensified political pressure on the state, overwhelming American governmental institutions. At a later moment, however, the continuing, downward spiral of the economy and the retaliatory responses of foreign trading nations only extended the crisis and served to delegitimate tariffs as an appropriate response to depression.[42] In both cases, policy change followed economic crisis. At one point, economic crisis unleashed the play of private groups; at another point, economic crisis created opportunities for government officials to reform the policymaking process and shift trade policy authority out of congressional hands.

---

39. Hirschman notes the importance of crisis as an inducement for institutional change in his studies of economic policymaking in Latin America. Economic or political crisis may serve to concentrate attention on problems. That is, change may fail in "ordinary times" not for "lack of knowledge, nor even for lack of motivation, but simply for lack of attention." "Experience also shows that crisis may make it possible to take required actions against powerful groups that are normally well entrenched and invulnerable; finally, crisis may stimulate action and hence learning on a problem on which insight has been low and which for that very reason has not been tackled as long as it was in a quiescent state." Albert O. Hirschman, *Journeys Toward Progress: Studies of Economic Policy-Making in Latin America* (New York: The Twentieth Century Fund, 1963), pp. 260–61.

40. See Lake, *Power, Protection, and Free Trade,* chaps. 5 and 6. See also David A. Lake, "Export, Die, or Subsidize: The International Political Economy of American Agriculture, 1885–1939," presented at the annual meeting of the American Political Science Association, 28–31 August 1986, Washington, D.C.

41. E. E. Schattschneider, *Politics, Pressures and the Tariff* (Hamden, Conn.: Archon, 1963), p. 284.

42. See Judith Goldstein, "The Political Economy of Trade: Institutions of Protection," *The American Political Science Review* 80 (March 1986).

In a later period, after World War II, the United States was in a position to perceive and act upon the new set of international demands and opportunities created by the destruction of the war. The crisis of war and the subsequent emergence of Soviet–American hostilities had catalytic effects on the institutions and powers of the state. An entire set of foreign and economic policy institutions were created, and they have persisted even as the international events that triggered these efforts at state-building have changed. Franz Schurmann, for example, argues that there are systematic linkages between war, ideology, and executive power. The crisis of war acted to "increase the power of the executive levels of organization." At the same time, the unrivaled international position of the United States in the later stages of the war and its aftermath allowed President F. D. Roosevelt and Harry Truman extraordinary opportunities to articulate a broad "ideological vision" that also strengthened the role of the executive.[43]

The focus on historical junctures has larger theoretical implications. Internationally generated interests and opportunities, for instance, may only be perceived and acted upon at moments of crisis. Put another way, the international economic and political structure may continually present a set of interests that states might best abide by, but those interests may only be perceived and acted upon at rare moments when crisis generates enough institutional and political fluidity. Such a conclusion would modify, for example, Lake's argument that states are continually monitoring and responding to the evolving national position within the international economic structure.[44]

The impact of these institutions on mediating societal demands or international interests can be of two types. The institutions can influence the way that the actors involved perceive *interests,* domestic and international. For example, the presence of executive agencies, such as the Special Trade Representative, or of administrative trade rules may continue to bias policy in liberal directions even when international competitive circumstances generate increasing pressure for protection.[45] More generally, organizational characteristics can bias the way in which the imperatives of the international system are perceived and acted upon.[46] Also, domestic institutions can influence the *capacities* of government officials to carry out policy. For instance, United States government officials today may want to pursue more

43. Franz Schurmann, *The Logic of World Power* (New York: Pantheon, 1974), pp. 8, 21–22.

44. See Lake, *Power, Protection, and Free Trade.* To the extent that a rational choice perspective can explain the outcomes, the salience of this point would diminish. Stephen D. Krasner, "State Power and the Structure of International Trade," *World Politics* 28 (April 1976), pp. 317–43.

45. Goldstein presents a variant of this argument.

46. See Barry Posen, *The Sources of Military Doctrine* (Ithaca: Cornell University Press, 1985). On the way institutions influence the perceptions of their incumbents, see Mary Douglas, *How Institutions Think* (Syracuse, N.Y.: Syracuse University Press, 1986), especially pp. 91–109.

activist industrial policy, but are unable to develop the necessary types of institutional mechanisms and policy tools. In both these ways, a set of institutional capacities and relationships that only change in fits and spurts may structure the role of societal groups, international pressures, and state officials themselves.

Issue-areas, institutional arenas, and foreign economic policy

Variations in the role of society and state-centered variables may also flow from the characteristics of issue-areas.[47] According to this view, differences in the properties of policy itself give rise to differences in the organization of politics and, consequently, in the role and influence of societal and governmental actors. Turning traditional analysis on its head, Theodore Lowi has argued that policy determines politics.[48] Extending this line of analysis, we can delineate the circumstances under which societal groups are likely to dominate the policy process and when state officials are likely to possess more autonomy.

The importance of issue-area characteristics is most evident when analysts compare trade and monetary policy. Krasner, for example, argues that U.S. commercial policy is an area where power is fragmented and diffused. Monetary policy, on the other hand, is an area that allows government leaders "a relatively free hand."[49] The implication of this observation is that overall characteristics of societal or state structure may have little to do with the power of groups and government officials as they struggle over policy.

There are three major ways that characteristics of an issue-area appear to influence the power of state and society. First, the location of decision-making may influence the activity and success of societal groups. While authority for trade policy spreads across congressional and executive organizations, monetary policy is confined to a small and more insulated arena. For this reason, societal groups have more opportunities to penetrate the decision-making process and influence politicians and officials in the trade area than in monetary policy.

---

47. The issue-area approach does not have much to say about international-centered theory. To the extent that state elites dominate policy and act in terms of systemic constraints and opportunities, however, the international explanations also become relevant.

48. Theodore J. Lowi, "American Business, Public Policy, Case-Studies, and Political Theory," *World Politics* 16 (July 1964), pp. 677–715. See later refinements and extensions by Wilson, *Political Organizations,* chap. 16; William Zimmerman, "Issue Area and Foreign-Policy Process: A Research Note in Search of a General Theory," *The American Political Science Review* 67 (December 1973), pp. 1204–12.

49. Stephen D. Krasner, "United States Commercial and Monetary Policy: Unravelling the Paradox of External Strength and Internal Weakness," in Katzenstein, ed., *Between Power and Plenty,* p. 66.

Second, the ability of groups to determine what interests they may have at stake in the policy decision may differ. The interests that particular groups have in international monetary policy would appear to be more obscure and less palpable than commercial policy. However, these "intellectual barriers to entry," as Gowa argues, are often not as high as commonly assumed. Many associations and firms have sophisticated views of the relationship between monetary policy and group interests.

Third, as Gowa reasons, the incentives for collective action vary. From this perspective, the nature of the good that a particular policy provides is important. Monetary policy exhibits the properties of a public good, and problems of collective action emerge quite readily. A policy of currency devaluation, for example, generates profits for exporters that cannot be selectively distributed only to those who contributed to its production. Nor is it likely that the benefits of exchange rate adjustments will be large enough for particular interest groups to justify the costs of seeking the public good.[50] Trade policy, on the other hand, provides many opportunities for excludability. Tariff legislation, for example, can be narrowly drawn, with protection extended to only a particular industry or even a single firm. "As a consequence," Gowa argues, "interest groups are far more active in it, and the trade policy process appears more fragmented than does its financial counterpart."[51] In other words, because trade policy provides opportunities for a public good (such as a tariff or voluntary export agreement) to be turned into a partly excludable good, the problems of collective action is less severe.

A focus on the logic of collective action uncovers a variety of factors that constrain or facilitate interest group activity over trade policy. Several scholars, for example, have cast this problem in terms of the "market for protection," finding that the costs of organizing effective lobbying efforts vary across industries.[52] For example, the more an industry is regionally concentrated, the more likely it is that an interest group will be successfully organized. Also, the larger the industry, the easier it is to organize support because of scale economies involved in efforts to persuade voters and politicians to adopt policies of protection.[53] Arguments of this sort provide an elaborate specification of the conditions under which particular societal groups can or will demand protectionism.

The public character of political goods, however, is not an inherent and

50. Gowa, "Public Goods and Political Institutions," p. 27.
51. Ibid., p. 22.
52. Kym Anderson and Robert E. Baldwin, "The Political Market for Protection in Industrial Countries: Empirical Evidence," World Bank Staff Working Papers, 1981; Helen Hughes and Jean Waelbroeck, "Foreign Trade and Structural Adjustment—Is There a Threat of New Protectionism?" in Hans-Gert Braun, et al., eds., *The European Economy in the 1980s* (Aldershot, Eng.: Gower, 1983). For an overview, see Douglas Nelson, "Endogenous Tariff Theory: A Critical Survey," unpublished paper, World Bank.
53. Hughes and Waelbroeck, "Foreign Trade and Structural Adjustment," p. 17.

immutable characteristic of a policy area. Issue-areas and their "public content" are defined subjectively and, therefore, can be shaped by political elites and prevailing institutional structures.[54] Specific policies, even within a common substantive policy area, are likely to differ widely in this regard. Such differences, which bear directly on the opportunities for collective action, generate important variations in the power of societal and state actors. The implications of the character of the political good for the power of various actors can be seen in several foreign economic policy cases.

In the case of East–West trade during the early postwar period, the character of the political good influenced the state's ability to pursue a strategy of international economic closure. Michael Mastanduno argues that the strength of the state, which was much greater than in other areas of foreign economic policy, emerged because, in addition to the small economic costs of the policy for most business interests, this area of trade policy was directly related to the conditions of military security. He concludes that "state officials may derive and enjoy considerable domestic strength at times, or in issue-areas in which economic affairs are understood to have direct national security significance."[55] The authority of the executive is strengthened by its ability to link trade to the larger circumstances of national security. As a result, Mastanduno notes, state officials encountered little domestic opposition. The American business community acquiesced in the policy and Congress provided political support.

While East–West trade was easily defined as a public good, this was not the case for American oil pricing policy. In the oil decontrol episode, the nature of the political good provided was deeply contested, and executive officials actively sought to reshape how the public perceived the issue. For most of the 1970s, oil pricing politics was dominated by interest group and congressional efforts to use public policy to protect distributive gains or prevent losses associated with higher energy prices. In Gowa's terms, oil price controls presented multiple opportunities for excludability and, consequently, interest groups easily overcame collective action problems. Since price controls existed prior to the first oil shock, the interests of consumers would be readily apparent and collective action, facilitated by Congress, would be straightforward. At the same time, executive officials found themselves involved in efforts to alter the character of the political good. By embedding the pricing policy in a larger set of foreign economic policy commitments, the position of the executive was strengthened.[56] A societal consensus on the character of the political good was never achieved, but

---

54. On the cognitive definition of issue-areas, see Robert O. Keohane and Joseph S. Nye, *Power and Interdependence: World Politics in Transition* (Boston: Little, Brown, 1977), pp. 64–65.

55. Mastanduno, "Trade as a Strategic Weapon," this volume, p. 124.

56. Ikenberry, "Market Solutions for State Problems."

perceptions in Congress and elsewhere were sufficiently altered to eventually sustain the executive's policy preference.

In another case, multilateral trade negotiations present interest groups with a variety of barriers to entry, thus enhancing the role and influence of state officials. These obstacles to entry relate to the publicness of the political good, but also concern intellectual and institutional barriers. During the Tokyo Round negotiations, for example, factors related to the institutional mechanisms of negotiation and congressional ratification insured that interest group involvement would not dominate policy. Since the policy was designed to implement an international agreement, executive officials would be able to control private groups' access to policymaking. Executive officials were authoritative agents of negotiation, and they wielded control of information. Consequently, they managed commercial groups more easily in the policymaking process than in other trade policy issues.

Accounts of the relationship between government representatives and the trade advisory committees suggest that executive officials were able to use this mechanism to build a domestic consensus on the emerging trade package.[57] In this case, state officials were able to build on their special position as authoritative spokespersons in trade negotiations to control access to the policymaking process. This institutional advantage allowed the executive to construct an elaborate set of advisory committees, and, by so doing, bureaucratize private interests and regularize government-business relations. This episode is a counterpoint to the conventional view of American interest groups in the policy process. From the conventional perspective, as one analyst notes, "there is no institutional way to regulate the access of interest groups to decision-making in the United States . . ."[58] Because of the multiple points of entry to the decision-making process, incentives do not emerge for interest groups to develop hierarchical and monopolistic associations. The Tokyo Round case reveals, however, that even in the United States, opportunities to control information and maintain discretion can emerge, particularly when government-business relations are a part of ongoing international negotiations. Executive officials gained some control over trade negotiations, shaping and influencing the role of business groups more effectively than observers might otherwise have expected.

During the ratification process of Tokyo Round agreements, institutional factors also facilitated state control of policy. A unique set of congressional

57. Gilbert Winham, *International Trade and the Tokyo Round* (Princeton, N.J.: Princeton University Press, 1986), chap. 8; John Ikenberry, "Manufacturing Consensus: The Institutionalization of American Private Interests in the Tokyo Round," Princeton University, 1986. See also Joan E. Twiggs, *The Tokyo Round of Multilateral Trade Negotiations: A Case Study in Building Domestic Support for Diplomacy* (New York: University Press of America, 1987).

58. Graham K. Wilson, "Why Is There No Corporatism in the United States?" in Gerhard Lehmbruch and Philippe C. Schmitter, eds., *Patterns of Corporatist Policy-Making* (Beverly Hills: Sage Publications, 1982), p. 225.

decision rules, set out in the Trade Act of 1974 to insure prompt congressional approval, tied the entire set of trade agreements together into a bill that was subject to a single up or down vote by Congress. This arrangement, equipped with its "fast-track procedure," diminished the effectiveness of individual industry lobbying efforts and ad hoc congressional obstruction.[59]

Clearly, the external involvement of states may heavily influence the nature of domestic restraints on state autonomy. Paradoxically, when states become enmeshed in international commitments or negotiations, these external constraints may loosen domestic obstacles and impediments; for this reason, states may even seek these external commitments. Stanley Hoffman notes that negotiations during the 1970s between the International Monetary Fund and the British and Italian governments resulted in a set of commitments on social and budgetary policy that "partly liberated these governments from the grip of left-wing socialist ideologies in one case, and a host of pressure groups in the other."[60] As with the cases of American oil decontrol and East–West trade, state officials can turn international constraints or imperatives into domestic opportunities.

The focus on the properties of issue-areas usefully differentiates the opportunities and obstacles to collective action that arise from the nature of the policies themselves. This was the seminal observation of Lowi. However, as we have argued, even in a particular policy area, such as trade, the way that policy is defined as a political good (public or private) may vary widely. Two conclusions follow: First, this observation leads to the need for much more fine-grained analysis of differences within, and between, policy areas. These differences will have important implications for the role of societal groups and state officials in influencing policy. When policy is articulated as a public good, executive officials have greater autonomy to influence policy outcomes. Second, because the publicness of policy is not simply intrinsic to a policy area, but is a product of how that policy is framed and its institutional context, a broader analysis is needed to determine how policy is defined and presented for political debate.[61] As Gowa notes, the "pattern of incentives" for collective action can only be understood in light of the political institutions that create and sustain those incentives.[62] The important political struggle may not be over specific policies, but over the institutions and rules within which those policies are conceived and debated. This conclusion moves the discussion away from the properties of policy and rein-

---

59. See note 19.

60. Hoffmann, "Domestic Politics and Interdependence," in Hoffman, *Janus and Minerva: Essays in the Theory and Practice of International Politics* (Boulder: Westview Press, 1987), p. 274. First published in Organization for Economic Cooperation and Development, *From Marshall Plan to Global Interdependence* (Paris: OECD, 1978).

61. See the discussion of agenda setting in John W. Kingdon, *Agendas, Alternatives, and Public Policies* (Boston: Little, Brown, 1984).

62. Gowa, "Public Goods and Political Institutions: Trade and Monetary Policy Processes in the United States," in this volume.

troduces the larger issues of the structures and dynamics of state and society relations.

Conclusion

Social science, according to Max Weber, tends to take one of two forms. It can involve the causal analysis of individual actions, structures, and personalities—what he called "history." Or it can involve the construction of concepts and typologies and the discovery of general laws of events—what he called "sociology."[63] The research presented in this volume suggests that, as Weber himself demonstrated, the two aspects of social science inquiry are complementary. Aside from the article by Gowa, the authors in this volume share a view that an understanding of American foreign economic policy is best pursued by theoretically based historical inquiry. The empirical cases tend to focus on historical turning points or transformations in the international position of the United States. Rather than testing grand deductive theories, the chapters begin with historical problems or puzzles and build inductively around a cluster of theoretical reference points.

Many of the authors' specific arguments can be subsumed within the institutional approach. The three contending approaches to studying foreign economic policy—namely, the system-, society-, and state-centered perspectives—can also be reconciled with each other, at least in part, through an institutional approach. Yet, the institutional analysis of foreign economic policy, I must emphasize, is an approach and not a theory. It presents a set of problems and variables, but it does not pretend to provide the basis for a formal and parsimonious set of propositions that researchers can test in a simple fashion. For those interested in more axiomatic social science theory, the institutional perspective will be grossly inadequate. The defense of an historical focus on institutional structures, and their workings within periods of social change, is based on the types of questions that the approach generates. The crucial issues, from this perspective, concern the large-scale, shifting sets of constraining and enabling conditions within which individuals and groups are situated.

In his classic, polemical attack on the grand theorizing of the 1950s and passionate defense of historical sociology, C. Wright Mills noted that "we more readily become aware of larger structures when they are changing, and we are likely to become aware of such changes only when we broaden our view to include a suitable historical span."[64] When one admits that social

---

63. Weber, *Economy and Society*, edited by Guenther Roth and Claus Wittich, vol. 1 (Berkeley: University of California Press, 1978), p. 19.

64. Mills, "The Uses of History," in *The Sociological Imagination* (New York: Oxford University Press, 1959), p. 149.

and international structures are themselves historically bound and subject to change, the virtue of the institutional approach is in its necessity.

Nonetheless, in terms of explaining foreign economic policy, the institutional approach can provide only some of the answers. The approach focuses on the structural constraints that confront social and governmental actors in the process of policymaking. Yet while constraints tell us what is not possible, they provide less guidance concerning what is.

Understanding when and how individuals and groups can overturn or transcend their structural setting has occupied scholars for generations. An avenue of investigation that has increasingly occupied the attention of social scientists is the role of political ideas or ideology that, in complex interaction with social and political structures, occasionally provides openings for policy innovation and institutional change. Goldstein's work on trade policy provides important insights into the centrality of ideas in American foreign economic policy. In his study of U.S. monetary policy, John Odell also finds the role of ideas crucial in explaining the direction of new policy.[65] Their attention to the role of ideas in policy innovation is consistent with the broad outlines of the institutional approach. Ideas are never completely disembodied from the complex of professional and governmental institutions within which they emerge. Indeed, the institutional setting of policymaking is likely to be crucial to the location and shape the ideas themselves are likely to take.

Another promising line of inquiry concerns the interactive relationship between international regimes and domestic political process. Several scholars have recently argued that theories of international cooperation can benefit from opening the "blackbox" of domestic politics.[66] A systematic understanding of the institutional position of state officials reveals the variety of constraints upon and incentives for participation in international regime agreements. For example, as Stephan Haggard and Beth Simmons note, the rise of the "voluntary export agreements" and "orderly marketing agreements," in violation of GATT (General Agreements on Tariffs and Trade) norms, is propelled by efforts to respond to domestic political pressures while also limiting the severity of protectionism.[67] Departures from regime norms, and the substantive evolution of the trade regime, are driven

65. John Odell, *U.S. International Monetary Policy* (Princeton, N.J.: Princeton University Press, 1982).

66. Joanne Gowa, "Anarchy, Egoism, and Third Images: The Evolution of Cooperation and International Relations," *International Organization* 40 (Winter 1986), pp. 167–86; Stephan Haggard and Beth Simmons, "Theories of International Regimes," *International Organization* 41 (Summer 1987); Robert D. Putnam, "The Logic of Two-Level Games: International Cooperation, Domestic Politics, and Western Summitry, 1975–1986," paper delivered at the annual meeting of the American Political Science Association, 28–31 August 1986, Washington, D.C.; Douglas Nelson, "The State as a Conceptual Variable: Another Look," World Bank, unpublished paper.

67. Haggard and Simmons, "Theories of International Regimes."

by a complex set of domestic compromises between state officials and societal interests. Change in the international trade regime is bound up with the evolution of domestic-level relations between the state and configurations of social interests.[68] In other cases, state officials may find international cooperation or participation in regime agreements to be a useful means of building domestic support or diffusing pressure. As I have noted earlier, the effort to alter the domestic balance of political forces led the Carter administration into the 1978 Bonn Summit package agreement on oil pricing and macroeconomic policy. By relaxing the divisions between domestic and international political processes, and appreciating the special position state officials occupy at the intersection of these spheres, political outcomes within each become more explicable.

The study of American foreign economic policy has become a prominent field of inquiry largely because the United States continues to occupy the dominant position in the international system, but also because foreign economic policy provides the bridge between domestic and international politics. In this arena, societies and states make choices between independence and interdependence. The central claim of the institutional approach is that the institutional structures mediate the interests and capacities of individuals and groups within them—by the large-scale and historically evolving organizational structures of state and society. Understanding the nature of these constraining and enabling circumstances, and the historical dynamics of institutional change, remain vital issues of study.

68. Charles Lipson stresses the importance of the evolving domestic position of the state relative to the international standards and practices of protection of foreign capital. *Standing Guard: Protecting Foreign Capital in the Nineteenth and Twentieth Centuries* (Berkeley: University of California Press, 1985), especially pp. 19–26.

Cornell Studies in Political Economy

EDITED BY PETER J. KATZENSTEIN

Library of Congress Cataloging-in-Publication Data

The State and American foreign economic policy.

  (Cornell studies in political economy)
   1. United States—Foreign economic relations. I. Ikenberry, G. John.
II. Lake, David A. III. Mastanduno, Michael. IV. Series.
HF1455.S8 1988   337.73   88-11858
ISBN 0-8014-2229-9
ISBN 0-8014-9524-5 (pbk.)